USING EVIDEN
HOMELESS

Edited by
Lígia Teixeira and James Cartwright

With a foreword by
David Halpern

First published in Great Britain in 2020 by

Policy Press
University of Bristol
1-9 Old Park Hill
Bristol
BS2 8BB
UK
t: +44 (0)117 954 5940
pp-info@bristol.ac.uk
www.policypress.co.uk

North America office:
Policy Press
c/o The University of Chicago Press
1427 East 60th Street
Chicago, IL 60637, USA
t: +1 773 702 7700
f: +1 773 702 9756
sales@press.uchicago.edu
www.press.uchicago.edu

British Library Cataloguing in Publication Data
A catalogue record for this book is available from the British Library.

Library of Congress Cataloging-in-Publication Data
A catalog record for this book has been requested.

ISBN 978-1-4473-5286-0 paperback
ISBN 978-1-4473-5287-7 ePub
ISBN 978-1-4473-5410-9 OA PDF

The right of the Centre for Homelessness Impact to be identified as the editor of this work has been asserted by them in accordance with the Copyright, Designs and Patents Act 1988.

Cover design by Robin Hawes
From cover image: iStock/fi lo

Contents

List of figures

Notes on contributors

Stephen Aldridge is Director for Analysis and Data at the Ministry of Housing, Communities and Local Government. A government economist by background, Stephen was previously Chief Economist and then Director of the Strategy Unit in the Cabinet Office. Stephen is a member of the National What Works Advisory Council; a member of the international advisory board for the UK Collaborative Centre for Housing Evidence; and other bodies. He is a fellow of the Academy of Social Sciences and a continuing fellow at the Centre for Science and Policy at the University of Cambridge.

Jo Bibby is Director of Health at the Health Foundation. Jo is responsible for developing and leading the Foundation's Healthy Lives strategy to address the wider social and commercial determinants of health. Joining the foundation in November 2007, Jo initially led the development of the foundation's influential portfolio of work in patient safety and person-centred care. Jo has worked in healthcare at local and national level for 25 years, including ten years at the Department of Health. As Head of NHS Performance, she oversaw the implementation of the policy agenda set out in the NHS Plan. At the NHS Modernisation Agency, Jo led an international quality improvement initiative – Pursuing Perfection.

Bob Blackman is the Conservative MP for Harrow East and serves as Joint Secretary of the prestigious 1922 Committee within Parliament. He was elected London Assembly Member for Brent and Harrow in 2004 and was a member of Brent Council for nearly 24 years. During that time, he led the Conservative Group for 20 years and the Council for 5 years. Since being elected as MP for Harrow East in 2010 Bob has been able to bring his extensive experience in local government to bear on many of the issues facing the government today through his work on the Communities and Local Government Select Committee. In 2016, Bob was drawn in the Private Member's Bill ballot, which gives backbench MPs a chance to put forward a piece of primary legislation. Bob put forward the Homelessness Reduction Bill with the support of the homelessness charity sector, particularly Crisis, which was one of the final pieces of legislation given Royal Assent before the 2017 general election. The Act was backed with £91 million of investment from the government, the Homelessness Reduction Act is the most well-funded Private Member's Bill on record alongside being the longest and most substantial at 13 clauses. It is the only Bill of its kind to be explicitly backed by the work of a Select Committee. The Act came into force in April 2018 and the 'duty to refer' in October 2018. The Act is recognised as the biggest reform in legislation in assisting the homeless in more than 40 years.

Jonathan Breckon has been Director of the Alliance for Useful Evidence since it was created at Nesta in 2012. Formerly Director of Policy and Public Affairs at the Arts and Humanities Research Council, he has had policy roles at the Royal Geographical Society, the British Academy and Universities UK. He is a member of the Cabinet Office What Works Council and a director of the Department for Education's What Works for Children's Social Care. His research and professional interests cover politics and psychology, particularly the ever-awkward relationship between evidence and policy-making. He is a visiting professor at Strathclyde University and a visiting senior research fellow at King's College London's Policy Institute.

Tracey Brown has been the Director of Sense about Science since 2002. Under her leadership, the charity has turned the case for sound science and evidence into popular campaigns to urge scientific thinking among the public and the people who answer to them. It has launched important initiatives to expand and protect honest discussions of evidence, including AllTrials, a global campaign for the reporting of all clinical trial outcomes, and the Ask for Evidence campaign, which engages the public in requesting evidence for claims. It has challenged opinions and changed the behaviour of governments, media and corporations in the use of scientific evidence. Tracey leads Sense about Science's work on the transparency of evidence used by governments in policy, to ensure that the public has access to the same evidence and reasoning as decision-makers. This has included drafting the Principles for the Treatment of Independent Scientific Advice, which were adopted into the UK Ministerial Code in 2010, the creation of a public interest defence to libel in the Defamation Act 2013 and the Evidence Transparency Framework, used to audit UK government in 2016 and 2017 and adopted by government audit agencies around the world.

James Cartwright is an associate at the Centre for Homelessness Impact, where he consults on editorial and communications strategies to enable the Centre to achieve its goals as quickly and effectively as possible. He is a writer, journalist and the editor of *Weapons of Reason*, a social sciences publication that uses the power of storytelling and data to communicate and address the most pressing global issues.

Neil Coyle is the Labour MP for Bermondsey and Old Southwark and was elected to Parliament in 2015. As the co-chair of the All-Party Parliamentary Group on Ending Homelessness, he is currently working to introduce mandatory safeguarding reviews for homeless people who have died on the streets and is leading the 'A Safe Home' campaign to ensure that anyone fleeing domestic abuse is provided with automatic priority need for permanent housing. Neil also serves on the Work and Pensions Select Committee and has been pressing the government on welfare reform for Universal Credit and PIP payments; he set up the All-Party Parliamentary Group on Foodbanks and was a councillor for the London Borough of Southwark from 2010–2016, serving as the Deputy Mayor of Southwark between 2014–2015. Before being elected to Parliament, Neil ran a charity helping half a million disabled people and carers every year.

Dennis Culhane is Dana and Andrew Stone Chair in Social Policy and Co-Principal Investigator, Actionable Intelligence for Social Policy at the University of Pennsylvania. Dr Culhane is a social science researcher with primary expertise in the area of homelessness and assisted housing policy. His work has contributed to efforts to address the housing and support needs of people experiencing housing emergencies and long-term homelessness. Most recently, Culhane's research has focused on using linked administrative data to gain a better understanding about the service utilisation patterns of vulnerable populations, including youth exiting foster care and/or juvenile justice, as well as the individuals aged 55 and older who are experiencing homelessness. Culhane's research also focuses on homelessness among veterans. From July 2009 to June 2018 he served as Director of Research at the National Center on Homelessness Among Veterans, an initiative of the US Department of Veterans Affairs, Culhane also co-directs Actionable Intelligence for Social Policy (AISP), an initiative that promotes the development, use and innovation of integrated data systems by states and localities for policy analysis and systems reform.

Danny Dorling is Halford Mackinder Professor of Geography at the School of Geography and the Environment, University of Oxford. He was previously a professor of geography at the University of Sheffield. He has also worked in Newcastle, Bristol, Leeds and New Zealand, went to university in Newcastle upon Tyne and to school in Oxford. He has published, with many colleagues, more than a dozen books on issues related to social inequalities in Britain and several hundred journal papers. Much of this work is available open access. His work concerns issues of housing, health, employment, education and poverty. He is an academician of the Academy of the Learned Societies in the Social Sciences, was Honorary President of the Society of Cartographers from 2007 to 2017 and is a patron of Roadpeace, the national charity for road crash victims.

Matt Downie MBE is Director of Policy and External Affairs for Crisis. Matt has led award-winning teams at Action for Children, the National Autistic Society and Crisis. Political successes include the Autism Act 2009, stopping the extradition of Gary McKinnon to the US on charges of computer hacking, establishing a multi-million pound government savings scheme for children in care and the introduction of a new criminal offence of psychological child abuse. Most recently he led a campaign to achieve the Homelessness Reduction Act which came into force in 2018. Matt was awarded an MBE in the 2019 Queen's birthdays honours list, for services to tackle homelessness.

Caroline Fiennes is Director of Giving Evidence, which encourages and enables *giving* based on sound *evidence*. She advises people and companies on giving well to charities and is one of the few people whose work has featured in both the scientific journal *Nature* and *OK!* magazine. She frequently speaks and writes in the press and has been an award-winning Chief Executive of the climate change charity Global Cool, which promotes green living. She has advised donors including the Emirates Foundation in UAE, Eurostar, the Ashden Awards, the Big Lottery Fund, the Sainsbury Family Charitable Trusts, professional tennis players, the Private Equity Foundation, BBC Children in Need, Booz & Co and Morgan Stanley. This work has spanned environment, health, education, international development, children's issues and other areas.

Suzanne Fitzpatrick is Professor of Housing and Social Policy in the Institute of Social Policy, Housing and Equalities Research (I-SPHERE), Heriot-Watt University. Suzanne completed her PhD on youth homelessness at the University of Glasgow in 1998. She subsequently held a number of posts in the Department of Urban Studies at the University of Glasgow, including ESRC Research Fellow in Housing and Social Exclusion and, latterly, Lecturer in Housing and Social Policy. From 2003 to 2010 Suzanne was Joseph Rowntree Professor of Housing Policy and Director of the Centre for Housing Policy at the University of York. Suzanne took up her research professorship in housing and social policy at Heriot-Watt University in July 2010. Suzanne specialises in research on homelessness and housing exclusion and much of her work has an international comparative dimension.

David Gough is Professor of Evidence Informed Policy and Practice and the Director of the Social Science Research Unit and the EPPI-Centre at University College London. He came to the unit in 1998, having previously worked at the University of Glasgow and Japan Women's University. Previously, he wrote on child protection and abuse, but now spends most of his time on the study of methods for research synthesis and research use.

Olly Grender is a former Director of Communications for the Liberal Democrats and a party life peer. Her career has spanned the world of politics, government and the voluntary and corporate sectors. She has run communications operations and campaigns in all four. She was drawn into the Liberal Party by community politics in 1981 and has worked for the Party locally and nationally since. She spent a year at Number 10 as the Deputy Director of Communications for the Government, where she co-ordinated the Liberal Democrats' communications operation on behalf of the Deputy Prime Minister, and was Director of Communications under Paddy Ashdown's leadership from 1990 to 1995. Prior to that, she was a speech writer and had responsibility for housing and transport policy in his office. She was elected by the Party to the Interim Peers Panel in 2006 and became a peer in 2013. Her private member's bill and campaign in 2016 to ban lettings fees for tenants who rent has resulted in a government bill.

David Halpern is the Chief Executive of the Behavioural Insights Team. He has led the team since its inception in 2010. Prior to that, David was the founding Director of the Institute for Government and, between 2001 and 2007, was the Chief Analyst at the Prime Minister's Strategy Unit. David was also appointed as the What Works National Advisor in July 2013. He supports the What Works Network and leads efforts to improve the use of evidence across government. Before entering government, David held tenure at Cambridge and posts at Oxford and Harvard. He has written several books and papers on areas relating to behavioural insights and wellbeing, including *Social Capital* (2005), the *Hidden Wealth of Nations* (2010), and is co-author of the MINDSPACE report. In 2015 David wrote a book about the team entitled *Inside the Nudge Unit: How Small Changes Can Make a Big Difference.*

Louise Marshall is Senior Public Health Fellow in the Healthy Lives team at the Health Foundation, where her work focuses on new approaches to generating and using evidence about population-level action on the wider determinants of health. Before joining the Foundation in 2014, Louise worked in public health roles spanning policy, practice and research during public health specialty training. Prior to this, she was a postdoctoral scientist in public health nutrition. Louise has a PhD from the University of Cambridge, and master's degrees from the London School of Hygiene and Tropical Medicine and the University of Cambridge. Louise is also an Honorary Consultant in Public Health at Oxford University Hospitals NHS Foundation Trust and is a Fellow of the Faculty of Public Health.

Campbell Robb is the Chief Executive of Nacro. Before joining Nacro, he was the CEO of the Joseph Rowntree Foundation and the Joseph Rowntree Housing Trust from January 2017. There he steered the organisation through a significant change and reform programme, introducing an outcome-focused approach to change, new values and focus on working alongside those with lived experience of poverty. Before this, Campbell was Chief Executive of Shelter for seven years. As Chief Executive, he led the organisation through one of the most challenging periods in its history. This included building a sustainable, fundable model of integrated advice and support that is helping more clients than ever before, a growth in independent income and leading the organisation's response to some of the biggest changes to housing and welfare policy in generations. Prior to joining Shelter, Campbell was the first Director General of the Office of the Third Sector, an adviser to the Treasury and was previously Director of Public Policy at the National Council for Voluntary Organisations (NCVO).

Jon Sparkes has been Chief Executive of Crisis, the national charity for homeless people, since 2014. Previously he was Chief Operating Officer of UNICEF UK and Chief Executive of SCOPE, the national disability charity. Jon also had a successful commercial career as Human Resources Director of the international technology firm the Generics Group. He is a non-executive director of South Yorkshire Housing Association and a Trustee of the Centre for Homelessness Impact, has Chaired both the Scottish Government's Homelessness and Rough Sleeping Action Group and the Welsh Government's Homelessness Action Group, and is a member of the UK Government's Rough Sleeping Advisory Panel and the Scottish Government's Homelessness Prevention and Strategy Group.

Emma Taylor-Collins is Senior Research Officer at the Wales Centre for Public Policy, a research centre based at Cardiff University, which aims to improve policy-making and public services by supporting ministers and public service leaders to access and apply rigorous independent evidence about what works. Emma leads social justice research projects at the Centre on issues such as gender equality, social security and looked-after children. Emma's background is in the charity sector, and she is currently working towards a PhD on youth volunteering at the University of Birmingham's Third Sector Research Centre.

Lígia Teixeira is Chief Executive of the Centre for Homelessness Impact. She set up the Centre in 2018 and led the feasibility study which preceded its creation while at Crisis UK. Lígia is bringing the 'what works' methodology to homelessness: the use of reliable evidence and reason to improve outcomes with existing resources. In 2019, Lígia was conferred the Award of Fellow of the Academy of Social Sciences (FAcSS) for her contribution to social science. In 2016, she was awarded a Clore Social Fellowship on Housing and Homelessness, funded by the Oak Foundation. Lígia was previously at Crisis UK, where over a period of nine years she led the organisation's evidence and data programme - growing its scale and impact so that it's now one of the largest and most influential in the UK and internationally. She joined the charity in March 2008 following stints at the Young Foundation and the Refugee Council. Lígia was awarded a PhD from the Government Department of the London School of Economics in 2007. She has also worked in research roles for David Held, founder of Polity Press, for sociologist Helmut Anheier, who founded and directed the LSE's Centre for Civil Society, and for the International Labour Organisation where she covered issues including human trafficking, child labour and women's rights.

Dan Treglia is a Postdoctoral Fellow at the University of Pennsylvania's School of Social Policy and Practice. His research focuses on improving life for vulnerable populations, particularly those experiencing homelessness, through collaborative and innovative research that engages governments, non-profits, and people with lived experience. His recent work centres on the overlapping healthcare and other social service needs of homeless populations, and he is a recognised leader in methodologies for estimating the size and needs of unsheltered homeless populations. Dan also developed and piloted a technology-based street homelessness intervention called StreetChange and works with the United for ALICE project to improve national measures of income insufficiency. Prior to coming to Penn, he managed research and evaluation at New York City's Department of Homeless Services. Dan has a PhD in Social Welfare from Penn's School of Social Policy and Practice and a Masters in Public Policy from Harvard's Kennedy School of Government.

Julia Unwin is an experienced, well-known and respected senior strategic leader, with extensive professional leadership experience in the voluntary and public sectors and corporate social responsibility. Julia has experience in the regulatory environment having served at a very senior level at the Housing Corporation, Charity Commission and, as Deputy Chair and later Chair, of the Food Standards Agency and, until December 2016, Chief Executive Officer of the Joseph Rowntree Foundation.

Howard White is the Chief Executive Officer of the Campbell Collaboration. He was previously the founding Executive Director of the International Initiative for Impact Evaluation (3ie) and has led the impact evaluation programme of the World Bank's Independent Evaluation Group. Howard started his career as an academic researcher at the Institute of Social Studies in the Hague, and the Institute of Development Studies, University of Sussex. As an academic, he leans towards work with policy relevance and working in the policy field believes in academic rigour as the basis for policy and practice.

Foreword

David Halpern

The world has many problems, many of which seem like we ought to be able to fix. Homelessness is one of those problems. It has a Dickensian cruelty that feels as out of place in a modern society as 19th-century smogs.

There are serious and determined people trying to address homelessness. These include authors of chapters of this book, as well as social activists, volunteers and policy-makers. Yet as one chapter after another gives testament to, even leading experts are not sure 'what works', particularly when getting into the detailed choices that confront practitioners.

Historically, doubt has been seen as weakness in the political and practitioner world. To parody, it was presumed that the last thing that a voter, patient or parent wanted to hear from a politician or practitioner was 'I'm not sure'. But acknowledging the limits of our knowledge – what will work, when and for whom – opens the door to a powerful and pragmatic approach to dramatically increase the impact of our efforts.

This is what the 'What Works' movement is about. What Works Centres embody three key activities: the generation and synthesis of evidence; translation of this evidence for the key audiences; and building the capacity of those actors to utilise this evidence.

The parallel is often made to medicine (including by Lígia Teixeira and by Louise Marshall and Jo Bibby in this book). We now take it for granted that when our doctor prescribes a treatment, it has good evidence behind it. Yet the body that assembles that evidence for medicine, NICE, itself a What Works Centre, only just passed its 20th birthday. The comparable bodies for education and policing are less than a decade old. For many areas of policy and practice, the journey is only just beginning.

It can be surprisingly hard to distinguish between what is plausible and what is true. Many people that doctors treat get better, but how many would have got better anyway? Similarly, governments and foundations spend billions, but often the evidence base on which this spending is based is remarkably thin about the marginal effectiveness of that spend or whether and which better solutions exist.

Details matter too, as illustrated in the Behavioural Insights Team's work. Back in 2010, it was considered a radical and contested idea to test deliberate variations in how we asked people to pay their tax bills; how we prompted people to look for work; or which mobile text prompts might help a young person perform better in school. When these types of tests were run, it was found that small variations could lead to significant improvements in outcomes. Adding into a reminder letter that 'most people pay their tax on time, and you are one of the few yet to do so' led to a 15 per cent increase in the number of late payers paying off their tax bill within a month without further prompts. Encouraging jobseekers to think about what jobs they would look for next week, rather than asking them what they looked for the previous week, shaved on average two or three days off how fast people got back to work. Similarly, asking young retake students to nominate 'study supporters' – a parent, sibling or friend – to receive regular prompts from their college on how to have conversations with the student about their studies, boosted pass rates by nearly 30 per cent.

Whatever we are trying to do, from prime ministers to frontline practitioners, we face choices. Very often, we do not know which of these will work better or for who. But with humility, determination and better methods, we can answer these questions.

The same is true of the choices we face around housing and homelessness. Some of these choices will be around big policy and spending decisions. Are we better off addressing housing shortages through rental subsidies or direct capital investments? What are the best ways of addressing 'upstream' the causal drivers of poverty and disadvantage (that Campbell Robb rightly highlights in this volume)? Other questions may hinge more on the subtle details of how, rather than what. Confronted with a person with multiple and complex issues, and perhaps a history of being let down by those who could have done more, how can a social worker begin to win that person's trust and help them find a path back to a better life? How can a teacher or carer motivate and support a troubled young person to strive at school and away from drugs or alcohol?

In the 1970s, during Archie Cochrane's great battles to get medics to adopt more empirical methods, he noted that while he had been hard on his fellow medics, in other areas the fight had not even begun: 'What other profession encourages publications about its error, and experimental investigations into the effect of their actions? Which magistrate, judge, or headmaster has encouraged RCTs into their " therapeutic" and "deterrent" actions?' (Cochrane, 1971: 87)

It may have taken us nearly half a century for these words to sink in, but they have. The new Centre for Homelessness Impact has joined ten other What Works Centres in the national What Works Network.

It will not be easy. There are formidable methodological barriers to answer the disarmingly simple question 'what works?' There will often be resistance from those who already think they know the answer – resistance rooted not in malice, but in passion and a presumption that what we are already doing is effective and we just need to do more of it. Even as the evidence begins to build up, that is only the start of the journey. Policy-makers will want to know not just what works, but also at what cost, and the relative cost-effectiveness of options. Finally, there can be as much of a struggle to figure out 'what works' in getting practitioners and policy-makers to adopt 'what works', as to generate the primary evidence.

In the end, our challenge is not just to answer the immediate questions in front of us on homelessness. We need to build a system of practice and learning that asks and answers ever more specific questions, as well as going back to deeper causes and, in so doing, change what we do to make the world we share better.

Reference

Cochrane, A.L. 1971. *Effectiveness and efficiency: random reflections on health services.* Nuffield Provincial Hospitals Trust.

The Impact Manifesto: doing the right things to end homelessness for good

Lígia Teixeira

The problem of extreme complexity

It is the challenge of our age: How do we end homelessness for good?

For the last 50 years, a lot of smart, well-resourced people and institutions have been trying to work out how to end homelessness in the UK and elsewhere. Billions of pounds have been invested in programmes and organisations with the mission of helping people who are at risk of or experiencing homelessness. They have studied issues like housing, social security, employment and asset-building, and then introduced or advocated for policies and programmes to support the most at-risk groups. They have written reports and columns and given passionate speeches, decrying the fact that the weakening of our social safety net is pushing more and more people into homelessness, even though we know that prevention is better than cure. These efforts have helped. But they are not enough.

Too many people remain without a home in the 21st century. They are not just sleeping rough on our streets, but also living in overcrowded housing, hostels and other temporary accommodation. Our best programmes do make a difference, but their impact has not changed significantly since homelessness first entered the national consciousness as a major concern in the mid-1960s.

In recent years, increased homelessness in many areas has again put a spotlight on the issue. At times like these, homelessness returns to the public's attention, leading to renewed political action and the provision of more resources. As a result, the number of people experiencing homelessness goes down temporarily, but in time the cycle repeats. It is therefore no wonder that recent commitments to ending homelessness have been met with scepticism by the public – it is not enough to reduce the number of people affected by homelessness if we cannot sustain that change.

In this environment, what can government leaders and advocates do to make lasting change in ending homelessness? In the following chapters we argue that one way to break this cycle and rebuild the public's trust is by focusing on 'what works' – by finding and funding solutions backed by evidence and data and by seeding experiments with the potential to produce outsized social returns. Existing approaches are proving insufficient to truly crack homelessness, so we need to experiment and find new approaches to create breakthrough change.

One simple idea: how can we use our resources to do the most good?

I was born and grew up in one of the poorest regions in Portugal. Although I did not grow up in poverty it was a close neighbour. It was not until I came to London as a young academic that I first came across destitution and street homelessness. I lived in Holborn at the time and, on my walk to the LSE each morning, I would often see people who were sleeping rough, especially in Lincoln's Inn Fields. After a while I mustered sufficient courage to stop and talk to them, and that is how I began to learn about their journeys into homelessness. Hearing individual stories and looking at the wider figures, one would be forgiven for thinking that the UK is not a wealthy nation.

These early interactions made me pay attention. They made me want to do something to help the people I spoke with. I have now worked with and learned from people affected by or at risk of homelessness for more than ten years. I have campaigned for the strengthening of the social safety net, which protects individuals and families on low incomes from falling into homelessness. I have worked with individual people experiencing homelessness who manifest hope and promise, despite the complex challenges they sometimes face in Jobcentres, public spaces and specialist services. I have advocated for change in how we talk about homelessness so the public understand that it is an issue that can be solved because what is broken is our approach to solving homelessness, not the people who experience homelessness themselves.

I joined Crisis in 2008 because it was a great opportunity to place evidence at the heart of our efforts to help people at risk of, or experiencing, homelessness. While major forward strides have been made since then, I continue to be surprised by the limited use of evidence-based practices in policy-making in the UK and beyond. Only a small fraction of government spending is backed by reliable evidence that taxpayers' money is being spent wisely.

Yet progress is within reach. We have more information than ever about the root causes and consequences of homelessness. Advances in legislation, research developments and the work of bold third-sector leaders and social entrepreneurs point the way to solutions. But too often we continue to do what we have always done in the past, without using evidence about what works (and perhaps most importantly, what does not) expecting that the same actions will yield different results. This is not a problem unique to homelessness.

This is why the time has come for a 'what works' movement in homelessness. What do we mean by this? 'Homelessness impact' is about using evidence and reason to figure out how to help people who are at risk of, or experiencing, homelessness as much as possible at a societal level, and taking action on that basis. It means acting promptly on the best available knowledge, while being aware of the limits of what we know. And, like evidence-based medicine, 'homelessness impact' can help us figure out what works and what does not, allowing us to reject the dangerous half-truths that can pass for wisdom.

Why are the ideas of 'what works' in homelessness important?

The 19th-century French physician Pierre-Charles-Alexandre Louis put a lot of leeches out of business. For centuries before his research, doctors believed that removing a few pints of a person's blood would help cure all types of ailments. In the 1830s, doubting bloodletting's alleged benefits, Louis carried out one of the first clinical trials. He compared the outcomes of 41 pneumonia victims who had undergone early and aggressive bloodletting to the outcomes of 36 pneumonia victims who had not. The results were clear: 44 per cent of the bled patients subsequently died, compared to only 25 per cent of the patients who remained leech-free (Morabia, 2006). Louis' discovery helped convince physicians to abandon bloodletting and his study became a touchstone of the modern evidence-based medicine movement, which trains physicians to conduct, evaluate, and act according to research.

Today, as then, the experimental, empirical approach matters. It matters because many attempts to do good fail – even those with a high profile. Scared Straight is a good example of misguided intuition passing for wisdom: a programme that takes kids who have committed misdemeanours to visit prisons and meet criminals to confront their likely future if they continue to offend. The concept proved popular not just as a social programme but as entertainment; it was adapted for both an acclaimed documentary and a TV show on A&E, which broke ratings records for the network upon its premiere. There is just one problem with Scared Straight: multiple studies have found that the programme actually increases rates of offending among its participants (see, for example, Washington State Institute for Public Policy, 2004).

More recently, teenage pregnancy prevention programmes that use 'magic dolls' to simulate the needs of a new baby have been found not to work, according to a study in *The Lancet* (Brinkman, S. et al, 2016). More than 1,000 teenage girls who took part in programmes in Western Australia were more likely to become pregnant than girls who did not. Similar programmes are still used in schools in 89 countries, including the US.

Research shows that many attempts to do good are like Scared Straight and Magic Dolls. When tested with rigorous randomised controlled trials, nearly 80 per cent of individual interventions do not work. Between 1 and 10 per cent have negative effects.[1] But while many attempts to do good fail, some succeed, and the best examples of success are exceptional. Consider the evidence-informed provision of bed nets in sub-Saharan Africa, where malaria is one of the leading killers of children. Long-lasting insecticide-treated nets (LLINs) effectively prevent deaths and many other non-fatal cases of malaria. They are also relatively inexpensive – about $5 per net.[2] The charity evaluator GiveWell estimates that a donation of $7,500 to the Against Malaria Foundation will save someone's life.

In other areas of policy, giving cash grants to people living in poverty in low-income countries has the strongest track record of success. Cash transfers – directly transferring money to poor individuals – are a priority programme of GiveWell as they allow individuals to purchase the things most necessary to them. Strong evidence indicates that cash transfers lead recipients to spend more on their basic needs (such as food) and may allow recipients to make investments with high returns, with no evidence of large increases in spending on items like alcohol or cigarettes, in spite of what many unhelpful stereotypes would lead us to assume.[3]

Homelessness has yet to find its direct cash transfers or insecticide-treated mosquito nets. Housing First is one of the few interventions to have rigorous evidence behind it, but even here there are not enough studies to provide reliable cost-effectiveness data. People are not aware of the best ways to help end homelessness for good, and so miss opportunities to make a tremendous difference. No wonder then that in lieu of evidence, leaders often base their decisions on dearly held ideologies, the actions of others and strategies they have used in the past. As a result, we inadvertently risk causing harm in the manner of Louis' bloodletting doctors.

What are the origins of the movement?

None of these challenges are unique to homelessness. As David Halpern remarks in *Inside the Nudge Unit* (Halpern, 2016): 'The dirty secret of much government policy and professional practice is that we don't really know whether it is effective at all.'

To counteract this and help find more ways to link research to practice, a whole movement has emerged in health, international development, education and policing. From the 1990s onwards, whole ecosystems of organisations, individuals and networks have grown around this movement. Some of them are wide-ranging like the Cochrane and Campbell Collaborations, the National Institute for Health and Care Excellence (NICE) or the Africa Evidence Network. Others are grassroots, like the Society for Evidence-Based Policing, researchEd, Evidence for the Frontline and the Coalition for Evidence-Based Education. In the UK, there has been a push for new organisations to synthesise actionable research for decision-makers through the What Works Network.

Also positive is the fact that, until recently, none of these organisations, at home or internationally, had a focus on homelessness. But we now have the Centre for Homelessness Impact (CHI) – one of the nine-strong What Works Centres – to act as a catalyst for evidence-led change in the field and recognise that a new approach is needed.

What past social movements does this echo? The What Works movement in the UK bears a number of similarities to evidence-based medicine, and in homelessness we have combined this with some insights from the movements of effective altruism and design thinking.

One of the strengths of evidence-based medicine is that it realises the limits of our rationality. It acknowledges that we are in fact *very* bad at working out how to maximise expected utility through abstract reasoning. We should therefore test things empirically to find out what works.

An important lesson from the effective altruism movement is an awareness of the importance of prioritising the most pressing challenges if we are to magnify impact ('the multiplier effect'). Design thinking provides a powerful tool to understand fully the challenge we are trying to address and whether it is the *right* challenge to address, putting a spotlight on the importance of diversity and creativity to achieve breakthrough solutions.

What has been the journey in homelessness?

On the first day of class, the deans of many medical schools greet their first-year medical students with this sobering statement: 'Half of what we know is wrong. The problem is, we don't know which half.' Why is this an important message for us all to bear in mind? Because to achieve step change in homelessness, we too must act with knowledge while simultaneously doubting what we know. This entails striking a balance between arrogance (assuming you know more than you do) and insecurity (believing that you know too little to act). With this attitude, those working in or around homelessness can take action now but continue to learn along the way.

In homelessness, modesty is often in short supply and absolutes abound − in recommendations as to what to do, in conclusions about what affects performance and in beliefs about what works. Interestingly, it seems that the less developed the evidence infrastructure is in a particular field, the more prevalent these things appear to be.

But it is not all bad news. Circumstances have improved significantly since I first started working in homelessness. We have a much richer understanding of the causes and consequences of homelessness and the need to address its root causes instead of its symptoms (see, for example, MHCLG, 2019b; Fitzpatrick, S. et al, 2011–19). The types of services offered to individuals and families experiencing housing instability have changed for the better in the past few decades. For example, there has been a shift towards a model of support that prioritises immediate housing and away from the traditional model of requiring preconditions such as sobriety and employment before obtaining permanent housing. Evidence played an important role in building support for this shift, with several randomised evaluations showing that a 'housing first' approach could more effectively house people experiencing chronic homelessness than hostel-based approaches.

Evidence also played a key role in the move from a crisis-driven approach to prevention to a more strategic and targeted methodology. In the UK, post-devolution Scotland took the bold step of strengthening its statutory safety net for those affected by homelessness, culminating in the ambitious commitment to house all those deemed to be homeless.[4] More recently it took the decision to provide people with support from their local authority regardless of whether they have a local connection with them or are intentionally homeless. In England and Wales, local authorities now have a duty to help prevent homelessness regardless of a person's level of priority, and the period during which a person is deemed to be 'threatened with homelessness' has been extended from 28 to 56 days.

Also welcome is the increase in the number of rigorous studies on homelessness in recent years. Prior to 2000, there were fewer than two studies published per year, an average of four per year from 2000 to 2009 and, since 2010, nearly ten per year. CHI's Evidence and Gap Map of effectiveness studies demonstrates that there is now an evidence base on which to build an infrastructure for evidence-based policies. With the exception of legislation, there are studies we can learn from in most outcome areas. The largest concentrations of studies are on health and social care interventions, followed by accommodation-based approaches.

There is a caveat, however; most studies are currently from North America – 227 versus 12 UK studies. In the UK there has been very limited use of rigorous systematic reviews and examples of evaluation using experimental and quasi-experimental methods are still rare. But that is beginning to change. The Ministry for Housing, Communities and Local Government (MHCLG) recently published the first Rough Sleeping Initiative (RSI) impact evaluation, which provides good evidence that the RSI is having a positive impact in reducing the number of people sleeping on the streets of England (MHCLG, 2019c).

Developments in data are also moving in the right direction. In England, the Homelessness Reduction Act 2017 included a new requirement for case-level data to be returned to the MHCLG through their new H-CLIC data collection system

(MHCLG, 2019a). The richer data being collected by local authorities will in time provide a much deeper understanding of how the population is affected and the ways in which people flow through services.

Data linkage presents important opportunities and progress on this front is encouraging. In 2018, the Scottish Government linked homelessness and health datasets for the first time at a national level to explore the relationship between homelessness and health, revealing that at least 8 per cent of the Scottish population had experienced homelessness at some point in their lives (Waugh et al, 2018).

Also vital are ongoing efforts across the Government Statistical Service to improve the comparability and coherence of statistics on homelessness and rough sleeping in the UK, up to and including the 2021 census. And technological developments mean it should be possible to gather information from a larger fraction of the population affected or at risk. Businesses are at the forefront of collecting and making effective use of big data. It is time for the public and non-profit sectors to catch up.

I am often asked whether in the past there have been successful methods that we can learn from. But I am inclined to think that history is more instructive about what not to do. If we stopped doing what was ineffective, the impact would be quick and significant.

Policy-makers must have good information on which to base their decisions about improving the viability and effectiveness of government programmes and policies. Today, too little evidence is produced to meet this need. This is partly due to the absence of a tradition of robust evaluation. Very few programmes have been adequately evaluated anywhere in the world. Process evaluations are sometimes conducted but, while valuable, these are not enough to inform decisions about how to do the most good. We have a richer tradition of enumerating the scale of the issue and the characteristics of those at risk or affected by it, but our methods are slow and costly, and we are yet to take full advantage of the opportunities presented by technological developments.

It is also possible that the best interventions in an area are not based on current evidence – rather they might involve creating and testing new interventions (innovation has not been strong in homelessness; we have not taken many risks).

There is also plenty of reason to think that our decision-making competence is currently less than perfect. A whole host of cognitive biases affect judgements and decisions as psychology research over the past few decades has documented. Though these are not specific to homelessness, the sector has no reason to believe that it is any different. We are also regularly overconfident in our predictions – it is human nature.

Homelessness, like other social issues in the world, is incredibly complicated, requiring an understanding of complex interrelated systems, an ability to predict the outcomes of different actions and to balance competing considerations. That means there is all the more room for errors of judgement to slip in. And let us not forget that the organisations best placed to solve homelessness are often bureaucratic, meaning that decision-makers face many constraints and competing incentives, not always aligned with better decision-making. Improving the decision-making competence of key institutions may be particularly crucial to our efforts to end homelessness sustainably, as the challenges we face become more complex.

Where do we go from here?

The experimental methods being spread by the What Works movement bring with them something new and deeply important to policy and practice: humility. As Richard Feyman quipped, 'Science is the belief in the ignorance of experts'. As experimental studies have shown, we are all prone to overconfidence (Halpern, 2016: 296). We need to recognise this and our dangerous assumption that what we know is 'right'. We need to follow in the footsteps of Archie Cochrane, Richard Feyman and David Halpern and embrace doubt. We need to test, learn and adapt.

It is time to approach one of the seemingly intractable challenges of our time in a new way. If we do not, we risk lagging further behind than other fields, further losing the public's trust and, most importantly, missing an important opportunity to create a better society for all. It will not be easy, but when it comes to addressing an issue like homelessness, it is absolutely the right thing to do.

After over ten years of building links between evidence, policy and practice in homelessness, I have come to understand that we are in the business of capturing hearts and minds. Key to this is to ask what problems decision-makers are trying to solve, building demand for more data-driven decision-making and not overselling the availability of evidence-based practices or underestimating what it takes to scale them.

If we want to gain momentum for evidence-based approaches with a view to ending homelessness for good, we need to start routinely testing the effectiveness of intervention while taking a bird eye's view of the issue. Only then can we figure out how to achieve breakthrough results at population level and use data to drive improvement on an ongoing basis.

What would this approach look like?

1. Ask the right questions and prioritise the needs of evidence users

Understanding a problem is essential to working out how best to solve it. Typically, we rush straight to solutions without gathering the necessary evidence about why a problem exists or whether it is the most pressing problem we could be focusing on. We select strategies based on their assumptions about the nature of the issue. Various theories may be based on research evidence, making them seem evidence-based to decision-makers. But without better data to diagnose the problem within a specific context, proposed interventions may not, in fact, apply, and may cause people to waste precious time and money solving a problem they never actually had.

2. Gather better data and evidence

There are limited resources for evaluation and other evidence-building activities, which too often are seen as 'extras'. Developments in data and evidence give us the tools to better understand social problems like homelessness. With better understanding, we will be able to zero in on better questions to measure the effectiveness and long-term impact of our interventions.

Many programmes at the local, national and UK level have minimal information to use for performance management and assessing impact and even fewer staff with the skills required to use it effectively. We need to figure out what data is needed to support evaluation, research and development, and programme management, and advocate for collecting it.

3. Invest in the infrastructure of evidence

In fact, building systems to better use data and implement evidence-based practice is likely to require additional funds.

As a field, we have paid little attention to the infrastructure and capacity building necessary to be more data and evidence driven. Many programmes lack the resources – including a strong coaching workforce – needed to implement these practices well. Also, current implementation of evidence-based practice undervalues the need for ongoing monitoring and continuous improvement. Our 'what works' conversations are too static and act as if interventions found to be effective once or twice will be effective for all time and in all contexts.

4. Promote ongoing improvement

Given that an evidence-based practice may not be effective in all places or contexts, it is absolutely critical that decision-makers have and use local data to monitor their progress. Continuous improvement in homelessness requires lots of types of information, including data on how well a programme reaches its target population, whether the needs of that population are changing, whether interventions have been implemented effectively and whether outcomes are moving as expected.

There is an inherent tension between using data for accountability and using it for programme improvement. When there is a risk of being defunded for showing weaknesses, no one is going to speak candidly about the need to improve. And yet continuous improvement is going to be key to getting to outcomes at scale. To move forward and for it to work in homelessness, we will need to figure out how to be strategic about funding in a way that does not stifle innovation and improvement.

5. Focus equally on systems and practice

For millions of people in the UK, the struggle for stable housing shapes and is shaped by numerous factors, such as financial stability, employment opportunities, wages, housing market dynamics, access to health care and involvement with the care system. The scope and complexity of housing instability and homelessness highlights the need for rigorous evidence on the effectiveness of strategies to prevent and reduce homelessness at population level, rather than just person by person.

Improvements in systems without changes in practice will not deliver the outcomes we need, but without systems reforms, evidence-based practices will have difficulty scaling up. This means we need to attend to evidence, data, and decision-making at many different levels. Effectiveness matters, but so do cost, population and context.

6. Embrace creative confidence and an experimental mindset

To date in homelessness, our appetite for experimentation and risk has been low, even as we trumpet our desire to make big bets. But we are yet to end homelessness for good. We must therefore experiment and find new approaches to create breakthrough change. This will require a fundamental shift in mindset; developing a deep appreciation for failure, iteration and learning.

Fear of uncertain outcomes creates a barrier to creativity and confidence. We often think that if we spend enough time on a problem and collect as much data as possible that we can find a solution. But taking measured risks is an essential part of cultivating innovation. Some funders are recognising this, and, instead of just supporting proven, incremental solutions, they focus on transformation – investing in approaches that may have a higher risk of failure, but the potential to be lasting and truly game-changing if they succeed. For example, in addition to distributing LLINs to reduce the spread of malaria, a funder might also pursue research to genetically alter mosquitos so they cannot transfer the parasite (an effort the Gates Foundation is now actually exploring).

We all want to end homelessness for good. But it took us a long time to build the current system and it will take time to right the ship. If there is one thing we should learn from other fields, it is that there are no silver bullets. If we let our desire to move quickly jeopardise our focus, we risk scepticism about the benefits of evidence-based policy-making altogether. And that would be a missed opportunity.

Using evidence to end homelessness

The following chapters offer a blueprint for how we might go about righting the ship by outlining the current scope and scale of homelessness in the UK before exploring various 'what works' methodologies that will enable us to address it. It is a first step in bringing together disparate voices to unite behind a movement for evidence in homelessness.

In Chapter 2, Jon Sparkes and Matt Downie, of Crisis, explore the current and historic barriers to the adoption of evidence by policy-makers, commissioners and funders in homelessness. They suggest that political will is held back by public understanding; that current UK human rights legislation on homelessness does not go far enough; that society gives itself moral licence to tolerate some forms of homelessness; and that we are wilfully blind to policy change because of systemic complexity. We must address all four challenges to move forward.

Olly Grender looks at the mismanagement of the private rented sector in Chapter 3, and the role it plays in exacerbating homelessness in the UK. Currently, the loss of a private tenancy is the single biggest cause of homelessness in England and, while the UK's other administrations have made some progress in this area, evidence-based reform is urgently required.

In Chapter 4, Danny Dorling makes the case for a new, evidence-informed approach to housing in the UK by looking at the recent sharp rise in the deaths of people experiencing homelessness – particularly in some of the nation's wealthiest regions. Current policy, he says, is failing people of all ages and backgrounds by continuing to treat the symptoms of homelessness for short-term gain.

Poverty is Campbell Robb's focus in Chapter 5, which looks at the systemic factors that currently lock 14.3 million people into poverty in the UK. As one of the major causes of homelessness, addressing poverty is a key priority to drive lasting change. To do so, Robb proposes radical changes to the societal narratives around poverty and homelessness, drawing on detailed research about what does and does not work in effectively communicating about poverty and homelessness.

In Chapter 6 we hear from Neil Coyle, chair of the All-Party Parliamentary Group (APPG) on Ending Homelessness who, since 2016, has been responding to rising homelessness by identifying, exploring and advocating for the best policy solutions to it. He looks specifically at two year-long inquiries into prevention and rapid responses to homelessness that saw the APPG collect written and verbal evidence from key stakeholders from across the homelessness, housing, health, domestic abuse, justice, immigration and young people's sectors, as well as hearing from people with personal experiences of homelessness.

Chapter 7 looks specifically at the extant literature in homelessness from the UK and US, the contrast between the types of studies produced by each country and the drivers of that difference. Dennis Culhane, Suzanne Fitzpatrick and Dan Treglia note that while the US has typically commissioned quantitative 'impact' studies, the UK has, until recently, been more qualitative and conceptual in its research. This has had profound implications on both countries' ability to answer pressing policy and practice questions. Culhane, Fitzpatrick and Treglia then propose shared priorities and opportunities for future co-development.

Chapter 8 zooms out to look at the importance of evidence in a number of different areas of social policy, while also explaining the limitations of certain types of evidence and intervention. Jonathan Breckon and Emma Taylor-Collins of the Alliance for Useful Evidence outline how best to use evidence effectively and draw on examples from the What Works Network to illustrate their thesis.

In Chapter 9, Jo Bibby and Louise Marshall of the Health Foundation define homelessness as a complex social problem. Like public health, they suggest, a complex systems model could be used to conceptualise homelessness as an outcome of a multitude of interdependent elements within a connected whole and set out strategies through which the movement could bring about lasting change.

Stephen Aldridge of the MHCLG uses Chapter 10 to look at the opportunities of data and evidence in UK public policy, outlining the ways in which government is already engaging in complex data linkage in homelessness and other areas of social policy, and how to make evidence-based the 'new normal'. He also makes the fiscal case for using evidence in policy-making to ensure that programmes and interventions are cost effective and deliver desirable return on investment.

In Chapter 11, David Gough and Howard White look at the history of evidence in UK social policy, tracing it back to the 1908 instigation of the Old Age Pensions Act as a result of the sociological writings of Charles Booth and Joseph Seebohm Rowntree. From there it looks at the origins of NICE and the current What Works Network, identifying important lessons in building the evidence architecture for a what works movement in homelessness.

In Chapter 12, Caroline Fiennes elucidates the role of charities and donors in evidence systems, casting research as a behaviour change exercise that must make use of human psychology in order to be effective. She outlines the importance of making evidence accessible and translating it for a particular audience in order to ensure that donors give effectively at each stage of the evidence system.

Following on from this, in Chapter 13, Tracey Brown explains the importance of transparency in enabling the uptake of evidence. Transparency, she says, is a prerequisite to assessing quality, and therefore anyone involved in the generation and use of evidence must be transparent in their motivations and methodology, outlining the best practice for doing so.

Concluding thoughts: bold goals seem impossible ... until they are not

Homelessness is one of the most tragic forms of poverty, and it blights rich countries as much as poor ones. It is one of a growing number of social and economic problems that belie the separation of the world into developed and developing. A new approach is needed that includes a commitment to improving people's lives through data and evidence as its centrepiece.

A huge amount of commitment and effort has only taken us so far until now. And history shows—whether dramatically reducing smoking, alcohol-related traffic fatalities or deaths from malaria—that bold goals seem impossible until they are not.

This effort will not be easy. The challenges facing local areas are complex. And evidence is never black and white. There will always be judgement calls about how to interpret and use data and evidence. But the authors of the chapters in this book believe, rightly, that we can achieve something substantial for everyone in our society – not just those affected or at risk of homelessness – if more and better information is used to guide the vital investments we make in children, their families, individuals and communities.

Now we are shifting gear, and the path ahead is fraught with obstacles, but the biggest leadership challenge for us is to resist temptations to slide off the ultimate goal of ending homelessness sustainably when the going gets tough. The fact that initiatives to end homelessness in the US and elsewhere have often come hand in hand with growing criminalisation of street homelessness should act as cautionary tales. And while there may be a role for enforcement, it should only be used as a last resort and alongside appropriate support.

There's an opportunity to learn from other fields and make lasting change happen. We should build on successes to date and commit to finding our own unique place in creating real change. There is no magic formula for ending homelessness, but we – individuals, the homelessness field and society more generally – should no longer be satisfied with business as usual. Good is no longer good enough when too many people are suffering because they do not have a home to call their own.

Notes

[1] But see the latest 80,000 blog on this topic: https://80000hours.org/articles/effective-social-program/#what-can-we-conclude-from-all-the-above.

[2] https://www.givewell.org/charities/amf.

[3] www.givewell.org/international/technical/programs/cash-transfers.

[4] Homelessness (Abolition of Priority Need Test) (Scotland) Order 2012: www.legislation.gov.uk/sdsi/2012/9780111018187.

References

Brinkman, S.A., Johnson, S.E., Codde, J.P., Hart, M.B., Straton, J.A., Mittinty, M.N. 2016. Efficacy of infant simulator programmes to prevent teenage pregnancy: a school-based cluster randomised controlled trial in Western Australia. *Lancet*, 388: 2264–71. www.thelancet.com/journals/lancet/article/PIIS0140-6736(16)30384-1/fulltext.

Fitzpatrick, S. et al. 2011–19. *Homelessness Monitor Series*. London: Crisis. www.crisis.org.uk/ending-homelessness/homelessness-knowledge-hub/homelessness-monitor/.

Feynman, R. 1966. What Is Science? Presented at the fifteenth annual meeting of the National Science Teachers Association, 1966, in New York City, and reprinted from *The Physics Teacher* (7)6, 1969, pp. 313–20.

Halpern, D. 2016. *Inside the Nudge Unit*. London: WH Allen.

MHCLG. 2019a. *Homelessness Case Level Information Collection (H-CLIC) Specification*. London: MHCLG. https://gss.civilservice.gov.uk/wp-content/uploads/2019/04/HCLIC-Data-Specification_v1.4.4.pdf.

MHCLG. 2019b. *Homelessness: Causes of Homelessness and Rough Sleeping*. London: MHCLG. https://assets.publishing.service.gov.uk/government/uploads/system/uploads/attachment_data/file/793471/Homelessness_-_REA.pdf.

MHCLG. 2019c. *Rough Sleeping Initiative 2018: Impact Evaluation*. London: MHCLG. www.gov.uk/government/publications/rough-sleeping-initiative-2018-impact-evaluation.

Morabia, A. 2006. Pierre-Charles-Alexandre Louis and the evaluation of bloodletting. *Journal of the Royal Society for Medicine*, 99(3): 158–60. www.ncbi.nlm.nih.gov/pmc/articles/PMC1383766/.

Washington State Institute for Public Policy. 2004. *Benefits and Costs of Prevention and Early Intervention of Programs for Youth.* Olympia, WA: Washington State Institute for Public Policy. http://www.wsipp.wa.gov/ReportFile/881/Wsipp_Benefits-and-Costs-of-Prevention-and-Early-Intervention-Programs-for-Youth_Summary-Report.pdf/.

Waugh, A., Clarke, A., Knowles, J., Rowley, D. 2018. *Health and Homelessness in Scotland: Research.* Scottish Government, Edinburgh. www.gov.scot/publications/health-homelessness-scotland/.

2

A new approach to ending homelessness

Jon Sparkes and Matt Downie

Fifty years after the homelessness sector was founded, in some ways our collective mission to end homelessness feels renewed. The problem of homelessness is once again of a scale and severity that demands we think more deeply about a solution. Together with advocates, decision-makers and our fellow service providers, we must remake a consensus to end homelessness.

In delivering and then reflecting on our own 50th anniversary year at Crisis, we have learned a lot about the critical factors of ending homelessness and the barriers we must overcome. This chapter collects many of those lessons and, in particular, seeks to ask why it is that when we know so much about how to end homelessness it is still not happening.

These are not simply theoretical questions. They pose real challenges of leadership that must be answered before the spotlight of political and media attention moves away from our issue.

What is 'ending homelessness' and why define it?

In 2018, Crisis published a landmark report called *Everybody In: How to End Homelessness in Great Britain* (Downie et al,

2018). The first of its kind, this report brought together the best-known evidence of solutions to the problem at home and abroad, and from academic, front line and lived experiences of homelessness.

Perhaps the most difficult and contested territory was the basic question of how to quantify what the problem is and how to precisely define 'homelessness ended'. To this end we ran a six-month consultation dedicated to the question of defining and explaining that definition.

Two things guided our discussions. First, the fact that strategies and definitions that are limited to ending rough sleeping at home and abroad are insufficient. They stop short of what is required to end rough sleeping itself, because to do so requires us to prevent other forms of homelessness too. They are also insufficient because an ambition to end rough sleeping alone is to admit defeat in tackling pernicious and completely solvable homelessness for people living in hostels, night shelters, bed and breakfasts, etc.

Second, our discussions were guided by a desire to push the boundaries of interest and responsibility for ending homelessness out of the limits of statutory homelessness services. To truly prevent homelessness, we must confront the fact that many public services and agencies, alongside housing providers, know full well that people they serve are at acute risk of having nowhere to live but take no responsibility or action to prevent it.

Discussions across the three nations of Britain helped craft a new definition. The definition extends ambition from residual approaches but stops short of the utopian 'absolute zero'[1] approach that many would view as impossible to achieve:

- No one sleeping rough.
- No one forced to live in transient or dangerous accommodation such as tents, squats and non-residential buildings.
- No one living in emergency accommodation, such as shelters and hostels, without a plan for rapid rehousing into affordable, secure and decent accommodation.
- No one homeless as a result of leaving a state institution such as prison or the care system.

- Everyone at immediate risk of homelessness gets the help that prevents it happening.

There are many reasons to detail and agree a definition, but one reason has become urgent.

It is often said that 'what gets measured gets done', and this is certainly true within homelessness. But what if we only measure a small fraction of homelessness? What if this leads to disjointed and even counterproductive policies that neither tackle the root causes nor provide long-term evidence-based solutions.

This is exactly what is going on in England, with a heavy and sometimes exclusive focus on rough sleeping, now backed by one singular target and definition; to halve rough sleeping by 2022 and end it by 2024. This is strikingly different from the approach in Scotland where the government has committed to end homelessness more widely, including rough sleeping (Scottish Government, 2018).

The politics of homelessness

Following the publication of our plan to end homelessness, we have sought to engage governments in England, Scotland and Wales in building a new shared ambition. Our hope is that politicians of all parties can be persuaded to adopt a full definition of 'homelessness ended', to establish a target for reaching this goal, and to work with our sector to produce an evidence-based strategy to achieve it.

We have a long way to go before political parties and governments are persuaded of this vision.

In the past, sharp rises in homelessness have led to new political pressure to tackle it, perhaps most famously with the rough sleeping initiatives (RSIs) in England and Scotland in the late 1990s. These led to two-thirds and one-third reductions in numbers respectively.[2] Then, as now, media and public concern about the most visible form of homelessness is high, and naturally politicians react to it.

Rough sleeping is of course unacceptable, and the personal danger faced by every person living on the streets should be considered an emergency. We have learned, however, that the political clamour for immediate results exclusively to reduce rough sleeping can in fact produce limited results. Unless these initiatives are accompanied by broader strategies to prevent all forms of homelessness, and to house and support everyone currently homeless, they do not achieve an end to rough sleeping, let alone to the wider definition of 'homelessness ended'.

It is rare for rough sleeping to be the first form of homelessness that an individual or household endures. Very often it occurs following, or alongside periods of transient 'sofa surfing' and short-term stays in emergency accommodation such as hostels, refuges and night shelters.

This means that strategies to simply address living on the streets are unlikely to resolve the reasons individuals become homeless in the first place. Moreover, if the solution provided to resolve rough sleeping is the provision of emergency accommodation, this is self-evidently not resolving homelessness, and risks an immediate return to the streets for many people for whom this approach does not work.

The success of rough sleeping reduction programmes in the 1990s and 2000s has been rightly highlighted and celebrated. But the cold reality is that these initiatives did not end rough sleeping or other forms of homelessness, and nor did they sufficiently tackle the root causes of the problem.

We must learn and bank the successful lessons of the past, but to repeat the same strategies will be to repeat the same limited and short-term results. There may be political quick fixes to the most obvious form of homelessness, but this cannot and will not be enough.

Evidence-based homelessness strategy

The good news is that the evidence about how to end and prevent homelessness much more effectively has improved in the last two decades. And in recent times the value of evidence-based policy and service provision has begun to be discussed in relation to homelessness. Of course, there is a long way to go until all gaps in evidence are completed, but we have come a long way.

The test of the coming few years is whether advocates can persuade decision-makers to take the opportunity of public pressure to adopt sustainable, long-term and evidence-based strategies.

We recently commissioned two major systematic evidence reviews; one into solutions to homelessness and another dedicated to rough sleeping (Social Care Institute for Excellence, 2018; Mackie et al, 2017). Without repeating the full conclusions of these reviews, some themes emerged that pose fundamental questions for our sector and for decision-makers.

One repeated frustration is that evidence of what works does not seem to lead to that evidence being adopted by policy-makers, commissioners and funders. For example, it has been known for some time that resettlement and discharge arrangements from hospitals, prisons and other state provision can both prevent and resolve homelessness (Homeless Link, 2015). Similarly, the provision of mental health specialism in outreach services is widely accepted as vital but has rarely been sufficiently backed or funded. Our own experience of supporting a large and successful private renting support programme is similar (Rugg, 2014). It works, it saves money, but ultimately falls by the wayside of policy change.

While these are good examples of programmes with some evaluative evidence, there is a similar frustration relating to those with the most rigorous evidence base. It has been known and proven for some time that housing-led approaches to solving homelessness are more effective than 'staircase' models that make requirements of homeless people to prove they are ready for mainstream housing.

The provision of homelessness services in the UK are not binary, with simple extremes of housing-led and staircase provision (unlike in some parts of North America and elsewhere). Yet, we are still a long way from realising the potential of an evidence base of housing-led approaches. For example, the potential cohort of Housing First tenants is 18,500, yet only around 400 people actually access this most evidence-based of all homelessness schemes (Blood et al, 2018).

Again, Scotland is emerging as an exception, with stated backing for housing-led and rapid rehousing approaches and the ongoing work of all local authorities to deliver rapid rehousing transition plans to make housing-led approaches the default instead of the exceptions. But until this reaches fruition, and particularly until this disparity between the evidence and the policy, funding and provision is addressed across Britain, we have to ask why an outdated and increasingly discredited default of emergency accommodation still prevails?

Can we work out why?

Pointing to the simple existence of evidence-based programmes, or of successful state-led strategies to eradicate homelessness internationally has not shifted policy on homelessness (at least in England and Wales). While we cannot assume the evidence base is complete, this is very frustrating for advocates in the sector. But simply being annoyed about it will not get us anywhere. We must think more deeply about why. What is it that sustains the gap between professional knowledge and public policy? Why is homelessness practice so difficult to challenge and reform?

In the next section are some suggested ways of thinking about these questions. None are sufficient in isolation. Each is intended to provoke new thinking that may help break the impasse we face. Each also presents a challenge to Crisis, and colleagues from across the housing and homelessness sectors, to do things differently.

1. Political will is held back by public understanding of homelessness

During 2017–18 the Frameworks Institute was commissioned by Crisis to conduct the largest UK study to date of public attitudes relating to homelessness (Nichols et al, 2018). But before asking what people consider the causes and solutions to the problem, the analysts first asked homelessness experts to explain what they would like the public to think. In other words, they compared what we are trying to say with what is being heard and understood.

If you consider politicians and decision-makers to be responsive in any sense to public opinion then this analysis matters. It matters more directly if politicians are responsive to the same materials and discourse as the public.

Our sector communicates about homelessness a lot. At Crisis alone we send out many millions of direct messages to our valued supporters via physical and digital means. Alongside many other organisations, we also employ communications experts to generate mass broadcast, print, online, and social media coverage of our issue. This is all vital to sustain the mixed economy of voluntary income-funded services and to apply pressure to achieve positive policy chance. But what are the secondary effects and long-term trends of our communications?

The Frameworks Institute findings are stark. Our sector is seeking to explain the structural causes of homelessness in housing, welfare and social services policy, but the public are not hearing this. Instead they view the problem as individually driven by poor choices, behaviour or simple bad luck. We are also trying to explain the diversity of what homelessness is aside from rough sleeping, and of the range of people it affects, but the public almost exclusively equate homelessness with living on the street, and they have a narrow mental image of who is homeless – namely older men with substance addictions.

Over decades these cultural norms have been built up and sustained by the very people and organisations seeking to challenge or disagree with them. The analysis shows the disproportionate prevalence of rough sleeping stories in our communications. We have repeatedly provided stereotypical images that bolster existing cultural assumptions. And, perhaps most importantly, we collectively fail to tell stories that confirm the link between individual homelessness and structural policy causes.

This poses a strategic communication challenge. Our sector must find new and improved framing of homelessness that shifts public responses to a more productive understanding of our issue. We also have a responsibility to do this while continuing to grow our collective success in winning public and media support.

It will not be easy but, until we convincingly do so, we inhibit the potential of public support for the real political solutions to homelessness. To drive and sustain the right solutions, politicians need to feel the pressure of a different public understanding.

2. Homelessness is a human rights crisis

Human rights and homelessness have a complicated relationship in the UK. Working in homelessness you often hear people talk about housing as a 'basic human right'. In reality, while the Universal Declaration of Human Rights confers this right to housing, it is (alongside subsequent conventions) a non-binding treaty and, unlike other countries, the unwritten constitution of the UK does not protect or ratify this human right.

Meanwhile, the UK does have some of the most generous and 'rights-based' approaches to rehousing people experiencing homelessness anywhere in the world (Downie et al, 2018). Starting with the Housing (Homeless Persons) Act 1977, the UK led the way in enshrining legal entitlements for rehousing to groups of 'priority' homeless households. Since 1977 this legal entitlement has extended in different ways across the UK, with Scotland going furthest to extend it to all eligible homeless households in 2003.

This legal framework does not strictly give people a 'right' to rehousing, but an entitlement if local authorities deem them to have met strict criteria. More than four million households have benefited from this entitlement since 1977. The downside of this success is that there are catastrophic consequences for those that fail to qualify under the arbitrary tests set out in law and guidance for local authorities.

Hard-wired into this system is the idea of deserving and undeserving homeless people. Under a truly rights rights-based approach this should not be possible. Even in Scotland, the most generous of all statutory homeless systems, there are still winners and losers, and the concept of 'non-eligible' homeless people survives.

Recent criticism of human rights approaches to social problems points to the risk that the original purpose of tangible and material equality among citizens has been lost. Instead, human rights advocates are seen to have accepted a 'sufficiency' argument, limiting their aspirations for the poor to the basic minimum of shelter, warmth, etc (Moyn, 2018). This resonates in the UK, where our non-codified rights are rationed and reduced, leaving strategies that find it sufficient that some citizens will remain in slightly more favourable forms of homelessness such as night shelters, hostels, refuges, etc.

An often overlooked but crucial element of the Finnish success in reducing homelessness is the fact that in 1990 the Finnish Government incorporated the European Convention on Human Rights (ECHR) 'right to private [and family] life' within domestic law (Article 8). At a stroke this challenged the legitimacy of the most basic and services that seek to manage rather than end homelessness.

Perhaps we have a lesson to learn here. It is right to argue for a complete legal safety net of homelessness assistance, but maybe it is also time to take the argument further and to advocate a full expression of a 'right to housing'. This would lift collective aspirations, would require adequate housing supply and access, and would find it unacceptable to allow people to live in emergency and temporary accommodation.

The Frameworks Institute analysis provided strong evidence that when resolving homelessness is presented as a 'moral human right' people are more likely to support the policy changes needed to end homelessness. This could be a good place to start.

3. Do we give ourselves the 'moral licence' to tolerate some forms of homelessness?

Political speeches on homelessness normally follow a narrative arc that starts with a declaration that in 21st century Britain homelessness is unacceptable. They then go on to detail the initiatives that have been implemented or proposed to resolve an element of homelessness (normally relating to rough sleeping or a particular cohort such as youth homelessness). This mismatch between the complete conceptual problem and the residual practical solutions will vary in detail, but is persistently present.

Could it be that by demonstrating a commitment and some action (however successful) to resolve a portion of homelessness, that a 'moral licence' is granted to go no further in committing to a full and unequivocal end to homelessness?

Moral licensing[3] is the idea that by doing the 'right thing' in a limited sense the human brain (individually or collectively) is convinced it is absolved, or off the hook, for wider positive action. This is also sometimes referred to as the 'halo effect', where limited progress blinds us to the bigger picture or goal.

In relation to homelessness, this may relate to both a policy and service delivery. Does the provision of life-saving help, such as severe weather shelter, allow license to stop short of the evidence-based policies and programmes we know would resolve the issue sustainably?

In the grand scheme of policy-making, moral licensing may well explain why certain policies that directly contribute to homelessness – reduced housing benefits, benefit sanctions – are deemed tolerable. Recently, the National Audit Office pointed to the illogical reality of some departmental policies creating homelessness in England while other departments are charged with picking up the pieces (National Audit Office, 2017).

This idea resonates too when you consider how homeless people are compartmentalised into certain groups that receive assistance and others that do not. Dating back to the Vagrancy Act 1824, certain people experiencing homelessness are even deemed worthy of criminal punishment if they are somehow seen to have made a 'choice' to be homeless.

The licence we collectively accept – that some people will not be helped out of homelessness – is pernicious and harmful and will only result in the problem continuing until such time as we challenge this thinking.

4. Are we 'wilfully blind' to changing our approach

The social theory of 'wilful blindness' is perhaps the most sensitive and difficult to consider for our sector. The concept has its origins in 19th-century criminal law, where the accused was considered to be wilfully blind if they knowingly avoided salient facts about the legal framework that would otherwise render them liable for a crime.

More recently, the concept has been applied to a range of personal and professional life settings, and has become an established explanation of organisational dysfunction (Heffernan, 2012). Most famous was the Enron scandal where bosses were accused of shutting their eyes to obvious and available facts, and closer to home the conduct of News International in relation to phone hacking was also described as 'wilful blindness' (Heffernan, 2011).

The central idea is that groups of people will fail to fix a problem that they refuse to acknowledge. The reason for this is that we often surround ourselves with people who think like us and share our ideals and values. In turn, this allows us to construct a world that feels safe but can also blind us to valuable information, facts and behaviours that should alert us.

We stay silent when we should speak out or question for fear of being criticised, and often overlook threats and dangers that should otherwise be obvious. Our brains are wired to wilfully blind ourselves to evidence that contradicts our beliefs. And we can also block out the uncomfortable realities of life to save ourselves the hard evidence that contradicts our beliefs.

Could this theory help explain why it is so hard for homelessness policy-makers to see and act upon the evidence of what is driving and sustaining the problem? After all, there will always be confirmation on offer that credits any progress in tackling homeless is a good thing. Could it also help explain why it is so difficult to shift commissioning of homelessness services from interventions with little or no evidence, to those with a compelling proof of success?

It is important to state that choices in policy and practice are by no means simple and binary. It is also important to recognise that nobody involved in policy-making or service provision is actively choosing to create or sustain homelessness.

Nonetheless, a key lesson we have learned in the last year is that when bold and evidence-based solutions on homelessness are presented, there are powerful forces at play that stop or slow progress. The conformity to existing approaches, to maintaining or even growing the provision of services that demonstrably are not ending homelessness, is a real problem.

At Crisis, we know very well that changing service models that have existed for many years is difficult. It can be difficult, traumatic even, to accept that wholesale change is necessary. Understanding the concerns people have about change and applying a sensitive approach to managing it are paramount.

By seeking out other perspectives and questioning the evidence used to back our choices, we can avoid falling into complacency and conformity.

The art of the possible

Talk of ending homelessness on a national scale can be daunting, especially in these times of smaller and still shrinking budgets for many public bodies and sector agencies. It is also easy to understand why politicians are cautious to over-commit. They know it would take years to redress the erosion of social housing in England and the restatement of housing benefits at the levels required across Great Britain.

This is why our plan to end homelessness sets out a ten-year agenda for achieving it. Not ten years from today, but ten years from the publication of a strategy to achieve the aim, including all the necessary measures.

As we have already done in Scotland through our work to support and chair the Homelessness and Rough Sleeping Action Group in 2018, we stand ready to help build the strategy for an end to homelessness in England and Wales. We want to help governments and political parties make bold choices, not to accuse decision-makers of getting it wrong. We are not alone in this. Our sector is full of willing specialists in every area, from housing supply, rapid rehousing, prevention, migrant homelessness, and Housing First, to trauma-informed services, specialist outreach any many more specialist topics.

We will continue to make the case for national strategies. But until these are in place there are also other measures we can take to help demonstrate success at a smaller scale.

This is why we worked together with Glasgow Homelessness Network to create the Centre for Homelessness Impact (CHI), and it is our sincere hope that CHI will play a crucial role in demonstrating the potential of individual programmes that tackle homelessness. Perhaps more important though is the role the Centre can play in spreading the value and use of evidence-based policy and practice itself. This is why we have been so keen to invest in CHI and will continue to champion its unique role as an independent and impartial new What Works Centre.

We have also been working with a number of local authorities to establish the principles and policy changes of our plan to end homelessness within local areas. This has led to new partnerships to produce and deliver ten-year strategies to end homelessness. These partnerships will work to our definition of 'homelessness ended'. They will also involve a significant investment of new staff from Crisis, and a commitment to trial and refine evidence-based approaches to housing and supporting for every homeless person in those areas.

By investing heavily in service-delivery, and through a rights-based approach, we hope to provide lessons that demonstrate the art of the possible.

Conclusion

Publishing a plan to end homelessness was a bold move. We are aware that nobody asked us to do it and that we occupy no greater right to do so than anyone else.

The lessons we have learned since publication have not been that the content of our plan is incorrect – even the boldest legal and policy reforms have not been challenged. Instead, it has quickly become clear that we do not yet have the social consensus needed to make the necessary reforms a reality across all of Britain.

The people experiencing homelessness that we seek to serve demand that we sort this out. We do not need a recycled consensus that mirrors incomplete solutions of the past, but a new one, backed by evidence, rigour and unshakable resolve.

The opportunity to end homelessness exists only if we consciously acknowledge that we have failed to date and allow an honest discussion as to why this is the case. Fifty years after our sector was formed, after *Cathy Come Home* first shook public and political consciousness, we could form a new and powerful movement to end homelessness for good.

This requires us to root out any semblance of wilful blindness or moral licensing, and to frame the issue in positive solutions, not deficits and stereotypes of 'the homeless'. Let us stop talking about our work to 'tackle' homelessness and instead describe and act on our obligation to help people exercise their rights. If we do not talk and act in this way how can we expect politicians to do so?

A new approach to ending homelessness needs better data and evidence and positive social policy, but much more than these it requires passionate people who never compromise or dilute our aspirations. This could be the beginning of a new movement.

Notes

[1] https://homelesshub.ca/sites/default/files/Absolute-Zero-Turner-Albanese-Pakeman_0.pdf.

[2] https://webarchive.nationalarchives.gov.uk/20120919233902/http://www.communities.gov.uk/documents/housing/pdf/137995.pdf.

[3] http://adam.curry.com/enc/20140824153442_monin2010compasson morallicensing.pdf.

References

Blood, I., Goldup, M., Peter, L. and Dulson, S. 2018. *Implementing Housing First Across England, Scotland and Wales.* London: Crisis and Homeless Link.

Downie, M., Gousy, H., Basran, J., Jacob, R., Rowe, S., Hancock, C., Albanese, F., Pritchard, R., Nightingale, K. and Davies, T. 2018. *Everybody In: How to End Homelessness in Great Britain.* London: Crisis.

Heffernan, M. 2011. Wilful blindness – why we ignore the obvious at our peril. *New Statesman,* 8 August. https://www.newstatesman.com/ideas/2011/08/wilful-blindness-essay-news.

Heffernan, M. 2012. *Wilful Blindness: Why We Ignore the Obvious at Our Peril.* London: Simon & Schuster.

Homeless Link. 2015. *Evaluation of the Homeless Hospital Discharge Fund.* London: Homeless Link. www.homeless.org.uk/sites/default/files/site-attachments/Evaluation%20of%20the%20Homeless%20Hospital%20Discharge%20Fund%20FINAL.pdf.

Mackie, P., Johnsen, S., and Wood, J. 2017. *Ending Rough Sleeping: What Works? An International Evidence Review.* London: Crisis.

Moyn, S. 2018. *Not Enough: Human Rights in an Unequal World.* Cambridge, MA: Harvard University Press.

National Audit Office. 2017. *Homelessness.* London: National Audit Office. https://www.nao.org.uk/report/homelessness/.

Nichols, J., Volmert, A., Busso, D., Gerstein Pineau, M., O'Neil, M. and Kendall-Taylor, N. 2018. *Reframing Homelessness in the United Kingdom: A FrameWorks MessageMemo*. London: FrameWorks Institute.

Rugg, J. 2014. *Crisis Private Rented Sector Access Development Programme: Year Two to April 2013*. York: University of York.

Scottish Government. 2018. *Ending Homelessness Together: High Level Action Plan*. Edinburgh: Scottish Government. www.gov.scot/binaries/content/documents/govscot/publications/publication/2018/11/ending-homelessness-together-high-level-action-plan/documents/00543359-pdf/00543359-pdf/govscot%3Adocument.

Social Care Institute for Excellence. 2018. *A Rapid Evidence Assessment of What Works in Homelessness Services*, London: Crisis.

3

Reform in the private rented sector

Olly Grender

In all discussions of homelessness, the circular debate about where the blame lies for lack of investment and housing supply is rehashed again and again in the political world. Meanwhile the targets for social housing become greater and even less tangible in the minds of the numerous policy-makers who have heard these pleas for decades and failed to make measurable progress. Indeed the evidence and data regarding the need to build more homes suitable for people on the lowest income is not disputed, but the financial ask from politicians is significant, beyond their wildest expenditure imaginations.

Always the poor relation in this whole sorry argument is the tenant, who rents privately, in a country and culture that was never designed with their interests in mind. Evidence regarding this wide and varied community is scant. No wonder then that the policy response to renting has been piecemeal and reactive, rather than evidence-based and strategic.

Surely that has to change as the number of renters grows? Significant change for tenants in recognition of their growing numbers is still at best a work in progress. Add to that the fact that almost a fifth of MPs are declared landlords – which does not include any additional work with interests in property firms[1] – and the picture becomes bleak. It is telling that, with the best will in the world, the people that form policy in the UK tend to be people with mortgages, property owners or landlords and not those experiencing the insecurity of renting. That is why an evidence-informed agenda in this sector is long overdue.

If, as latest information suggests, half of all babies born in the UK start their lives in a rented home[2] it is worth understanding just how secure and safe those children are. In just ten years, the number of families with children in the private rented sector (PRS) has risen by 94 per cent. That would be fine if the UK had a history of renting like other countries with a lengthy stay, stable rents, and equal value in society. But it does not. The loss of a private tenancy in England is now the single biggest cause of homelessness. This is the recipe for a perfect storm.[3]

The constant drive throughout all the nations in the UK for more than two generations has been about property ownership. Ownership is an aspiration that, culturally, runs deep and means that people in their 30s and 40s who live in rented accommodation today are unlikely to be there out of positive choice. According to the Resolution Foundation, due to 'falling home ownership and a shrinking social rented sector, four out of every ten 30-year-olds now live in private rented accommodation – in contrast to one in ten 50 years ago' (Corelette and Judge, 2017). The argument is often used that private renting gives younger people freedom and flexibility, but only 6 per cent (in England) give that as the main reason they rent.[4]

Compare that to elsewhere in Europe – Germany, for instance, where rents are kept low and evictions are difficult. More people rent, raise their children in rented accommodation and see them through school before downsizing to somewhere more suitable. It is seen as a long-term option. By contrast, in England if you rent you are six times more likely to move than someone who owns their own property.

Defining a tenant in the PRS

Part of the problem is defining with clarity who in the PRS needs help and identifying the greater rights that could help them. The vast mix of demographics among tenants means that generic policy-making is difficult in this area. A tenant could be an extremely wealthy individual in a penthouse overlooking the Thames or an economic migrant living in an illegal slum rental, bed-sharing with 15 others in an unventilated room. Between those two extremes runs a gamut of students, people in temporary accommodation, tenants on housing benefits, young professionals and families. The wider use of big data and machine learning presents an opportunity to improve this lack of definition and allow government to be more targeted in future.

I first arrived in Parliament in Autumn 2013. At the same time two friends who rented were going through a tough time. One was in the PRS, with two children in primary school and a landlord determined to evict them as a result of her requests to improve the state of the property – a classic retaliatory eviction. Another was in a council flat, whose rights to be self-employed were severely restricted by the leasehold arrangements of the council. It was striking how both were in different ways being treated as second-class citizens. Both felt they had little power over their own futures: one doing exactly what the state wanted and seeking self-employment but then hampered by the state because of the terms of her lease; the other being advised to wait until she was evicted so that she could then be clearly defined as statutorily homeless – a ridiculous Catch 22 for someone with two school-age children.

If you are cash rich and upwardly mobile, your rights as a tenant are less significant. But if you are on a low or average income and living in the PRS, you live on a permanent cliff edge of insecurity.

The connection between a PRS tenancy and homelessness inevitably affects those caught in that sector who should really be in social housing. The PRS is caught between owner occupation and social rent and includes individuals at either end of that spectrum who do not want to be in the PRS.

The long pathway to rational change

For at least a decade the case was made that fees to lettings agents in addition to rent, utilities and council tax were prohibitively expensive, in particular for those on low or medium incomes.

I introduced a Private Members Bill in 2016 that sought to ban the fees. I made the case that, unlike the relative stability of the owner-occupied market, a quarter of current private renters moved last year, they are six times more likely than owner-occupiers and three times more likely than social renters to move (MHCLG, 2017).

Each time they move, the up-front costs are often significant. In London, the median amount that renters must pay before moving is £1,500,[5] and in many cases the cost is several thousand pounds. It goes up disproportionately for those on low incomes, who are viewed as a higher risk and so may be required to provide several months' rent in advance. Indeed, of those who rent on a very low budget, a third have to borrow or use a loan to pay up-front fees and 17 per cent have to cut down on heating and food to cover the up-front cost of moving.

Some examples from Shelter of the types of fees charged were £45 for the procurement of a dustpan and brush; another £200 to remove a set of saucepans left for the next tenant. The real rip off – often used – was the mark up on reference and credit checks – examples of £500 and more. Citizens Advice had seen an 8 per cent increase in complaints about lettings agents. One tenant had described to them a fee of £180 to renew a tenancy agreement with no work at all. Generation Rent estimated from a volunteer research project on more than 1,000 agents in England that the cost was over £400 for a new tenant (Parsons, 2016).

At the time, the Government's argument was that the number of lettings agencies who over-charged tenants was limited and that existing consumer protection legislation meant that details of fees must be prominently displayed or lettings agencies would face a fine. They argued that rents would rise and the impact on the lettings agencies industry would be negative.

There was little interest shown in the change in Scotland in 2012 to ban fees beyond rent and a refundable deposit. The only research that existed was by Shelter, which showed negligible impact on rents or lettings agencies (Shelter, 2014). Had more research been conducted into the progress of the change in Scotland – perhaps by the Scottish Government – it is possible that we would not have waited until 2019 for this change in England. The consequence of lack of analysis is that the significant numbers who were overcharged fees continued at least for another six years, and, in some cases, for ten years.

In the 2016 Autumn Statement, the Government responded to public pressure and campaigns led by journalist Vicky Spratt, among others. The desire to fulfil the original aims of Theresa May when she first became prime minister and pledged to fight against burning injustice was also significant. The Government changed their minds and announced a ban on lettings fees. They consulted from April to June 2017. The snap general election of 2017 and the impact of Brexit on government meant significant delay on delivering this promise. But the bans finally started on 1 June 2019 and private renters will no longer have to pay a fee for a new tenancy in England. Refundable holding and security deposits will also be capped. There is also an obligation of greater transparency when a holding fee is not returned.

As this ban becomes law, there will be claims and counterclaims about its impact – will rents rise as a result, will the lettings agency industry decline with resulting job losses? It will be critical that this legislation is rigorously monitored and evaluated to ensure that it does, as intended, help precarious renters.

End of tenancy, start of homelessness

In the PRS, the prohibitively expensive up-front fees, a rise in rent, an eviction and the short-term nature of a private rented tenancy can be reasons someone leaves a rental and ends up in serious debt or, worse, homeless.

A significant impact over recent years has been the shortfall in funding for those on benefits including local housing allowance (LHA). An investigation in *The Times* by Rachel Sylvester and Alice Thomson revealed a gap between housing benefit and rents in 95 per cent of England (Sylvester and Thomson, 2018). Housing benefit is still at 2011 rent levels and has been frozen since 2016, but rents have risen by an average of 16 per cent since 2011. Despite the fact that housing benefit is due to be unfrozen in April 2020, this measure on its own does not go far enough.

Tenants who are in the PRS and receiving benefits are stigmatised by both the financial shortfall and cultural assumptions – that they do not work hard, that they do not pay rent in full and on time. These opinions contradict the evidence. Landlords are currently able to specify 'no DSS' when advertising. Research by Shelter and the National Housing Federation exposed discriminatory practices, showing that six in ten landlords prefer not to rent to tenants receiving housing benefit (Shelter, 2018). The same research shows that the leading factor in discrimination against housing benefit tenants is advice from letting agents.

The connection between benefit shortfalls and homelessness are clear. All available evidence points to LHA reforms as a major driver of this association between loss of private tenancies and homelessness. These reforms have also demonstrably restricted lower-income households' access to the PRS. The number of housing benefit/universal credit claimants who are private tenants is now some 5 per cent lower than when the LHA reforms began in 2011, despite strong continuing growth in the PRS overall. This policy has also, as intended, had a particularly marked impact in inner London.

In 2016, the BBC broadcast a documentary by Sarah Montague called *After Cathy*, 50 years on from Ken Loach's *Cathy Come Home*. It featured the audio diaries of three people experiencing homelessness over the course of a year. One of them, Zara (not her real name) from London, a teacher and mum of two children aged 11 and three, had lived in the same private rented home for six years when her landlord put up her rent. She could not afford to move to cheaper accommodation because she could not afford the up-front costs of moving. This teacher was homeless and had been living in emergency accommodation with her children for a year – a teacher. She had sensibly left a tenancy she could not afford and found a cheaper rental, but the prohibitive up-front fees meant that she could not afford to move in.

The lack of social housing and affordable housing means that a significant number of people are living in the PRS when they really need a safety net of subsidised housing with full support.

The Help to Rent programme, like the one run by Crisis, aims to overcome this lack of support. They provide funding to ensure secure long-lasting tenancies in decent properties. From 2010, government funding helped deliver more than 10,000 private tenancies for people experiencing homelessness, a scheme the Government ended in 2016 but has revived in 2017 with £20 million of funding. It could be argued that the lack of rigorous evaluation at the time this programme was introduced resulted in its suspension in 2016.

Low income renters: second-class citizens

Take two people – Ms Owner Occupier and Ms Private Renter. They earn similar incomes (roughly the current median wage £28,677). Ms Occupier has defaulted a couple of times on her mortgage. It is at an extremely high level, but she spends just 19 per cent of her income on housing, whereas Ms Renter spends 41 per cent of her income (based on government housing survey averages). She already pays more than 10 per cent higher than what is defined as affordable and double that of Ms Occupier. They both want to buy a fridge but neither has ready cash so they need to buy it on hire purchase. Even though Ms Renter – rather typical of over 90 per cent of all renters – is not in arrears and has always paid her rent in full and on time, she will end up paying anywhere between £300 and £1,000 more than Ms Occupier as she is thought to be a higher risk. Unequal and unfair.

The Big Issue Invest's Rental Exchange programme is trying to turn this kind of situation around for social renters. Since launching in 2010, more than 1.5 million tenants across the UK have been represented by the scheme using rent and council tax data to generate a financial footprint for renters. In more than 80 per cent of cases, tenants gain an improved credit score when their rent data is shared and the evidence shows a jump from 39 to 84 per cent in their digital identity where rent data is included in credit files.

Thus, renters become 'valued customers'. As the Financial Inclusion Commission report published in September 2018 said: 'lower cost lenders could be willing to lower their income thresholds for loans if they had access to additional information on household income and earnings. Lowering the threshold from £15,000 to £12,000 per annum could make an additional 4.8m consumers more attractive to mainstream and lower cost lenders.' That is, the 4.8 million consumers who currently struggle to access normal levels of credit for no logical reason. At present, those same renters are in the poverty trap so common to people who rent on low or middle incomes.

Conditions, evictions and enforcement

The link between poor conditions in the PRS and the danger of retaliatory evictions is all too obvious. Ask anyone in the sector about problems and many of them think twice or never about complaining for fear of facing a rent increase or eviction. Karen Buck MP introduced the Homes (Fitness for Human Habitation) Act 2018 with all party support. Since 20 March 2019 newly let properties must be fit for human habitation at the start of and throughout the tenancy.

As the Communities and Local Government Committee in the House of Commons concluded in April 2018, while most of the PRS is an adequate standard 'a significant minority of private rented accommodation is shockingly inadequate'. The percentage of inadequate properties has fallen, but the absolute number has risen to 80,000, more than in 2006. Government statistics showed that, in 2016, there were approximately 800,000 private rented homes in England with at least one category one hazard, as identified by the housing health and safety rating system (HHSRS).[6] They also concluded that:

> [T]here is a clear power imbalance in the private rented sector, with tenants often unwilling to complain to landlords about the conditions in their homes for fear of retaliation. In our view consumer rights are meaningless without the guarantee that tenants will be able to use them in practice without fear of retaliation.

There is still considerable evidence that tenants are reluctant to be their own enforcers, in which case the responsibility falls to the local authority. Current data suggests that local authorities are equally unable to fulfil this role. In 2013–14 fewer than 2 per cent of all PRS properties were inspected. While that has improved in recent years, it is still woefully low. Indeed the Residential Landlords Association (RLA) report *The Postcode Lottery of Local Authority Enforcement in the Private Rented Sector* suggests that while greater powers have been afforded to local authorities along with the use of civil penalty notices up to £30,000, the enforcement is sporadic with '67% of local authorities not commencing a single prosecution against a private landlords in 2017/18'. Their research also found that 89 per cent of local authorities reported they had not used the new powers and over half did not have a policy to use them (Simcock and Mykkanen, 2018). Contrast that with the London Borough of Newham, whose much more proactive approach to enforcement is responsible for 60 per cent of all prosecutions in London and 50 per cent in England.

As a result of their report, RLA call for greater resource for local authorities and simplification of the different systems that impact the PRS, including the HHSRS and the decent homes standards. Over the next two years it will be critical to monitor how often local authorities are using the enforcement and how much income they are making from the enforcement. Otherwise the 'chicken and egg' conundrum will continue – until local authorities start to enforce and use civil penalties they will not be able to get the income to boost their enforcement policies.

The future of security for tenants

Now that lettings fees are successfully banned and tenancy deposits capped to five weeks, the spotlight is naturally falling on the issue of security for tenants to stay in a home. The use of section 21 of the 1988 Housing Act, under which the majority of tenants have short-term tenancies fixed for six months or a year – after which a tenant can be evicted with just two months' notice and without any reason, is cited as a significant factor in causing some of the worst cases of homelessness. In England this system of 'no-fault evictions' under section 21 is the reason so many tenants feel unable to improve the property or report problems. Generation Rent rightly has launched a campaign to abolish section 21. They argue that section 21 can mean constant anxiety and insecurity, particularly for the 1.8 million renter households with children. They refer to the German system where tenancies are indefinite and properties are often bought and sold with tenants included. The situation in England is partly exacerbated by the fact that so many landlords are individuals or couples – nearly 90 per cent in 2010 – with a real mix of motives as to why and how they rent their property. This was best explained in a detailed study of the PRS by the University of York (Rugg and Rhodes, 2018).

The Government launched a review 'Overcoming the Barriers to Longer Tenancies in the Private Rented Sector'[7] in July 2018. The main proposal by the Government is to introduce three-year tenancies. The evidence request has closed and in April 2019 the Government announced a review to end 'no-fault' evictions. The review into section 21 is not straightforward and will inevitably require an evidence-based review of how rents are set. A significant hike in rent would provide a loophole to get round the end of section 21. The Housing, Local Government and Communities Select Committee are expected to examine this issue in the same way they conducted a pre-legislative review of the Tenants Fees Bill.

Scotland introduced a dramatic change to tenure in December 2017 – the private residential tenancy. It is open-ended, rents are more predictable – there are protections against excessive rent increases and rent caps can be introduced – and there are 18 specified circumstances that allow landlords to regain possession – too many some would argue. This change was introduced after a stakeholder-led group was set up in 2013 to review private tenancies – a consultation followed.

Shelter Scotland published a study, *An Evaluation of Rent Regulation Measures within Scotland's Private Rented Sector*, in March 2018 (Robertson and Young, 2018). They concluded that much greater data was needed on private rents. This ties in with University of York recommendation for a central register of landlords and lettings agents introduced in Scotland in 2006.

A significant struggle continues to be finding where people are renting and who they are renting from. Newham Council was the first to start a compulsory licensing scheme for all landlords. Their enforcement programme identified additional rogue landlords with a £30,000 fine for failure to register. In the end they had more than five times the numbers of private landlords they had originally estimated. In other words detailed data on this form of tenure is likely to be an underestimate, particularly in London and other cities. If underestimated, then policy-formers will be unaware of the extent of the need to enforce people's rights to live somewhere safe and secure.

What does the future look like in the PRS?

The good news is that the PRS is now a large consumer group, which if it acted as a homogenous whole could ensure the policy-makers sit up and pay attention. At the same time the balance to ensure that good landlords, of which there are many, stay in the market place is difficult, given that no-one would start from the current set of rules and regulations.

Encouraging signs include new emerging players in the market that are highly consumer friendly and use technology to provide a cheap and responsive service – companies like OpenRent. co.uk that have open and transparent costs. They started up in 2012 and from their inception they did not charge additional administrative fees to tenants. They are now the UK's biggest letting agent, competing with the more traditional lettings agencies like Foxtons.

The advent of artificial intelligence can help in the field of homelessness, from apps that alert outreach teams if someone is sleeping rough to apps that empower the tenant with more information and input. This is a good step forward. The benefits of big data currently held by local authorities to apply algorithms to predict people at risk of homelessness is achievable.

The counter to that are the emerging problems of slum rentals that are illegal – several organisations recommend that a national register of landlords, such as the one introduced in Scotland, would help. New and emerging issues, such as short-term lets like Airbnb, are something that the Government is looking into

– there are concerns that these short-term lets are removing decent rentals from the market. While there are restrictions of 90 days per annum for this type of rental, a recent investigation by Channel 4 suggests that loopholes are being found to this.

Property guardians – people who pay to stay in an empty property – is a new issue, where there is a lack of clarity about how applicable the law is. A recent undercover investigation by ipaper[8] revealed several local authority-owned properties that were let out by property guardian companies with safety issues. Most property guardians have to sign a contract saying they will not contact the local authority or the media about the conditions of the property. Eviction can be swift and the hazardous conditions of some properties mean that the Government will shortly try to clarify the current law and probably introduce new regulations. While current estimates suggest this affects 5,000–7,000 residents, the Property Guardian Providers Association has projected that as many as 100,000 could be housed in this way. The London Assembly report *Protecting London's Property Guardians*, which includes recommendations based on experience in the Netherlands, has embraced this form of private rental and introduced kitemarking and a regulator of the properties (London Assembly, 2018).

In every main political party, there are advocates of post-war Macmillan style levels of investment in social housing. Until that is achieved, the private rented sector will be used by people who have little alternative. The more vulnerable in the private rented sector will need support to ensure they do not fall through the net and straight into homelessness. The Institute for Fiscal Studies points out the stark facts – the number of social houses has declined by half from the 1980s when they housed a third of all families, mainly due to the failure to replace Right to Buy.

Once in power, the conditions for politicians to make that herculean shift are as rare as a total lunar eclipse. It would need the economy to be on the rise, a political party with a large majority, sufficient public funds to spare and an ideological belief in the role of the state to provide a safety net of housing. Unfortunately, the last time a government was in that situation it blinked and the decline in social housing continued.

So in the meantime it is incumbent on all policy-makers at local and national level to ensure that the private rented sector is as fit for purpose as it possibly can be. That means incremental change, such as the Tenants Fees Act 2019, the Homes (Fitness for Human Habitation) Act 2018, selective local licensing schemes and other incremental changes to ensure that the PRS is fit for purpose for everyone in it. For that to happen, a greater understanding through research and data is essential, including into how the raft of recent changes in the law are working for people who rent.

To fail in that endeavour would be to fail the most vulnerable in society. Until the housing crisis is solved, the PRS must be treated as part of the answer.

Notes

1 https://www.channel4.com/news/factcheck/almost-one-in-five-mps-are-landlords.
2 Royal London Insurance from Family Resources Survey and English Housing Survey https://www.bbc.co.uk/news/education-47723672.
3 https://www.gov.uk/government/statistical-data-sets/live-tables-on-homelessness#statutory-homelessness-and-prevention-and-relief-live-tables.
4 YouGov, survey of 3,978 private renters in England, online, weighted July–August 2017.
5 This is the combined median amount that renters spend on moving costs, excluding those who did not spend anything. YouGov for Shelter, base: London renters: 739. Survey conducted between 22 June and 13 July 2015.
6 17 per cent of private rented dwellings had at least one category one hazard: Department for Communities and Local Government, English Housing Survey 2015–16: Headline Report, March 2017, para 4.15.
7 https://www.gov.uk/government/consultations/overcoming-the-barriers-to-longer-tenancies-in-the-private-rented-sector.
8 https://inews.co.uk/news/long-reads/hidden-housing-crisis-property-guardians/.

References

Corelette, A and Judge, L. 2017. *Home Affront, Housing Across the Generations*. London: Resolution Foundation. https://www.resolutionfoundation.org/publications/home-affront-housing-across-the-generations/.

Housing, Communities and Local Government Committee.
2018. *Private Rented Sector: Fourth Report of Session 2017–19.*
London: House of Commons. Retrieved from: https://
publications.parliament.uk/pa/cm201719/cmselect/
cmcomloc/440/440.pdf

London Assembly. 2018. *Guardians in Occupation: Holding the
Mayor to Account and Investigating Issues That Matter to Londoners.*
London: London Assembly.

MHCLG. 2017. *English Housing Survey 2016/17*, Table
FA4121. London: Ministry of Housing, Communities & Local
Government. www.gov.uk/government/statistical-data-sets/
new-households-and-recent-movers.

Mykkanen, N. 2018. *The Postcode Lottery of Local Authority
Enforcement in the Private Rented Sector.* Manchester: Residential
Landlords Association. https://research.rla.org.uk/wp-
content/uploads/post-code-lottery- enforcement-prs.pdf.

Parsons, A. 2016. *Letting Fees: What We Know And Why They
Need To Go.* London: Generation Rent.

Robertson, D. and Young, G. 2018. *An Evaluation of Rent
Regulation Measures within Scotland's Private Rented Sector.*
Edinburgh: Shelter Scotland.

Rugg, J. and Rhodes, D. 2018. *The Evolving Private Rented
Sector: Its Contribution and Potential.* York: University of York.
http://www.nationwidefoundation.org.uk/wp-content/
uploads/2018/09/Private-Rented-Sector-report.pdf.

Shelter. 2014. *Lessons from the Scottish Lettings Market.* London:
Shelter.

Shelter. 2018. *Stop DSS Discrimination. Ending Prejudice Against
Renters on Housing Benefit.* London: Shelter.

Simcock, T.J. and Mykkanen, N. 2018. *The Postcode Lottery
of Local Authority Enforcement in the Private Rented Sector.*
Manchester: Residential Landlords Association. Retrieved
from: https://research.rla.org.uk/wp-content/uploads/post-
code-lotteryenforcement-prs.pdf

Sylvester, R. and Thomson, A. 2018. Landlords pushing up
rents to exploit housing benefit shortfall. *Times*, 9 November.
www.thetimes.co.uk/article/landlords-pushing-up-rents-to-
exploit-housing-benefit-shortfall-bpvht6lbg.

4

Houses, not homelessness

Danny Dorling

'The death of Sharron Maasz, though the subject of a coroner's inquest, would probably otherwise have passed unnoticed. I knew Sharron well. I taught her when I was head of her middle school. Her father, a single parent, was a friend and was for a number of years a governor. Sharron was a bright, lively and sensitive girl. She was a keen cyclist and an all-round athlete. This may be her only obituary.

She is quoted as saying: "I just want to get my life sorted ... I always wanted to get clean."

She didn't get sorted or clean. Instead, she died in a short-term home, a last refuge provided for those in desperate need. She had been living alone on the freezing streets of our leading university city.

I do not have solutions. I only know that the dreams that Sharron, a lovely child, had until her death, have perished in the wreckage of an austerity programme that has literally killed her and her like.' (Roger Pepworth, Headteacher, Marston middle school, Oxford 1983–91)

This letter, one of many in recent years, was published in *The Guardian* newspaper on 3 February 2019 (Pepworth, 2019). It stands out because, unlike the majority of articles or obituaries written about people who have died while experiencing homelessness, Sharron Maasz was named.

Anonymising people who have died while experiencing homelessness, or shortly after having been homeless, has become commonplace, but is a practice that does more harm than good. Understandably, the families of the deceased do not want their loved ones to be remembered for having died on the streets or in a halfway house, but while we name those who have died in almost any other circumstance, we attempt to forget those for whom society has failed to provide adequate safety and security.

Furthermore, these deaths are often attributed to proximal causes, not the underlying pervasion of poverty or severe lack of adequate housing that evidence suggests create and exacerbate other health problems that lead to death. In doing so, we fail to recognise that UK housing policy has exacerbated homelessness by creating an environment of precarious inequality. Acknowledging this is the first step towards making progress. From there, we can use evidence and data to reverse the policies that have created the current situation. If we do not, there is a great danger that simply monitoring the situation (and reporting the numbers) is perceived as action that will only continue to support the status quo. Roger Pepworth, Sharon's former teacher, ends the letter that opens this chapter by saying, 'I do not have solutions ...'. He should not have to; others should already be putting them in place. We know from other social policy fields that better use of evidence and data can lay the foundations to create tangible change.

Understanding the numbers

On 31 January 2019, the Ministry for Housing, Communities and Local Government (MHCLG) reported that an estimated 4,677 people were now sleeping rough on any one night in England, almost three times as many as in 2010 (MHCLG, 2019a). These figures have long been disputed, with the true number estimated to be at least twice as high. In the same timeframe, the number of families housed by local authorities in temporary accommodation rose significantly, but at a lower rate, from 50,000 in 2010 to 78,000 in 2018. In London alone, there are 225,000 'hidden homeless' people aged 16–25 arranging their own temporary accommodation with friends or family (Fransham and Dorling, 2018).

Reporting on its own rough sleeping initiative (RSI) in the same publication, MHCLG claimed: 'There were 2,748 people recorded as sleeping rough across the 83 RSI areas in autumn 2018, this is a decrease of 639 or 23% from the 2017 figure of 3,387 (MHCLG, 2019a). As the total figure for England hardly changed over this time period, there will have been a similar rise in those areas where the initiative was not undertaken. This could have been for many reasons, which might include people being displaced away from the 83 RSI areas to be homeless in other areas of England. MHCLG's report on itself continued:

> An evaluation of the Rough Sleeping Initiative will be published this year to help understand the impact of the range of activities in these areas on the number of people sleeping rough. There are a range of other factors that may impact on the number of people sleeping rough including the weather, where people choose to sleep, the date and time chosen and the availability of alternatives such as night shelters.

The government ministry did not mention its overall approach to housing as a potential problem, let alone that it is in fact one of the most significant factors. This is not surprising. Had they realised, they would surely have done something about it by now – unless the view of the ministers in charge is that some level of homelessness is necessary or inevitable. Later in 2019 the same government ministry produced another report in which their researchers wrote:

> The data collected for this study was informed by the previous literature on the drivers of rough sleeping and drew particularly on a recent Rapid Evidence Assessment for MHCLG and DWP. This suggested

that individual factors such as mental health and relationship breakdown were more likely to be the reasons for people sleeping rough than structural factors such as unemployment levels, poverty and housing affordability. However, more recent literature acknowledges that structural factors create the conditions that cause some people with personal problems to be more vulnerable, and to end up rough sleeping. (MHCLG 2019b, p 9)

Presenting a story that suggests there is a rapid change in our understanding and that the structural factors were only newly discovered is misleading. It has long been known that some people in some countries at some times are more likely to suffer relationship breakdowns and poor mental health as a consequence of the society in which they live. It is possible that the researchers writing this report did not know this, hence their reference to 'more recent literature'. However, if that is the case, then we have to ask why reports such as this are being written by researchers not aware of what is generally understood by social scientists.

This is not a phenomenon limited to the 2019 MHCLG. In 2018, there were estimated to be 726 deaths of homeless people in England and Wales (ONS, 2018), a 22 per cent increase since the time series began. When the Office for National Statistics (ONS) first reported these numbers in December 2018, and said that

Understanding a problem is the first step to solving it, and producing these statistics will help society make better decisions to tackle homelessness and stop homeless people dying in our communities (Brimblecombe *et al.*, 2019). These statistics aren't just numbers, behind each death is the story of some of the most vulnerable members of society. (Humberstone, 2018)

So what is the next step? Counting the rising number of deaths with increasing accuracy is certainly essential, but only illustrates how large the underlying problem has become. It does not tell us where the causes of that problem lie or what can be done to prevent it from happening again. The same can be said of the focus on rough sleeping. Read the quote from the ONS again and think whether you notice anything strange about the wording.

The phrase that struck me as most odd is, 'stop homeless people dying in our communities'. Implicit in that phrase is an apparent assumption that people who are homeless have always been with us. But when I was a young boy living in Oxford, there were almost no people experiencing homelessness. What has changed in that time?

While officially supporting the target of 'halving rough sleeping by 2022 and ending it by 2024', in truth, policy-makers are unlikely to meet these goals if the default is to blame the weather (recent warmer winters mean that the weather has not been the cause) and suggest that a few more night shelters could help. Despite acknowledging that street homelessness is just the tip of the iceberg, in England the decision was taken not to focus on the root causes. In Scotland, the approach is different and takes all forms of homelessness into account, not just rough sleeping. Neither of these two UK governments go into detail about evidence underpinning their plans or how the impact of policies will be evaluated – a missed opportunity. These government documents are an important source of evidence for other parts of the sector, and their choice of language and areas of focus affect which issues are dealt with or ignored.

Unexplained but not suspicious

In general, policy suggestions on homelessness only address the most precarious and heart-wrenching cases. While this is useful to galvanise sympathy, it unintentionally implies that by helping those whose need is greatest, the problem can be eradicated. This is wrong. It can also create negative side effects among the wider population who, when confronted with endless terrible individual stories, begin to feel that things will never change, becoming apathetic, desensitised and fatalistic.

In spring 2018, in one of the streets where I used to play as a child, a homeless man died in a council-funded hostel. The newspaper report was brief: 'The 61-year-old was found dead in a room in Marston Street in East Oxford on April 20. The city council said it believed there was nothing suspicious about the man's death' (Staff Reporter, 2018).

In autumn 2018, the same paper reported:

> A homeless man who was found dead in a graveyard had been sprayed with paint three days earlier in a separate assault ... someone uploaded a video onto social media of the homeless man being sprayed, with a voice in the audio that could be heard saying: 'This is how we deal with beggars on the street' (Press Association, 2018).

Just before Christmas 2018, a homeless man in his 30s was found dead on the main thoroughfare between Oxford rail station and the city centre. Four days earlier, a man who had been homeless died in the centre of town, in McDonald's, where local school children go to meet. The same code words were used as in previous reports that imply nothing unusual has happened: 'Police said on Monday that his death was being treated as "unexplained but not suspicious"' (Roberts, 2018).

Sharron Maasz died in January 2019 (Aziz, 2019), and two more deaths were reported in the month after. The only thing that connected the three was that they were all experiencing homelessness. We have long become accustomed to such deaths, and an unhelpful tradition has developed whereby it is deemed sufficient to express shock and horror instead of using these tragedies as an opportunity to learn, improve and prevent similar deaths in the future.

Perspective matters, because unless we can be confident that we are framing the challenge in the right way, we may be misusing vital resources and wasting precious time and energy. To achieve real, lasting change it is vital that we take a much wider view of homelessness, one that considers the bigger picture of the drivers and root causes of the issue as informed by current evidence and an historical context and understanding.

In 2018, the Centre for Homelessness Impact advocated exactly this approach in a report that went on to suggest that we must also better understand 'how housing equity is connected to opportunity and life chances' (Teixeira et al, 2018).

We have come to approach homelessness as a question of how to mitigate, subdue, and tidily deal with the symptoms of our social illness. We have learnt to cope saying these deaths are not suspicious, when in fact they are. We express horror and spend ample time 'raising awareness', but this is not good enough.

To achieve a step change in our efforts, a new evidence-based approach to homelessness is needed, one that aggregates evidence from other countries and our own former successes in addition to generating new research. What did we do in the past that meant fewer people were once homeless, and do we have all the evidence we need to address the most pressing questions that need answering today? What are the impact of our current interventions and what would have happened without them?

Luck matters most

Generating and utilising the right kind of evidence also requires that we ask more complex questions, like why it is that more men die homeless. The superficial reason is that there are simply more men 'sofa surfing', in hostels and on the streets. And the reasons for that? Women are more likely to be parents with young children and thus have a right to be housed, while men are more likely to take to drinks and drugs to an extent that leads to homelessness. But the explanations are more complex still.[1]

The number of people dying while experiencing homelessness is now so high that it is possible to break the figures down by the characteristics of those who die and the immediate, if not underlying, cause of death. Only one in six of those who die while experiencing homelessness are women, but the women in England and Wales who die while experiencing homelessness are, on average, two years younger than the men (42 rather than 44 on mean average). Some 21 years ago, as homelessness was starting to become normalised in the UK, Mary Shaw and I made similar calculations and found that the death rates of male rough sleepers aged 16–29 years were almost 40 times higher than those of the general population. For all men aged 16–64 years, this number is about 25 times greater (SMR=2587). Very little has changed in these death rates even while the numbers of people experiencing homelessness fell, and then rose (Shaw and Dorling, 1998).

The picture for women is a little different. Back in 1998 there were too few women on Britain's streets to be able to calculate their mortality rate by age. The latest data suggests that the number of younger homeless women is on the rise. Homeless men die 34 years earlier than most men, homeless women 39 years earlier than most women. People who are homeless are at highest risk of death where they are most numerous: in London and the conurbations of the north-west of England and, more recently, in Oxford. In early 2019, Oxford had the second highest mortality rate for homeless people in the UK,[2] with the majority of those who died having grown up and gone to school in the city or a village within a ten-mile radius (Brimblecombe et al, 2019; ONS, 2018, 2019).

A third of the deaths of people experiencing homelessness in the UK are now attributed to drug poisoning. Doctors know that the cause they write on the death certificate is not the true underlying cause. If they knew the person and were permitted to write a more nuanced description, a few might write something far more useful. Like Roger Pepworth's obituary for Sharron Maasz and Shaista Aziz's later tribute and explanation (Aziz, 2019), this could give a human face to people who would otherwise become statistics and present a more honest picture of the structural causes of death for people experiencing homelessness. Here is a hypothetical example:

> Died of drug poisoning after intermittent spells without a safe home. An imaginative young man who did well at school. A chance event aged 16, lead to the loss of his nearest sibling in a car crash. The resulting family breakdown began the path to heavy drug use and periods of living on the street. But he survived for some time. Had he been luckier, his overdose would not have happened. Had his local rehab centre had just one extra free space, he

would not be dead now, but its funding was cut. Had he been born a few years earlier, before heroin reached his home town, he might have resorted to drink instead and not suffered this overdose. Had he been born in another European nation under otherwise identical circumstances, there is a good chance he would still be alive. But he was born in England, in the mid-1970s, and is now dead, aged 44, coincidentally at the exact mean age that people die nationally. He had rotten luck.

Luck matters above all else to individuals, but at the aggregate level all the good and bad luck is ironed out. At the aggregate level the evidence is not about luck at all. At the aggregate level it is perception that matters most and the biases inherent in the interpretation and presentation of statistics. This is *always* the case. Individuals all operate with a worldview that they carefully structure their evidence to support. This means that simply gathering more evidence is not enough. To accelerate progress, the sector must be prepared to put its basic assumptions to the test on an ongoing basis, and to ask whether what it is doing is fundamentally improving the situation or instead is perpetuating a bad system, while superficially appearing to help.

What constitutes good evidence?

Just a few centuries ago it was possible to amass a large quantity of evidence to show that the Earth was at the centre of the universe. Just like the moon, the sun appeared to revolve around the earth, so too the planets and the stars orbiting us reassuringly in the night sky. What it took to change that view was not simply a better telescope, it was a better way of thinking. Rooting oneself in a mode of thinking can only sustain the prejudices of your times and place.

The current pervading narrative places the responsibility for homelessness on the individual. But the causes of homelessness do not lie with the people that it affects. Consequently, the solution to the underlying problem is not just intervention on the streets. Neither is it limited to the 'payment by results' of 'local social enterprises', or the issuing of 'social bonds'. Individual interventions may be well-meaning, but they can often be merely only superficially and very short-term successful. That is why it is vital to both address the dearth of causal evidence (as highlighted by the Centre for Homelessness Impact's Evidence and Gap Maps), while also ensuring we take the bird's eye view of homelessness and what really causes it to rise.

We know from other fields, such as public health, that to truly use evidence to drive improvements at a population level, taking a systematic and wide approach is crucial. The fitting of gastric bands, for example, may solve obesity in individual cases, but it does not have any effect at the societal level. Obesity will not be eradicated until the whole environment that makes a population fatter is dealt with.

When the ONS released their first estimates of the number of homeless people dying on the streets on 20 December 2018, section seven of their report was titled 'Proportion of deaths of homeless people that are due to drug poisoning has increased by 51 percentage points relative to the overall number of drug deaths over five years'. The next day the title of that section was changed to, 'Drug-related deaths of homeless people increased by 52 per cent over five years'.[3] This attention to detail and correction of a single statistic by one percentage point gives the impression that what matters most when gathering evidence is statistical exactness, and then issues such as drugs – the precise drug that lead to death is identified in individual cases. In 2018, the ONS notes that one person experiencing homelessness died from smoking cannabis, while 115 died while under the influence of opiates.[4] The fact that somewhere a doctor noted cannabis consumption as a potential cause of death while homeless is not a particularly useful piece of information.

The ONS should not be singled out here. The same could be said of much of the literature on homelessness. A report from Housing First England (2019) cites 'A long history of alcohol dependency, heroin and crack use and anti-social behaviour' as the main cause of homelessness for one of its service users.

The language used by leading sector organisations matters. Simple statements can, when repeated again and again in aggregate, frame a story, shifting focus from the causes to the symptoms of a problem. With homelessness, the emphasis is so often on how the people affected suffer from alcohol or drug misuse, have 'high/complex needs' or all of the above, while forgetting that the evidence suggests most people affected by homelessness never come into contact with the homelessness system, and can therefore not easily be labelled under any of these categories. They are in so many ways no different from you or me.

In its 2018 annual accounts, Homeless Link describes roughly £5 million of spending in a year and begins:

> The Government's commitment to halve rough sleeping by 2022 has set the policy agenda during the year. Homeless Link has made a full contribution to the Government's process of developing a strategy to implement this commitment, with representation on the Rough Sleeping Advisory Group and all five 'Task and Finish' groups set up to work on components of the strategy. We welcome the appointment of Jeremy Swain, who steps down as a Homeless Link Trustee, to lead the Government's Rough Sleeping Initiative and we are confident that the sector will play its part in reversing the shocking increases in rough sleeping we have seen in recent years. However, these worthy commitments can only be achieved with significant additional resources and we look forward to the publication of the finalised Government strategy later in the summer. (Feilden, 2018)

The call for 'significant additional resources' is a recurrent refrain in the sector, when in fact the significant injections of funding every decade or so may well have contributed to the problem. While adequate resources are key, throwing money at the problem does not necessarily mean those affected by homelessness will benefit. In the last 50 years, the homelessness system has grown in complexity and is more costly than ever, yet the impact of the work has not reduced the scale of the problem. For this reason, new types of data and evidence are needed – particularly causal and comparative – in addition to greater accountability and transparency to ensure policy-makers are indeed drawing on bodies of knowledge when developing policy. We know from other social policy fields like international development and education that better use of data and causal evidence can help accelerate progress and help target resources more effectively.

Progressing policy

Preventing homelessness in the UK requires significant reformation of housing policy. In most areas, it is currently not fit for purpose. It is not just those who are homeless who suffer as a result. Millions of others pay exorbitant rents for low-quality homes over which they have insecure rights.

In this instance, we would do well to draw on evidence from the past and look at similar failures in public policy where an emphasis on the symptoms, not the causes, has prevailed. Acknowledging systemic problems is a rare occurrence in current UK public policy and government often focuses on treating the symptoms of a problem for short-term gain.

In the past, the UK government has tried to address the prevalence of babies with low birth weights by focusing on the health and wellbeing of individual mothers, rather than addressing the systemic factors that mean that the UK has one of the worst records for underweight infant births and highest neonatal mortality rates in western Europe). The British government has looked at the individual cases of children excluded from school, instead of the wider social issues that mean school exclusions are rare elsewhere in Europe and were quite rare in the UK in past decades; but no longer. It has designed measures to address poverty that mitigate only the worst effects of living on a low income, rather than acknowledging that it is tolerance and exacerbation of high levels of income inequality that is fueling the problem. The British government, from 1979 continuously through to 2019, has treated the issue of long-term unemployment and sickness as if it were the result of work-shy individuals who should be sanctioned for not trying hard enough, rather than understanding that its organisation of the national economy results in greater sickness and wastes human resources.

Without new mechanisms to instigate change, this status quo will prevail. In a complex system, better use of evidence to identify how to prioritise things that do the most good and stop doing what does not work (or causes harm) is vital.

What is to be done?

It is not just housing policy, but social policy in general that has exacerbated homelessness by creating an environment of precarious inequality. Reliable evidence at the micro and macro levels needs to be collected and acted upon more promptly. We need to know what works in the short term, but also keep our eyes on the long-term prize. A piecemeal approach that seeks to improve one area will have little overall effect if other areas of public life are not also improving.

There are opportunities to learn from what we did better in the past, from other areas where social policy has been effective, and from other European countries with more successful social policies than our own (Dorling, 2016). While we may look back and idealise solutions that would no longer be effective, like the mass provision of traditional council housing, an evidence-based approach would clarify exactly why this is the case. Council housing worked so well at first because of a slum sector that existed below it from which a council house provided an escape. Those are no longer the times we live in, but we can learn from knowing that. It is vital it is to learn faster and fully embrace technological and social developments, what people will need in the future will be different from what worked well for their grandparents in the past, for instance because people now live longer we need far more dwellings without stairs in future. There is a danger that the timings of research seldom work for practitioners and policy-makers. To give another example that would have meant little in the recent past, many young people, including young people who are homeless, will go without food before they go without phone credit. Knowing that is useful.

In the UK, we seem unable to scale up promising interventions, largely because there is often no mechanism and they are thus so often never subject to rigorous evaluation, meaning that projects then close down as and when the fashion passes. The root causes of new homelessness are almost never treated as a political priority. In England, there are a few new schemes being piloted that have fared well in Nordic nations, like 'Housing First'. In Finland, 'Housing First' as a policy was successful predominantly because of Finland's stronger social safety net – one that the UK has now largely lost. We do not yet know if it will work in the UK, but the omens are not good given the cuts that have occurred to other services.

We should recognise that all European countries now have lower income inequality than the UK and also enshrine more tenant rights into law. Rent regulation is a vital part of that. It is the only defence against arbitrary eviction.[5] In Germany half of all householders rent privately. Often they rent using standard leases, which permit tenants to live in a property for the duration of their lives (Hickey, 2016). Rent caps are enforced to stabilise rates for all tenants, and closely monitored to ensure they do not increase too quickly. Tenants' groups organize to complain when landlords are not penalised for breaking the law.

In Sweden, private sector rent levels are set through negotiations between representatives of landlords and tenants in a very similar way to how trade unions and employers negotiate pay. In 2014, the whole of Stockholm was limited to increasing rents in a year by only 1.12 per cent as a result. In the Netherlands, monthly rental fees are fixed by government. Government officials inspect properties for quality and decide rents accordingly. Denmark has two forms of rent regulation and does not suffer homelessness on the scale of countries with a supposedly more 'free market'.

In France, a new set of rent regulations came into force in the capital in August 2015, stating that private rents 'must be no more than 20 per cent above or 30 per cent below the median rental price for the area'. Of course, the rules prompted anger among property agencies and landlords, who claimed they would deter investment. But the evidence from less equal countries is clear: landlords charging whatever rent they choose does not result in more housing becoming available. The USA and its enormous rate of homelessness amply demonstrates what leaving housing to the free market produces. In contrast in the European mainland these controls have helped reduce rent inflation as firms and European agencies move parts of their workforce to Paris during the Brexit process.

The dominant narrative in Britain, and especially in England, remains one that always focuses on the apparent deficits and perceived failures of people who become street homeless. Victim-blaming is an area in which much of western society excels, but at which the most economically unequal societies such as the UK and USA excel the most. Thankfully, there is now growing evidence that this may be changing, and that attitudes in the UK are finally beginning to alter (Dorling, 2018). Changing old habits will not be easy, but nurturing a learning sector that acts more promptly on existing knowledge and tests its assumptions about what works will improve the positive impact of our efforts. Much more importantly than that, though, is having a government made up of people who both care and understand.

Sharron Maasz was one of so many who could, and should, be alive today.

Notes

[1] The consultant child and adolescent psychiatrist Sabastian Kraemer collated the evidence and has found that in a surprising large number of aspects of life men might be more likely to 'succeed', be promoted and be higher paid, but they are also more likely to do badly as compared to women. His examples ranged from male humans being more likely to being miscarried as a foetus, to failing to gain any qualifications at school, through to dying earlier. In the detailed notes to his analysis he made it clear that women often do very badly too and suffer systematic discrimination in society. Sabastian summed up the fundamental difference as 'Men die, women suffer' (Kraemer, 2017).

[2] On 25 February 2019, the BBC reported that Blackburn had the highest death rate among people who were homeless by area, followed closely by Oxford and then Camden (BBC News, 2019).

[3] Section 7 'Drug-related deaths of homeless people increased by 52 per cent over five years' (ONS, 2018).

[4] Ibid, Table 1: Drug poisoning deaths of homeless people (identified) by substances mentioned, persons.

[5] This section is based on work done for the book *The Equality Effect* written by the author of this chapter published by New Internationalist (Oxford) in 2017; see: http://www.dannydorling.org/books/equalityeffect/.

References

Aziz, S. 2019. The death of Sharron Maasz shows why domestic abuse services are vital. *The Guardian*, 26 November. https://www.theguardian.com/cities/2019/nov/26/the-death-of-sharron-maasz-shows-why-domestic-abuse-services-are-vital

BBC News. 2019. Homeless deaths nine times higher in deprived areas. *BBC News*, 25 February. https://www.bbc.co.uk/news/uk-england-47357492.

Brimblecombe, N., Dorling, D., and Green, M. 2019. Who still dies young in a rich city? Revisiting the case of Oxford, *The Geographical Journal*, DOI:10.1111/geoj.12336, Accepted Article published online on 12 November, 2019. https://rgs-ibg.onlinelibrary.wiley.com/doi/abs/10.1111/geoj.12336

Dorling, D. 2016. *A Better Politics: How Government Can Make Us Happier.* London: London Publishing Partnership.

Dorling, D. 2018. *Peak Inequality: Britain's Ticking Time Bomb.* Bristol: Policy Press.

Feilden, P. 2018. Introduction to company account 25 July 2018 authored by Homeless Link: Reports and Financial Statements for the year ended 31 March 2018. https://assets.publishing.service.gov.uk/government/uploads/system/uploads/attachment_data/file/724952/CC_Annual-Report-Accounts-2017-18_A4_web.pdf.

Fransham, M. and Dorling, D. 2018. Homelessness and public health. *British Medical Journal*, 360. https://www.bmj.com/content/360/bmj.k214.

Hickey, S. 2016. Would a rent cap work for tenants facing £1000 a month rises? *The Observer*, 1 May. http://www.propertyinvesting.net/cgi-script/csNews/csNews.cgi?database=default.db&command=viewone&id=32624&op=t.

Housing First England. 2019. *Life Stories.* https://hfe.homeless.org.uk/life-stories.

Humberstone, B. 2018. ONS reveals the number of people dying homeless. https://blog.ons.gov.uk/2018/12/20/ons-reveals-the-number-of-people-dying-homeless/.

Kraemer, S. 2017. Notes on the fragile male. Extension of (2000) 'The fragile male' *British Medical Journal*, 321(7276): 1609–12. Extended notes online only: http://sebastiankraemer.com/docs/Kraemer%20notes%20on%20the%20fragile%20male%20 2017.pdf.

MHCLG (Ministry of Housing, Communities & Local Government). 2019a. *Rough Sleeping Statistics Autumn 2018, England (Revised)*. London: Ministry of Housing Community and Local Government. https://assets.publishing.service.gov. uk/government/uploads/system/uploads/attachment_data/ file/775089/Rough_Sleeping_Statistics_2018.pdf.

MHCLG (Ministry of Housing, Communities & Local Government). 2019b. *Impact Evaluation of the Rough Sleeping Initiative 2018, England*. London: Ministry of Housing Community and Local Government, https://assets.publishing. service.gov.uk/government/uploads/system/uploads/ attachment_data/file/831133/RSI_Impact_Evaluation.pdf.

ONS. 2018. *Deaths of Homeless People in England and Wales: 2013 to 2017*. London: Office for National Statistics. https://www. ons.gov.uk/peoplepopulationandcommunity/birthsdeathsand marriages/deaths/bulletins/deathsofhomelesspeopleinengland andwales/2013to2017.

ONS. 2019. *Deaths of Homeless People in England and Wales: 2018*. London: Office for National Statistics. https://www. ons.gov.uk/peoplepopulationandcommunity/birthsdeathsand marriages/deaths/bulletins/deathsofhomelesspeopleinengland andwales/2018

Pepworth, R. 2019. Harsh reality of life and death on the street below dreaming spires. Letters. *The Guardian*, 3 February. https://www.theguardian.com/society/2019/feb/03/harsh-reality-of-life-and-death-on-the-street-below-dreaming-spires.

Press Association. 2018. Homeless man found dead in graveyard had been sprayed in paint attack. *Oxford Mail*, 14 September. https://www.oxfordmail.co.uk/news/national/16861295. homeless-man-found-dead-in-graveyard-had-been-sprayed-in-paint-attack/.

Roberts, J. 2018. Man in thirties dies on Hythe Bridge Street, Oxford. *Oxford Mail,* 7 December. https://www.oxfordmail.co.uk/news/17284460.man-in-thirties-dies-on-hythe-bridge-street-oxford/.

Shaw, M. and Dorling, D. 1998. Mortality amongst street sleeping youth in the UK. *The Lancet,* 29 August: 743, http://www.dannydorling.org/wp-content/files/dannydorling_publication_id1455.pdf.

Staff Reporter. 2018. Homeless man found dead in Marston Street hostel, Oxford. *Oxford Mail,* 2 May. https://www.oxfordmail.co.uk/news/16196961.homeless-man-found-dead-in-marston-street-hostel-oxford/.

Teixeira, L., Russell, D. and Hobbs, T. 2018. *The SHARE Framework: A Smarter Way to End Homelessness.* London: Centre for Homelessness Impact. https://uploads-ssl.webflow.com/59f07e67422cdf0001904c14/5af4288fdebbda9d1a495a98_SHARE-framework_report_2018.pdf.

5

Loosening poverty's grip

Campbell Robb

Poverty is not just felt by the individuals experiencing it, but by society as a whole. Its social and economic costs cause lasting damage. In the past, as a country, the UK has shown that it can reduce poverty among those groups that have been most at risk. In the early 2000s, we achieved significant reductions in poverty among pensioners and children through a combination of rising employment, tax credits and help with housing costs. However, this progress has begun to unravel and poverty rates are now rising again in many parts of the country. One in five of us is struggling to make ends meet – and with that rise in poverty comes an increase in the number of people sitting at the brink of homelessness (JRF Analysis Unit, 2018). This is not an acceptable state of affairs.

For over a decade I have been working directly to combat poverty and homelessness, in government as head of the Social Exclusion Unit, and at Shelter, the Joseph Rowntree Foundation (JRF) and Nacro. Two things run through that time like letters through a stick of rock. The first is the devastating impact on the opportunities of people and communities when they are dragged into poverty or become homeless. The second is that, while we have some evidence about what policies work to get people off the streets, out of temporary accommodation, or off the sofas they are surfing on, we still are not doing enough to implement them or fill the gaps in our understanding of what works, where and for whom. That is why I am still passionate about working to address this injustice and believe so strongly that we must make better use of data and evidence to persuade the public, policy-makers and politicians alike that the problem of poverty can be solved.

We live in a society that takes pride in its compassion – a country that believes in justice, in doing the right thing and in supporting people in hard times. But right now, the very systems that should be protecting people from the damaging effects of poverty are making their lives harder and pulling them further into it. The social security system, which should act like an anchor and provide stability when times are hard, is often dragging people under.

Additionally, there are not enough affordable homes for people to live in (Soodeen, 2018) and, for those who do have a home, rising costs, low pay and the benefits freeze mean their lives are constantly precarious and under stress. It can take only a small change in circumstances to tip individuals into poverty. These malfunctioning systems are locking people into poverty and have been designed in a way that fails the people they were created to help. Now they must be redesigned to do the job they were made to do, using robust, reliable evidence to design policies that work.

If we achieve this, poverty and homelessness can be solved (Joseph Rowntree Foundation – various authors, 2016).

The current state of poverty in the UK

In the UK, 14.3 million people live in poverty – one in five of us are trying to cope with resources that are well below our minimum needs. To give you a sense of scale, that is more than the combined populations of London, Edinburgh, Cardiff, Belfast, Birmingham and Greater Manchester.

JRF's 2018 report on UK poverty (JRF Analysis Unit, 2018) highlights that both the number of children in poverty and the number of workers in poverty have risen by half a million in the last five years, with in-work poverty rising faster than employment.

There are some differences in poverty trends in the different nations of the UK. Although the poverty rate in England started to decline almost ten years ago, it has risen again to 22 per cent (JRF Analysis Unit, 2018). Figures (Fitzpatrick et al, 2018a) also reveal rising homelessness pressures across England, with 40 per cent of councils in London surveyed for the *Homelessness Monitor: England 2018* saying that the number of people seeking help from their local authority homelessness services had risen over the last year – 76 per cent in the Midlands, 70 per cent in the south and 62 per cent in the north.

The poverty rate in Wales has generally been higher than in England, Scotland and Northern Ireland for the last 20 years and this remains the case (JRF Analysis Unit, 2018). While there has been progress on worklessness, employment rates and adult skills, this has done nothing to decrease the number of people living in poverty – in fact, the risk of poverty has increased for working and workless households. Reductions to working-age benefits, rising living costs (especially for housing) and poor-quality work are responsible for rising poverty in Wales. The nation also has the highest poverty rate for disabled people in the UK – 39 per cent of disabled people live in poverty.

Scotland has generally had the lowest poverty rate of the UK nations for the last ten years, but that rate too is increasing. One in four children in Scotland lives in poverty[1] – often because their parents are restricted by a lack of work, mainly due to disability or the difficulties of juggling work and childcare.

While the overall poverty rate in Northern Ireland has fallen slightly in the last ten years, this improvement is not reflected across all groups. Working-age adults without children are now at a greater risk of living in poverty than ten years ago. Northern Ireland has higher worklessness and lower employment than in the UK as a whole and the proportion of people in poverty in workless households has increased slightly over time, in contrast with other parts of the UK.

Our data and analysis are crucial indicators of the scale of poverty, but to really understand the effects it has on people's lives, we have been working directly with people who have experienced it. In their stories,[2] it is plain to see how events in their lives have created powerful currents that pull them into poverty.

> 'I ended up in poverty through massive, catastrophic changes in my life that were beyond my control.'

> 'I live in a private rented house. My rent is £700 a month and I earn £700 a month from my job, so that just leaves me and my two kids with my tax credits for everything else.'

> 'Losing my job, losing my home, losing my marriage were all hard but it was poverty that sent me to the brink of suicide.'

> 'For about three years I was in and out of work. My son was the only thing that kept me going. I got into debt with nurseries for childcare. I split up with my boyfriend and I became really ill. I had to move back in with my parents for two months. I lost my purpose.'

People who are in poverty have very little financial resilience. With their benefits frozen, housing costs taking up the vast majority of their minimal income, and perhaps managing caring responsibilities or a disability, this unrelenting pressure increases their susceptibility to becoming homeless.

Destitution

Over 1.5 million people experienced destitution (Fitzpatrick et al, 2018b) in the UK at some point during 2017. This means that they could not afford to buy the bare essentials that we all need to eat, stay warm and dry, and keep clean. When we look into the causes of destitution, we see a familiar mix of issues combining to lock people out of the chance to build a decent, secure life:

• benefit delays, gaps and sanctions;

- harsh debt recovery practices (mainly by public authorities and utilities companies);
- financial and other pressures associated with poor health and disability;
- high costs of housing, fuel and other essentials;
- for some groups – including young people – even lower levels of benefits than for others and, for some migrants, no eligibility for benefits at all.

This tells us a story of destitution by design – a culmination of policy and service design flaws that can push people into destitution and tear apart the safety net that should prevent them falling further into dire need.

Homelessness is one of many interlinked issues that make up the picture of destitution and poverty in the UK. While rough sleeping may be the most visible sign of poverty, it does not account for many homeless households living in temporary accommodation (Fitzpatrick et al, 2018a) or living in other hidden homeless situations. Hidden homelessness refers to those who are omitted from official statistics and not receiving support despite not having access to a place to call home. They include people who are 'sofa surfing' or squatting. Rough sleeping is just the tip of the iceberg.

How the current system is failing

The moment someone becomes homeless is not an isolated incident that happens out of the blue. It is a milestone on a journey that could be prevented and halted at a number of junctures along the way. These are all seen and handled separately by different agencies. Unfortunately, every part of the system is failing in some way, but better use of data and evidence could help us achieve lasting results for those affected.

We need evidence of what is going on at each of these stages – who is involved, what is happening to them, what impact it is having on them, what is helping them, what is making things worse, where they go next, and how we can do the most good with limited resources. For example, we need better evidence on the experiences and consequences of people living in temporary accommodation. What happens to them and what system changes and improvements would help them relocate into secure accommodation?

Of course, evidence on its own is of little use unless it is reliable and people learn and act on it – something we have historically not been good at. There is an imperative need for more experimentation and innovation and for greater collaboration between agencies. There are many people working in homelessness – from researchers and policy-makers to practitioners and more – and our best services do have a positive impact. Despite all this great work, little has changed over the past 50 years, in many cases because we have no evidence of 'what works' and what does not. We do not yet have the causal evidence we need to improve decision-making, nor the capacity and mechanisms required to share these bodies of knowledge between agencies and individuals.

How evidence can help to solve homelessness sustainably

Evidence plays a crucial role in understanding the scale and experience of poverty and homelessness, as well as whether interventions work or not for different groups of people. To be effective, better data and evidence will need to be integrated throughout the whole system. It should be the fundamental basis of policy and practice and thus the foundation for change.

We have a long way to go to address this. The Centre for Homelessness Impact's Evidence Tools[3] are a great way to find causal evidence that already exists, but they do show that very little reliable evidence exists about how our most common interventions work. The vast majority of studies that do exist are from North America and are therefore not necessarily replicable in the UK. What works in one context often does not work in another. What the UK lacks is a comprehensive picture of the problems unique to our country and a full understanding of the solutions that will allow us to address them effectively.

To build a stronger evidence infrastructure, it is essential that we listen closely to the people providing and receiving services, as well as those who the system has failed and who have dropped out of it altogether. This will show us what does and does not work in practice, providing opportunities to expand and develop services that are having a positive impact or seem promising, and stop practices that are failing – or, worse, doing harm – and create new ones.

Over the last decade there have been significant cuts to legal aid and to the voluntary advice sector. We need to ensure that people on the brink of homelessness are getting the right advice, quickly and easily, at every stage, to stop them losing their homes. To be able to do this, we need causal evidence of what advice could be put in place, where, and how it should be provided, whether online, face-to-face, intensive support, on housing, debt management and benefits. Combining this approach with better use of big data will enable us to learn faster about what interventions could do the most good.

As benefits changes continue to be rolled out across different parts of the UK, we need to monitor closely how these affect people, whether they are already in poverty or at risk of being pulled into it, and improve how data and evidence is used across the system to continually improve people's experiences and outcomes.

If we are to end poverty and homelessness sustainably it is vital to persuade the public that it is possible to do so and compel them to act. But currently the public generally views homelessness as almost impossible to solve – it is seen as a pernicious problem that money, government policies or charity can mitigate but not cure.[4] Part of the issue is that when organisations and the media discuss the prevalence of homelessness or emphasise its urgency without offering solutions, they substantiate the public's fatalism about the issue, inadvertently sending out the message that homelessness is an unavoidable problem.[5]

To change attitudes, we must use evidence-informed communications to explain both the root causes of issues and why solving poverty and homelessness matters to society at large. Increasing investment in reliable evidence and a better use of evidence and data offers the opportunity to do this more effectively than ever before. These are not intractable problems.

Evidence-informed communication

For many years we have been researching the issues of homelessness and poverty, bringing facts and figures about the scale of the problem to the fore. Despite all this excellent work, the problem persists. Worse, the public still incorrectly believe that individual factors such as a person's character and personal choices, rather than systemic issues, are largely to blame. If we are to end homelessness for good, we need the public's belief and support that this can be achieved.

JRF, Crisis and others have been working with the FrameWorks Institute to understand the basis for public attitudes and how to use evidence to communicate more effectively with this in mind. By changing the way we talk about poverty and homelessness, we can build public support and political commitment for change.

We often make the mistake of assuming people's minds are empty vessels. But our research has shown that the public's ideas about poverty in the UK are shaped by a set of 'cultural models' – shared assumptions and patterns of thinking that are widely held across our population. It is possible to tap into the helpful cultural models that we share across our society, but we also have to be alert to triggering and reinforcing unhelpful beliefs. In other words, we need to take the same evidence-informed approach to our communications that is required for sound policy development and practice.

Beliefs and assumptions

We have to make conscious decisions about the impact we want to have with our communications and think through what we say and how we say it to achieve the impact we want. Before exploring the most effective ways to talk about poverty and homelessness, it is important to understand exactly what we are up against and how easy it is to accidentally trigger unhelpful stereotypes or fatalistic thinking in our communications.

JRF's study by FrameWorks (Hawkins, 2018) involved 20,000 people across the political spectrum and highlighted these deeply and widely held ways of thinking about UK poverty:

- People think that our society is prosperous and has progressed beyond poverty, so they dismiss its existence. Facts and stories that do not fit with this view simply bounce off them.
- There is a persistent idea that a person's situation is solely down to their motivation and choices and that trying harder and working more are the only solutions.
- People believe that nothing can or will change, because we are all at the mercy of elites who manipulate the system. This fatalistic way of thinking means people disengage completely from problems that we need their support to address.

If our messages trigger one of these ways of thinking, people are more likely to blame individuals for their problems, will be less concerned with the issue and less supportive of change.

FrameWorks' research for Crisis (FrameWorks Institute, 2017) found that the public widely share these beliefs about homelessness:

- Rough sleeping is the only form of homelessness.
- Homelessness is the result of poor choices and lack of effort – or a deliberate decision to live outside of society's rules.
- Homelessness cannot be prevented.
- Homelessness is an inevitable and unsolvable social problem.

Put another way, the study shows how the public sees the 'typical' homeless person as an outsider or victim – someone whose circumstances place them in a separate category of society. When asked about their expectations for the future, most see homelessness as an impossible problem that personal actions can do very little to solve. And this fundamental misconception may be preventing our work from progressing.

You can see from these two sets of beliefs and assumptions that there is a lot of common ground in how we think and talk about poverty and homelessness, reflecting the strong links between the two.

Telling a different story

This work gave us vital evidence-based techniques to tell our stories in ways that trigger more positive ways of thinking, some of which made us completely rethink how we communicate. For example, we learned that:

- Statistics on their own will not change someone's mind about an issue – the numbers need to be part of a story that gives more context, otherwise people will interpret figures in line with their own worldview. In fact, a big number on its own can trigger fatalistic thinking that nothing can be done.
- Myth-busting does not work. This is a tough one to come to terms with, but telling people they are wrong will not change their opinion – quite the opposite, in fact. The myth you are trying to bust is more likely to reinforce individuals' existing beliefs.

So what *does* work?

Values: Our society's shared sense of morals and values gives us a way to show why poverty and homelessness matter and explain the responsibility we all have for change. For Crisis, 'moral human rights' is a powerful value because it highlights that everyone has a right to dignity and respect and that these are part of our basic humanity. At JRF, we talked about the values of compassion and justice to highlight society's shared moral responsibility to ensure everyone has a decent standard of living.

Solutions: Without offering a solution, our stories can easily put across a fatalistic message that the problem is too big or difficult to fix. We should use reliable evidence to find and develop solutions to poverty and homelessness and we must include these in our stories whenever possible. For example, we talk about how the economy can be redesigned. The public sees the economy as something that is big, complicated and unmovable, but if we talk about it as a designed system, we can also show that it can be redesigned to work better for people in poverty and society more generally.

Metaphors: Poverty and homelessness are complex issues, but we can make them easier to understand by using metaphors. At JRF, we talked about how the economy 'locks' people in poverty and how poverty 'restricts and restrains' them, to demonstrate how poverty stops people choosing their own path in life. We also talked about 'currents' as a metaphor for how poverty works. For example: 'Our economy creates powerful currents that can pull people into poverty, like low wages or increasing living costs.'

These examples of framing the issue show the importance of evidence-informed communication that tells people's stories in the context of wider systems, taps into shared values, helps people understand the issues and ideally shows how the problem can be solved.

If the sector develops a shared understanding of how to do this, we can tell a new evidence-informed, consistent and compelling story that can change hearts and minds and inspire change. Ultimately, that will improve the lives of people experiencing poverty and homelessness. If we carry on doing what we have always done, we risk reinforcing negative attitudes and beliefs and causing further harm to the very people we exist to support.

How can we solve homelessness?

Homelessness is one of the most extreme examples of where the safety net has failed those in poverty. To really end homelessness we need smart, sustained investment in a safety net that catches people and we need to provide more homes that are truly affordable and in the right areas. If we fix those things and create a system that continually tests and improves itself, we can fix homelessness. In the past, we have greatly reduced rough sleeping, which shows it can be done. But the solutions to homelessness lie far further up the chain.

There are a series of choices that government – central, devolved, and local – need to make about their commitment to ending homelessness on a day-to-day basis and to driving prevention upstream. Others, from churches to businesses, campaigners and independent funders, also have an important role to play.

Evidence plays an absolutely vital role in shaping the best possible solutions and accelerating impact. Currently we know that change needs to happen but lack the types of evidence and data needed to drive it.

The following is a list of areas in which we know a what works movement in this space could make an enormous impact.

Evidence-informed approach to building the right type of houses in the right places for the right people

Where are people living? Is housing a cause or consequence of their poverty? We need better data and evidence about how social housing is allocated; on how many houses we build and where. We are not building anywhere near enough houses and, of those we do build, there is a dire lack of truly affordable homes in the right places. We see people being offered properties that are not suitable for them or their family and having to live in these unsuitable places because they have no other option.

We need reliable evidence about the best way housing can be used as a tool to alleviate poverty and improve lives – for more people to have suitable homes and fewer people to be homeless.

Increasing tenant rights in the private rented sector

We need an evidence-informed increase in tenant rights to make it harder for landlords to enforce eviction without good reason. Losing a home is traumatic, stressful and challenging for anyone, and compounds the problems for someone who's already struggling. One woman told us: "I've just got pressure on my mind the whole time, where am I going to go? What's going to happen to me? ... I tried to do away with myself three or four times because I didn't know what way my life was going to go." On 1 December 2017, new legislation was introduced in Scotland introducing private residential tenancies that supersede assured and short-assured tenancies. Three of the most important changes under this legislation were:

- no fixed-term tenancies;
- landlords cannot use section 33 (no-fault evictions) – instead they must use one of 18 grounds to regain possession of their property;
- rents can only increase once a year and a landlord must give a tenant three months' notice of any increase. If a tenant considers an increase unreasonable, they can make a referral to a rent officer, who will set the open market rent for the property.

Use evidence to use existing resources more effectively and to secure longer-term resources

To support the changes we need to see in society, local authorities and the third sector must become better at using reliable evidence to achieve the best possible results with existing resources. We know local authorities are struggling. *The 2018 Homelessness Monitor for England* (Fitzpatrick et al, 2018a) shows:

- The majority of local councils in England are struggling to find any stable housing for homeless people in their area, leaving them forced to place more and more people in unstable temporary accommodation.
- As housing supply dwindles and rents outstrip wages and benefits, 70 per cent of local authorities surveyed for the report said they had difficulties finding social housing for homeless people in the previous year, while 89 per cent reported difficulties in finding private rented accommodation.

The 2019 Homelessness Monitor for Scotland (Fitzpatrick et al, 2019) showed that local authorities are expecting homelessness to get worse:

- Local authorities generally believed that post-2010 welfare reform has exacerbated homelessness in their area, although almost all acknowledged that its impacts had been mitigated by the Scottish Government, particularly via discretionary housing payments.
- Three-quarters of Scottish local authorities anticipate that the full roll-out of universal credit will exacerbate homelessness in their area over the next two years. The consensus of concern is almost as strong with respect to the lowering of the benefit cap.

Greater use of reliable evidence

We desperately need to make sure that decision-making is underpinned by evidence and that it designs evidence and data across the system to improve impact. We need more causal evidence on the support that should be available before people become homeless. Evidence of successful prevention measures could have a very significant impact on the number of people affected by homelessness at each stage of the system, but we will also need evidence that reflects the state of homelessness at the population level.

The (voluntary, higher) living wage is an example of how evidence can be used well to create change and build a movement, with over 4,700 employers now paying a wage based on the cost of living.[6] It is calculated using the Minimum Income Standard (MIS),[7] developed in collaboration with JRF by the Centre for Research in Social Policy (CRSP) at Loughborough University. MIS is what the public have told researchers they need for a decent minimum standard of living and takes into account the differing needs of different groups, updated each year to account for rising costs and other factors (Davis, A. et al, 2018).

A shift in attitudes

For major social change to happen, we first need to build a movement of people demanding that change. This is something we can achieve, working together. Public opinion on poverty has begun to shift. We need to build on this momentum and new uses of data and evidence present an opportunity to help accelerate progress.

Conclusion

It is quite simply wrong that anyone should be homeless in the UK and it is possible to redesign the system so that it truly protects people from harm, and does not contribute to locking them in poverty. Progress on poverty has stood still and has now gone into reverse, but we can do something about this. We can solve poverty and homelessness if we embrace a learning mindset and use data and evidence in a more focused way to accelerate progress.

With a shared vision and united effort, we could have fewer people on the streets for less time and only a tiny handful of people homeless at any time. We can do something about the high housing costs and inadequate jobs that lock people into poverty and restrict their opportunities to make a better life. With more data and evidence we can begin to redesign the shredded safety net that no longer prevents people from dropping into destitution and homelessness.

If we design evidence across the system to address the gaps in our knowledge and understanding, frame our communications more effectively to change attitudes and drive continual improvement in our services, we can begin to imagine how we could improve the whole system and ensure it acts as a platform for better lives for those affected by poverty and homelessness.

Notes

[1] JRF press release, 2 October 2018: https://www.jrf.org.uk/report/uk-poverty-2018.

[2] First quote taken from JRF's podcast, Is Anyone Listening?, 30 October 2018: https://play.acast.com/s/isanyonelistening/solving-poverty-after-brexit-featuring-ayesha-haza; quotes 2–4 taken from Paul Brook's JRF blog, 4 December 2018: https://www.jrf.org.uk/blog/why-working-parents-are-struggling-repel-rising-tide-poverty.

[3] See https://www.homelessnessimpact.org/tools.

[4] www.feantsaresearch.org/download/think-piece-23459289098505715364.pdf.

[5] www.feantsaresearch.org/download/think-piece-23459289098505715364.pdf.

[6] Living Wage Foundation: https://www.livingwage.org.uk/.

[7] CRSP, Minimum Income Standards: https://www.lboro.ac.uk/research/crsp/mis/.

References

Davis, A., Hirsch, D. and Padley, M. 2018. *A Minimum Income Standard for the UK, 2008–2018: Continuity and Change*. York: JRF.

Fitzpatrick, S., Pawson, H., Bramley, G., Wilcox, S., Watts, B. and Wood, J. 2018a. *The Homelessness Monitor: England 2018*. London: Crisis/JRF. www.crisis.org.uk/ending-homelessness/homelessness-knowledge-hub/homelessness-monitor/england/the-homelessness-monitor-england-2018/.

Fitzpatrick, S., Bramley, G., Sosenko, F., Blenkinsopp, J., Wood, J., Johnsen, S., Littlewood, M. and Watts, B. 2018b. *Destitution in the UK 2018*. York: JRF. www.jrf.org.uk/report/destitution-uk-2018.

Fitzpatrick, S., Pawson, H., Bramley, G., Wilcox, S., Watts, B., Wood, J., Stephens, M. and Blenkinsopp, J. 2019. *The Homelessness Monitor: Scotland 2019*, London: Crisis. www.crisis.org.uk/ending-homelessness/homelessness-knowledge-hub/homelessness-monitor/scotland/the-homelessness-monitor-scotland-2019/.

FrameWorks Institute. 2017. *Our Common Experience: The Big Idea That Can Help End Homelessness*. London: Crisis. www.crisis.org.uk/media/238822/our_common_experience_summary_report_2018.pdf.

Hawkins, N. 2018. *How to Build Lasting Support to Solve UK Poverty*. York: JRF. www.jrf.org.uk/report/how-build-lasting-support-solve-uk-poverty.

Joseph Rowntree Foundation – various authors (2016) *We Can Solve Poverty in the UK*. York: JRF. www.jrf.org.uk/report/we-can-solve-poverty-uk.

JRF Analysis Unit. 2018. *UK Poverty 2018*. www.jrf.org.uk/report/uk-poverty-2018.

Soodeen, F. (2018) *Social Housing Green Paper: JRF and JRHT response*. York: JRF. www.jrf.org.uk/report/social-housing-green-paper-jrf-and-jrht-response.

6

A cross-party approach to homelessness

Neil Coyle and Bob Blackman

All-Party Parliamentary Group for Ending Homelessness

Over the last decade, all forms of homelessness have risen significantly across England. Research for Crisis found that 170,000 families and individuals are experiencing the worst forms of homelessness across Great Britain (MHCLG, 2013–19). If we carry on as we currently are, this is expected to rise substantially. Across the UK, in our very different constituencies, my parliamentary colleagues and I on the All-Party Parliamentary Group for Ending Homelessness (APPG) unfortunately see families living in unsuitable temporary accommodation, rough sleepers on our streets or 'sofa surfers' who are waiting on social or private housing. In my own surgeries this has included a cleaner in her 50s sleeping on night buses and a young woman sleeping with a different guy from bars each night to avoid rough sleeping.

Homelessness is a far more widespread issue than the more visible problem of rough sleeping though and affects far more people than most of us realise. People lose their homes for a variety of reasons. We know from government statistics that the greatest cause of homelessness in England is the loss of a tenancy in the private rented sector.[1] High demand for affordable housing and the freeze on housing benefit also mean people are increasingly struggling to keep up with housing costs. Sudden life events, such as losing a job or family breakdown can also quickly force people into homelessness.

The causes of homelessness can be varied and complex. However, we know that all forms of homelessness can be ended with holistic and system-wide reforms across a range of areas, including welfare, housing supply and immigration policy. A rapid rehousing approach for people with low–medium level needs can be very effective in ending their homelessness quickly and preventing repeat homelessness. Meanwhile, a housing first approach that focuses on getting those with more complex needs into permanent accommodation before addressing their wider support needs has proven effective in countries where it has been rolled out nationally, such as Finland. It is also essential that government focuses on tackling the root causes of homelessness by investing in social housing; ensuring that the welfare budget, which has seen cuts in funding since 2010, covers the cost of housing; and investment in sustained support for addressing mental health problems and substance abuse.

We set up the APPG in 2016 in response to rising homelessness and with the aim of identifying, exploring, and advocating for the best policy solutions to it. Alongside MPs and peers, the APPG works with a wide range of experts from within the homelessness and related sectors to enable the group to be fully informed on the debate and identify workable solutions. We have so far carried out two year-long inquiries into prevention and rapid responses to homelessness, during which we collected written and verbal evidence from key stakeholders from across the homelessness, housing, health, domestic abuse, justice, immigration and young people's sectors, as well as hearing from people with personal experience of homelessness.

We have developed strong cross-party support and provided a platform for people experiencing all forms of homelessness to inform the political dialogue surrounding homelessness. We aim to bring the voice of people with lived experience of homelessness and local organisations that work directly with people experiencing homelessness into the centre of our work by ensuring their stories are heard by parliamentarians and government officials through oral evidence sessions and case studies published in our reports.

Inquiries into prevention and rapid responses to homelessness

We believe homelessness should be rare, brief and non-recurrent. To this end, we have carried out two inquiries into prevention and rapid responses to homelessness. The best way to end homelessness is to stop it from happening in the first place. Not only would this protect people from the devastating impacts homelessness can have, such as physical and mental health problems; it is also the most cost-effective approach to tackling homelessness. A recent study, which interviewed 86 people, who had been homeless for at least 90 days, concluded public spending would fall by £370 million if 40,000 people were prevented from experiencing one year of homelessness (Pleace and Culhane, 2016).

Our prevention inquiry focused on high-risk demographics, including care leavers, prison leavers and survivors of domestic abuse. There seems to be an acceptance of an inevitability to the homelessness experienced by these three cohorts. They all should be known to services and therefore their homelessness should be preventable as there are obvious intervention points. Some of the key recommendations to emerge from this inquiry included extending automatic priority need for housing to all survivors of domestic abuse, exempting all care leavers under 25 from the shared accommodation rate (the maximum amount of housing benefit or universal credit housing costs available when renting a room in a shared house from a private landlord) and introducing integrated transition plans for all prisoners and measurable housing outcomes for community rehabilitation companies.

The human cost of homelessness is at its highest when it is continual or is recurrent. It is vital that action is taken to find people stable, secure housing as quickly as possible to prevent their support needs escalating and minimise the risk of repeat homelessness. Our rapid response inquiry focused on how homelessness can be ended more quickly for young people and migrants, both groups who face particular barriers to resolving their homelessness. It also looked at rapid rehousing models, such as critical time intervention (CTI) and private rented sector access schemes.

The report showed that with focused and evidence-based interventions, a person's homelessness can be ended quickly and effectively. Key recommendations included scrapping the no recourse to public funds condition for survivors of domestic abuse, care leavers and families with dependent children; the commissioning of CTI approaches for care leavers, prison leavers and survivors of domestic abuse with low-level needs; and ensuring each local authority has a 'homelessness hub' for young people to access the support they need in one place.

Since the APPG was established in 2016, we have seen a number of welcome commitments from government on homelessness. This includes a commitment to end rough sleeping and the publication of the Rough Sleeping Strategy, though we are united in wanting government to go further (MHCLG, 2018).

Government strategy focuses on prevention, intervention and recovery. We are pleased to see funding for pilots to help people leaving prison find stable and sustainable accommodation, as well as new funding for intensive support for care leavers with complex needs. Both prison leavers and care leavers were identified by the APPG, in our report on prevention, as two cohorts at particular risk of homelessness, but for whom homelessness should be easily preventable.

The 2017 budget also saw a focus on housing-led solutions. Government announced that there would be £20 million made available for private rented sector accommodation schemes and support over two years, for which it has now announced the allocations. While this is welcome, it is important that this funding is used to deliver good quality rapid rehousing approaches based on existing evidence of what works. The APPG will continue to call for this funding to be increased to meet the £31 million per annum that was identified as necessary to deliver private rented sector schemes to scale (APPG for Ending Homelessness, 2018). We will also continue to make the case for the funding to be accompanied by funding for a deposit guarantee service to make this expansion viable.

We have also seen significant changes to homelessness legislation in England that have made prevention a clear priority. The Homelessness Reduction Act 2017 introduced new legal duties for local authorities to step in earlier to prevent homelessness and to do so for more people. It also introduced a new requirement for some public authorities to refer people to the local authority if they are homeless or at risk of homelessness.

However, this could go further by strengthening the duty to refer, so public bodies have a responsibility to cooperate with one another to ensure homelessness is prevented where possible. The primary responsibility for preventing homelessness remains with local authorities, even though in many cases they will not be the first organisation that is aware when someone is at risk of homelessness.

Too many opportunities to prevent homelessness are currently being missed. This is especially true for people leaving the care of the state, including those leaving prison and the care system, as we found during our inquiry into prevention. Recent statistics show that 15 per cent of male and 13 per cent of female prisoners serving short sentences were released without a home to go to (HM Inspectorate of Probation, 2016). This was also the case for one in seven long-term prisoners (HM Inspectorate of Prisons and HM Inspectorate of Probation, 2017). Twenty-six per cent of care leavers had sofa-surfed since leaving care and 14 per cent had slept rough (Gill and Daw, 2017).

From both our prevention and rapid response inquiries, a very clear message emerged; that we need a joined-up, cross-government strategy to end homelessness that makes preventing and ending homelessness a priority across all government departments. To make this a reality, we need everyone from across the homelessness and related sectors to present strong evidence to each government department, including the Cabinet Office and prime minister, on why a joined-up approach to homelessness prevention is necessary and how it will benefit each department in the long run.

The responsibility to tackle homelessness crosses numerous policy areas, from education to immigration policy. As such, many government departments beyond the Ministry of Housing, Communities and Local Government (MHCLG) have a central role to play in preventing and ending homelessness. Through the APPG, we have used different methods and tactics to engage ministers from across different departments over the past three years.

Most recently, we held a meeting in parliament focused on recent research into homeless deaths, the latest iteration of which shows 798 homeless people have died over an 18-month period in the UK, or 11 people each week.

The meeting followed on from a private roundtable held with Public Health Minister Jackie Doyle-Price where it was agreed that homelessness is a public health issue. On the back of this meeting, we are engaging ministers in both MHCLG and the Department of Health on the need for a review to take place into the death of every homeless person, so we can learn the lessons from these tragedies and prevent future deaths.

Poor physical and mental health are both drivers and consequences of homelessness. There is a higher rate of mental health problems among the homeless population than the general population. The onset of mental illness can trigger, or be part of, a series of events that can lead to homelessness. Additionally, mental health issues might well be exacerbated or caused by the stresses associated with being homeless.

It is not surprising that sleeping on the streets, in hostels, in squats or in substandard or overcrowded accommodation can have a damaging effect on someone's physical wellbeing. Office for National Statistics data on homeless deaths revealed that the average age of death of a homeless person is 30 years lower than the national average. Many homeless people have co-existing problems, including poor physical and mental health and substance dependence problems. The data also revealed a significant contrast in the proportion of the general population dying from drug and alcohol abuse or suicide and the proportion of homeless people dying from these causes. Only 0.7 per cent of deaths among the general population were due to drug poisoning, compared to 32 per cent of homeless people. 1.2 per cent of deaths among the general population were due to alcohol-specific causes, compared to 10 per cent of the homeless population. 0.9 per cent of deaths among the general population were due to suicide, compared to 13 per cent among homeless people (Office for National Statistics, 2018).

This evidence makes clear the need to recognise homelessness as a public health issue. While the fact that the ONS was driven to release these statistics last year is positive, we need to ensure that this evidence continues to be collected and that reviews take place after the death of each homeless person so we can better understand the reasons for homeless deaths and prevent deaths in the future.

At the beginning of each APPG year, we hold an annual general meeting where we elect officers to the group and determine what the priorities for the APPG will be over the coming months. Officers and stakeholder members of the group are invited to put forward ideas for work to be carried out by the APPG based on recent research or events. This helps ensure we are focusing on the issues that matter to our members and that we have cross-party support for our work.

We are determined to ensure that the APPG for Ending Homelessness is an effective vehicle for change and is not simply viewed as a talking shop. We have therefore chosen to use this year to focus on campaigning for the implementation of some of our previous recommendations.

Domestic abuse and homelessness

The Domestic Abuse Bill presents a fantastic opportunity for us to move forward with one of the key recommendations to emerge from our inquiry into prevention; that automatic priority need for housing should be extended to all survivors of domestic abuse.

There is a clear link between homelessness and domestic abuse. Research carried out by the national homelessness charity Crisis in 2014 found that 61 per cent of women who were homeless had experienced domestic abuse from a partner (Mackie and Thomas, 2014).

Similarly, St Mungo's reported that half of their female clients have experienced domestic violence and a third of these women said domestic violence had contributed to their homelessness (St Mungo's, 2018).

During our prevention inquiry, we heard from a range of experts, including domestic abuse charities, refuges, local authorities and people with lived experience of both homelessness and domestic abuse. A very clear recommendation to come from that piece of work was that we need to change the law so that everyone made homeless as a result of fleeing domestic abuse is automatically in priority need for housing. This would mean that they would be entitled to an offer of settled housing, as is already the case for people who are homeless as a result of domestic abuse in Wales.

For people fleeing domestic abuse, access to safe, secure accommodation is vital. Without this, there is a risk that survivors will be left with no option but to return to a dangerous situation or sleep rough, putting themselves at risk of further abuse and exploitation. However, currently, unless a person experiencing domestic abuse can prove they would be 'significantly more vulnerable than an ordinary person would be if they became homeless'.[2] Then they would not be defined as being in priority need and eligible for an offer of settled housing.

Experiences show that domestic abuse in isolation is rarely considered enough to qualify someone as in priority need; particularly if they are without dependent children. In 2017, only 2 per cent of people were found to be in priority need and made an offer of settled housing because they were vulnerable due to domestic abuse.[3]

Of the survivors supported by the Women's Aid's 'No Woman Turned Away' project, which provides additional support to women struggling to access refuge places, 53 per cent were prevented from making a valid homelessness application by their local authority (Miles and Smith, 2018).[4] Nearly one quarter (23.1 per cent) of these women were prevented from making a homeless application because they were told that they would not be in priority need (Miles and Smith, 2018).

Providing evidence to demonstrate vulnerability can be traumatic and near impossible for people who have experienced domestic abuse. There is evidence of local authorities consistently failing to provide people fleeing from domestic abuse the help they need and of the 'vulnerability test' being used as a gatekeeping tool.

We argue that all persons who experience domestic abuse are, by definition, vulnerable and therefore they should be placed in the automatic priority need category.

We are calling on government to ensure that the forthcoming Domestic Abuse Bill makes provision to ensure that all survivors of domestic abuse have access to a safe home. This could be achieved by ensuring that everyone fleeing domestic abuse who is homeless is automatically considered in priority need for settled housing, rather than being subject to the vulnerability test to determine whether they qualify.

As part of this campaign, we will be engaging with ministers and civil servants in both MHCLG and the Home Office to demonstrate cross-party support for this amendment to the homelessness legislation that would see this particularly vulnerable group of people automatically given priority need for access to a safe, secure home where they can rebuild their life.

Migration and homelessness

Our inquiry into rapid responses to homelessness highlighted how essential it is that government address migrant homelessness if it is to achieve its goal of ending rough sleeping by 2024. As such, we are also focusing this year on campaigning for the extension of the 28-day move-on period for refugees to 56 days and scrapping the no recourse to public funds condition for survivors of domestic abuse, care leavers and families with dependent children.

Migrants with no recourse to public funds who are not considered vulnerable are ineligible for any support and left reliant on family and friends, or support from the voluntary sector and local faith groups. In 2016–17, 53 per cent of people seen sleeping rough in London were from outside the UK (Mayor of London, 2018).

There are many complex reasons and inter-related issues that result in people from outside the UK becoming homeless, which make it more difficult to resolve their homelessness. These can include difficulties resolving their immigration status, vulnerability to exploitation forcing them underground and barriers to accessing support. Errors and poor access to legal advice, alongside social isolation and a lack of access to support, have resulted in many people who could have their immigration status regularised facing ongoing destitution and homelessness.

We are calling on government to scrap the no recourse to public funds condition for victims of domestic violence, care leavers and any person applying for leave to remain under the family/private life rules when they have a dependent child.

The APPG's inquiry also found that an increasing number of refugees are facing destitution and homelessness as 28 days is not enough time for refugees to sort out welfare support, immigration status or find housing before the housing and financial support that was provided by the Home Office ends.

In London, the number of rough sleepers whose last settled base was asylum accommodation has increased over the past three years and in 2017–18 this accounted for almost 3 per cent of all new rough sleepers (Mayor of London, 2018). Crisis is also supporting an increasing number of people who became homeless because they had nowhere to live after leaving asylum accommodation. In 2016–17, 478 people (7 per cent of new clients that year) approached Crisis for help for this reason (Downie et al, 2018).

NACCOM, a charity that represents a network of organisations who provide accommodation and support to asylum seekers, refugees and other vulnerable migrants, reported that their members are accommodating a rising number of refugees. This includes people facing destitution after the end of the move on period. In 2017–18 NACCOM members accommodated 1,097 refugees. Of these, 37 per cent were known to be newly recognised refugees not yet in receipt of benefits/employment when they applied for accommodation (NACCOM, 2018).

The future of the APPG for Ending Homelessness

Unlike other APPGs, the APPG for Ending Homelessness was time limited to five years when it was established. By having a deadline, we hope the group can adhere to a strict timeline of activity that will ensure our activity and outputs are impactful.

This has helped focus our work on what we can achieve within this time-period, give our work and the issue of homelessness the sense of urgency it requires, and maintain momentum for change.

We have been robust with government about the causes of homelessness but remain constructive about solving the crisis. Homelessness is a social problem. The families suffering its consequences would not thank anyone seeking cheap political point-scoring rather than trying to deliver tangible solutions to end their hardship. We will continue to use the APPG as a platform for bringing together parliamentarians from all parties to unite and campaign on evidence-based policy solutions to homelessness.

Evidence gathering and policy-making remain important aspects of the APPG's work. However, a lack of a strong, accurate evidence base when it comes to the scale of homelessness and its impacts, especially in relation to more marginal groups such as migrants, has created an obstacle when it comes to fully understanding the key problems and solutions in relation to homelessness and the impact of policy decisions. This is why a more comprehensive collection of evidence and data is so vital to tackling homelessness. To complete our series of inquiries, we will be holding an inquiry looking at the sustainable solutions to homelessness, as without cross-party support for these there can be no long-term vision for ending homelessness. We hope that there will be an opportunity to work with the Centre for Homelessness Impact and other research organisations to identify where our focuses should lie with this inquiry.

Ultimately, only government, in partnership with public bodies who regularly encounter people who may be at risk of or experiencing homelessness and local authorities, can provide the leadership to end homelessness. We must draw on the expertise from every sector involved, including charities and people who have been or still are homeless, to build evidence-based sustainable solutions.

The APPG will continue to provide a unique platform for parliamentarians to discuss homelessness policy with key experts from within the homelessness and related sectors to provide a united voice in support of policy solutions based on evidence of what works. We will continue to make the case for government to take bold action across all departments to prevent and end homelessness in the UK by implementing a cross-government strategy to end homelessness. Once the group's self-imposed life span of five years has been reached, we hope it will leave a legacy of cross-party working and cooperation to ensure homelessness is a political priority.

Homelessness is not a given. By working together to promote long-term, sustainable solutions to it, we can ensure future generations are not at risk of the perpetuation of homelessness and end this national crisis.

Notes

[1] MHCLG, Homelessness Statistics, www.gov.uk/government/collections/homelessness-statistics#live-tables.

[2] Homelessness Code of Guidance for Local Authorities: www.gov.uk/guidance/homelessness-code-of-guidance-for-local-authorities.

[3] MHCLG (2013–19), Live Tables 773 and 774.

[4] Miles and Smith (2018)d. The analysis in this report is based on case work data from 264 women.

References

APPG for Ending Homelessness. 2018. *All-Party Parliamentary Group for Ending Homelessness: Rapidly Responding to Homelessness – A Look at Migrant Homelessness, Youth Homelessness and Rapid Rehousing Models*. London: APPG for Ending Homelessness.

Downie, M., Gousy, H., Basran, J., Jacob, R., Rowe, S., Hancock, C., Albanese, F., Pritchard, R., Nightingale, K. and Davies, T. 2018. *Everybody In: How to End Homelessness in Great Britain*. London: Crisis.

Gill, A. and Daw, E. 2017. *From Care to Where? Care Leavers' Access to Accommodation*. London: Centrepoint.

HM Inspectorate of Prisons and HM Inspectorate of Probation. 2017. *An Inspection of Through the Gate Resettlement Services for Prisoners Serving 12 Months or More*. Manchester: HM Inspectorate of Probation.

HM Inspectorate of Probation. 2016. *An Inspection of Through the Gate Resettlement Services for Short-Term Prisoners*. Manchester: HM Inspectorate of Probation.

Mackie, P. and Thomas, I. 2014. *Nations Apart? Experiences of Single Homeless People Across Great Britain*. London: Crisis. www.crisis.org.uk/media/20608/crisis_nations_apart_2014. pdf.

Mayor of London. 2018. *CHAIN Annual Report Greater London April 2017–March 2018*. https://data.london.gov.uk/dataset/chain-reports.

MHCLG (Ministry of Housing, Communities & Local Government). 2013–19. *Homelessness Statistics*. www.gov.uk/government/collections/homelessness-statistics#live-tables.

MHCLG (Ministry of Housing, Communities & Local Government). 2018. *Rough Sleeping Strategy*. London: MHCLG.

Miles, C. and Smith, K. 2018. *Nowhere to Turn, 2018, Findings from the Second Year of the No Women Turned Away Project*. Bristol: Women's Aid.

NACCOM. 2018. *Annual Report 2017–18*. https://naccom. org.uk/wp-content/uploads/2018/09/NACCOM-AnnualReport_2017-09-19_final-EMAIL.pdf.

Office for National Statistics. 2018. *Deaths of Homeless People in England and Wales 2013-2017*. https://www.ons. gov.uk/peoplepopulationandcommunity/birthsdeathsand marriages/deaths/bulletins/deathsofhomelesspeopleinengland andwales/2018.

Pleace, N. and Culhane, D.P. 2016. *Better than Cure? Testing the Case for Enhancing Prevention of Single Homelessness in England*. London: Crisis.

St Mungo's. 2018. *Rebuilding Shattered Lives, The Final Report: Getting the Right Help at the Right Time to Women Who Are Homeless or at Risk*. London: St Mungo's.

7

Contrasting traditions in homelessness research between the UK and US

Dennis Culhane, Suzanne Fitzpatrick
and Dan Treglia

You only need to take a quick glimpse at the Centre for Homelessness Impact's (CHI) Evidence Finder[1] to notice the contrast between the types of homelessness studies produced in the UK and the US. While in the US a large volume of quantitative 'impact' studies on homelessness has been generated over many years, homelessness researchers in the UK have tended to be concerned, at least until recently, with more qualitative and conceptual forms of exploration and evaluation. This has profound implications for our ability to answer pressing policy and practice questions, which often require mixed methods approaches that attain both breadth and depth of understanding.

This contrast between the US and UK extant homelessness literatures can be traced back to the different research traditions that have emerged over the years on opposite sides of the Atlantic (Fitzpatrick and Christian, 2006). In the UK, applied housing studies specialists have tended to dominate academic research on homelessness, with the important role played by domestic legislation in tackling homelessness in the UK also meaning that there is a strong tradition of socio-legal scholarship in this field (Cowan, 2019). More theoretical contributions in the UK, as in the US, often emerge from urban geography or sociology perspectives (Lancione, 2013), although a sharply contrasting conceptual approach within the UK now sees mainstream moral philosophy applied to the ethical challenges and dilemmas that abound in homelessness policy and practice (Watts et al, 2017). Health-orientated research on homelessness has generally been relatively marginal to the policy debate in the UK, not least because it is often very narrowly focused (for example on oral health or blood-borne viruses among specific homeless subpopulations). That said, there is now increasing engagement from UK-based public health specialists in the 'complex needs' of homeless people who face compounding problems of substance misuse, mental ill-health and/or involvement in the criminal justice system (Aldridge et al, 2018; Luchenski et al, 2018).

In the US, by contrast, psychological, sociological and medical perspectives have long played a central role in homelessness research, along with significant contributions from social policy and economics scholars. The prominence of these clinical perspectives, and a more quantitative approach in the social sciences more generally, has engendered a research tradition heavily slanted toward statistical research and policy and programme evaluation. This is not to minimise the extent, rigour or quality of qualitative research in the US but, on balance, it is quantitative analyses that have dominated research and policy conversations. This is due in large part to pressure from government and private funders alike to prove the efficacy and financial efficiency of homelessness programming, with robust evidence of success often required to justify increased spending on homelessness and other social policy priorities.

Regardless of any country's research traditions, a wide range of disciplinary perspectives have valid contributions to make in tackling homelessness, and more extensive engagement between scholars across the developed world in recent years has enriched our respective research traditions. One benefit of this international engagement has been to draw out ever more clearly the importance of striking a balance in research efforts such that we are able to stand back and identify the fundamental drivers of homelessness – and the broader societal and political context that allows this extreme form of disadvantage to persist – while simultaneously engaging in robust evaluation of targeted, practical responses that seek to prevent or alleviate homelessness in the here and now. This balance requires attention to both the macro and the micro scale, and to both qualitative and quantitative methods of analysis.

In the UK, however, a preoccupation with more theoretical and political concerns on homelessness has, at least arguably, meant a relative neglect of robust evaluative research on targeted interventions. Such micro-level initiatives proliferate in the UK homelessness sector, but very few have undergone rigorous evaluation, with cost–benefit and other quantitative techniques a particular rarity. Given the '80 per cent rule' – that most interventions when scrutinised closely turn out to be ineffective (White, this volume) – this is clearly a matter of concern.

In the US, on the other hand, the emphasis on quantitative impact evaluation has a tendency to limit the survival and proliferation of ineffective or financially inefficient programmes. Politicians and philanthropists alike boast about cost-savings and return-on-investment, and often require that grantees maintain an administrative database that allows the programme to report on utilisation and conduct – often through a third party – an outcome evaluation that may include comparison to a control group or incorporate some measure of cost–benefit analysis. Some funders, like the Robin Hood Foundation, have developed a reputation on this front, which includes collecting through primary or administrative records any data reasonably related to the programme being funded.

On a larger scale, the US Department of Housing and Urban Development (HUD) – far and away the largest funder of homelessness-related services – requires grantees to maintain and enter data into a Homeless Management Information System (HMIS), from which the federal government produces point-in-time and annual estimates of homelessness prevalence. Beginning this fiscal year, HUD is moving another step into the direction of national performance measurement, using a new longitudinal systems analysis (LSA) tool that will evaluate community-level performance in key homelessness metrics, such as number of placements into permanent housing and returns to homelessness. The focus on outcomes and performance metrics, however, often overshadows qualitative research that offers extensive depth into the experience of the lives and service needs of those experiencing homelessness.

There is therefore significant opportunity for improving the effectiveness of efforts to address homelessness through closer collaboration between disciplines and countries, improved data and evidential techniques and, where necessary, via a rebalancing of research investments. Here we explore the UK and US traditions with a view to identifying how new opportunities presented by developments in the field might help forge a path to better homelessness research and, more importantly, better homelessness responses.

The importance of mixed methods: the need for a rebalance in the UK

Historically, a lack of rigour in much British homelessness research has been associated with the highly policy-driven nature of much of this work, dominated by a plethora of small-scale projects closely tied to the (short-term) political objectives of either government or their opponents (Fitzpatrick et al, 2000). A great deal of this applied research on homelessness has been commissioned or conducted by pressure groups on a 'quick and dirty' basis for overt lobbying purposes. Paradoxically, but predictably, it has often had little credibility with policy-makers for that very reason.

At the opposite end of the scholarship – but not ideological – spectrum has been intensely and self-consciously 'academic' research, generally of a highly esoteric and abstract nature, that uses the predicament of homeless people as a vehicle for positing some bigger claim about the evils of capitalism, neoliberalism, and so on. Such so-called 'critical' research, far from being 'risky' to undertake, is now firmly embedded as the orthodox, almost compulsory, perspective to adopt in certain UK (and indeed European) academic circles. The urban and cultural geography milieu spring to mind in this regard and, so too, some variants of anthropology, where a voyeuristic fascination and lionisation of street homeless people's lifestyles seems to replace any urgency about addressing the immiseration they face. Sensibly, policy-makers, in the UK at least, seem largely oblivious to this kind of scholarship and, when they do encounter it, recognise it for what it is: self-referential agitprop.

However, it is also important to appreciate that, between these extremes, there is a long history of insightful, practically orientated qualitative research on the experiences, perceptions and priorities of people who are homeless in the UK (Fitzpatrick et al, 2000; Mackie et al, 2017). The lacuna has rather tended to lie in more fundamental or 'basic' quantitative research about the prevalence of homelessness and its underlying causes and drivers. Respectable statistical work, that is both conceptually informed and empirically robust, has therefore tended to be hard to come by. In particular, and despite all the insistence in the British academic tradition about the predominance of 'structural' causes of homelessness (Fitzpatrick et al, 2011), until recently, very little attempt had been made to demonstrate or test this proposition empirically (Alma Economics, 2019a; though see Bramley (1988) for an early exception). This may in part reflect the sense that the structural causation of homelessness is an indisputable a priori article of faith among some in the British academic community (Fitzpatrick, 2005). More prosaically, the quantitative research skills required to model and test the influence of macro-level structural factors on trends in homelessness, and relationships at aggregate level, have traditionally been in short supply among homelessness researchers in the UK.

This is now changing, with a series of more serious quantitative treatments of the scale, nature and impacts of homelessness in the UK emerging, to complement the richness of the predominant qualitative tradition. The growing engagement of health-related disciplines is helping enormously in this rebalancing endeavour (see also Marshall and Bibby, this volume). For example, the strong association between poor health and homelessness was emphatically underlined by the findings of a recent administrative data linkage study in Scotland (Waugh et al, 2018). This revealed that a sizeable minority of the whole of Scotland's population (at least 8 per cent) had been assessed as homeless or threatened with homelessness by local authorities between 2001 and 2016. This homeless cohort were shown to have a roughly five times higher chance of dying than people of the same age and gender living in the least deprived fifth of areas in Scotland (see also Aldridge et al, 2018 on excess morbidity and mortality among homeless people and other very excluded groups).

Another recent study has quantitatively tested the claim, or at least the implication, that homelessness risks are widely spread across the UK population – as encapsulated in the oft-repeated charity sector mantra that we are 'all two pay cheques away from homelessness' (Bramley and Fitzpatrick, 2017). Enabled by the existence of three large-scale survey datasets that contain questions about past experience of homelessness, this paper considered the inferences that can be reasonably drawn about the causes of homelessness from data on the characteristics and circumstances of people who have had this experience.

This work demonstrated that poverty, particularly childhood poverty, is by far the most powerful predictor of homelessness in early adulthood in the UK. Health and support needs, and adverse teenage experiences, also contribute to homelessness risks, but their explanatory power is less than that of childhood poverty. Social support networks are a key protective 'buffer', but again the link with homelessness is weaker than that with material poverty. The odds of becoming homeless are greatest in higher housing pressure areas, but these additional 'area effects' were considerably less important than individual and household-level variables. Two vignettes, drawn from either end of this risk spectrum, were presented to illustrate the point (see Figure 7.1).

Quantitative modelling of current and projected levels of homelessness in the UK, also developed by Glen Bramley (2017: 1), concluded that, alongside poverty, the other key drivers included:

> [the] availability and affordability of accommodation, the extent to which prevention measures are used, and the demographics of people experiencing homelessness. Using a series of 'what if' scenarios the model has shown that cessation of welfare cuts

and focused prevention activity can make an impact on levels of... homelessness but this is limited if not accompanied by investment in affordable and accessible housing supply.

UK government ministers do not necessarily accept this characterisation of the causation of rising homelessness in England, especially the link made with welfare reform. However, what is encouraging from an evidential perspective is that the Ministry of Housing, Communities and Local Government (MHCLG) and the Department for Work and Pensions have jointly commissioned a feasibility study to develop a new suite of quantitative, predictive models of homelessness and rough sleeping in England (Alma Economics 2019a, b, c; see also Aldridge, this volume).

There is, then, some progress with respect to this 'big picture' understanding of homelessness in the UK, but a major gap remains with respect to robust evaluations of targeted

Figure 7.1: Homelessness risks in the UK

White male	Mixed ethnicity female
Relatively affluent childhood in rural south of England	Experienced poverty as a child Brought up by a lone parent in London
Unproblematic school career	
Graduated from university at 21	Left school or college at 16
Living with parents at age 26	Living as a renter at 26
	Spells of unemployment
No partner	No partner
No children	Has children
Predicted probability of homelessness by age 30:	Predicted probability of homelessness by age 30:
0.6%	**71.2%**

Source: Bramley and Fitzpatrick (2017)

interventions (Mackie et al, 2017). CHI's Evidence and Gaps Maps work demonstrates that, while many qualitative evaluations of homelessness services exist in the UK, these tend to be small-scale and short-term in nature, and are very often conducted by those with a vested interest in demonstrating the value of a particular intervention (White et al, 2018). While these studies are generally characterised as 'process' or 'implementation' studies in systematic review exercises – in contradistinction to quantitative 'impact' or 'effectiveness' evaluations (White, this volume) – most do in fact make some attempt to analyse intervention effectiveness, even if these attempts frequently lack rigour. Qualitative evaluations conducted by independent researchers tend to have much greater integrity and robustness, for obvious reasons, and can provide rich insights into medium or longer-term outcomes when they contain a longitudinal component.

Nonetheless, rigorous quantitative evaluations are vital in enabling the sorts of research questions that require measurement – such as the cost-effectiveness or relative effectiveness of individual interventions – to be systematically addressed, and would allow the statistical generalisability of the existing qualitative findings to be tested. Yet, experimental and quasi-experimental approaches remain unusual in the UK homelessness sector, and even today it is rare for evaluations to include a comparison group or 'synthetic' controls (though there are some exceptions in recent evaluations of government-funded programmes, including the ongoing Rough Sleeping Initiative (MHCLG, 2019). Such comparison groups are essential in facilitating systematic assessment of the added value of homelessness interventions and the relative merits of different sorts of interventions. The outstanding example here is the tremendous international impact of the US-originating 'Housing First' model for addressing chronic homelessness, which can in large part be attributed to the robustness of the randomised controlled trial (RCT)-backed evidence base that supported this radical approach (Padgett et al, 2016).

The US tradition of homelessness research: balancing the methodological seesaw

Homelessness research in the US has found various disciplinary homes. Early research, from the tramp, Great Depression, and Skid Row eras from the 1890s through the post-Great Depression era, was largely the domain of sociologists (Lee et al, 2010). But as homelessness began to emerge as a public, and public health, concern in the 1980s, work on homelessness accelerated and spread and, with it, the methods used to understand its causes, demographics and solutions. In particular, as government became increasingly involved in the management and resolution of homelessness and required the systematic collection of data, homelessness research moved from a body of literature built on primary data to one built on the administrative data being collected in the course of business.

Anne Shlay and Peter Rossi's seminal 1992 article in *Annual Review* summarised the vast body of interdisciplinary homelessness research conducted through the 1980s and very early 1990s (Shlay and Rossi, 1992). This was, as Lee and colleagues wrote in 2010 and Shlay and Rossi wrote at the time, the 'new' research on homelessness – their summary included more than 60 empirical national and local studies of homelessness, all based on interviews with people in shelter and those on the streets. Within just a couple of years, it became clear that the nature of empirical homelessness research was fundamentally changing.

As managing and solving homelessness increasingly became the domain of local areas and the federal government, a better understanding of the scope of homelessness and characteristics of those experiencing it became increasingly necessary, spurring the development of HMIS (Poulin et al, 2008). New York City created the first such system of its own initiative in 1986 and the city of Philadelphia developed an HMIS as a way of tracking 'purchase of service' orders submitted by local shelters in 1990. Though this rolled out slowly – by 1999, HUD deemed only 12 jurisdictions as having adequate 'coverage' – the promise for operationally meaningful research became readily apparent (Culhane et al, 1994; Culhane et al, 1996; Poulin et al, 2008).

HUD, seeing the operational and research potential of this data, produced national HMIS data standards in the early and mid-2000s and by 2005, 93 per cent of jurisdictions receiving HUD homeless service funding had implemented, or were in implementation or planning stages of, an HMIS. HMIS is now required for funding by HUD.

The availability of data – largely a result of a metrics-driven performance management culture that became prevalent during the 1990s and 2000s – allows for a deeper understanding of the causes and dynamics of homelessness and provides information on how to end it. Research through the 1980s and 1990s on the impact of changes in the housing and labour markets on homelessness, among other macroeconomic forces, was largely speculative without an accurate accounting of flows through the shelter system. Precise measures of shelter utilisation in New York City in the 1990s and 2000s allowed Cragg and O'Flaherty (1999) and O'Flaherty and Wu (2006) to conduct time-series analyses tracking monthly shelter use rates in New York City against unemployment rates, broad-spectrum macroeconomic indicators, and shelter system policies. The collective findings of these two papers – that economic downturns, not the use of subsidised housing, result in net increases in homelessness – would not have been possible previously. O'Flaherty and Wu could even point to an uptick in shelter caseload in the immediate aftermath of the 11 September 2001 terrorist attacks (O'Flaherty and Wu, 2006; Poulin et al, 2008).

Shelter data have also been helpful for research and government-led efforts to describe the homeless population and how they use homeless services. The Annual Homelessness Assessment Report, produced annually for the US Congress since 2007, provides point-in-time and annual statistics on the extent of homelessness and the characteristics of those using homelessness assistance services. These national data have been critical in better understanding the disparities in homelessness risk. For example, African-American households are 4.7 times more likely to experience homelessness than a white household and women veterans are more than twice as likely to experience homelessness compared to other women (Montgomery, 2016; National Alliance to End Homelessness, 2019). This robust data collection has pointed towards the growing problem of young adult homelessness and guided efforts to address it.

The precision inherent in databases tracking homeless system entries and exits are the basis for our current understanding of how people use shelter, on which the federal government is building new capabilities and platforms. The typology of single adult homelessness created by Kuhn and Culhane (Kuhn and Culhane, 1998) and expanded to families by Culhane and colleagues (Culhane et al, 2007) helped to define the field's understanding of shelter use by demonstrating that the vast majority (approximately 80 per cent) of shelter users are 'transitionally homeless' meaning that they are generally homeless for one spell of two months or less, while only 20 per cent have more intensive homeless service needs. The difference between longitudinal analyses collected through administrative versus primary data are apparent in two papers published in 1997 by social welfare scholar Irene Wong. Analyses of administrative shelter records in New York City allowed for regression-driven predictors of shelter exit and re-entry among thousands of shelter users, while her work using interview data in Alameda County, CA was more limited in its ability to draw statistically robust conclusions. Beyond leveraging the work of researchers working with local data to understand these patterns, the federal government is only now creating its own tools – the longitudinal systems analysis (LSA) report – through which it and local service providers can understand how people are using their system of care. By quantifying, for example, shelter exits, re-entries, and long-term stayers, the LSA creates an opportunity for systems analysis and real-time system monitoring, inconceivable even ten years ago.

These same tools have proven invaluable in the development and testing of interventions addressing homelessness. Culhane and colleagues (Culhane et al, 2002) linked HMIS and mainstream social welfare system data in their effectiveness and cost–benefit analysis of permanent supportive housing in New York City. Using administrative data from multiple social service systems, they derived a statistically developed control group, assessed programme efficacy and provided the first estimates of the relative costs and cost offsets of PSH. Their work showed the promise of administrative data when fewer than 10 per cent of municipalities had functioning HMIS systems. These types of evaluations have become common within local and federal systems alike.

The Obama Administration expanded impact evaluations of federal homelessness programmes, particularly as part of efforts from the US Department of Veterans Affairs (VA) that reduced veteran homelessness by nearly 50 per cent (US Department of Housing and Urban Development, 2017). The Family Options Study, a multi-site RCT of four housing interventions for homeless families, was the largest and most comprehensive homeless programme evaluation commissioned by the federal government (Gubits et al, 2016). Despite their rigour and growth, efforts of this magnitude are still rare and it is now incumbent upon HUD and others to kickstart national-level evaluations using existing data; especially feasible with its recent movement toward longitudinal analysis.

All that said, the success and opportunities inherent in quantitative administrative data should not blind researchers to its limitations. Utilisation-based measures, by their very definition, exclude those who do not access services. Among other implications, it is important to consider how this impacts the US's annual point-in-time count. Only three jurisdictions – New York City, Washington, DC, and Massachusetts – have a right to shelter, meaning that estimates of sheltered homelessness are capped by capacity, and flaws in unsheltered homelessness estimates limit their utility. Building on analyses from Hopper et al (2008), Chris Glynn and colleagues convincingly argue to increase estimates of unsheltered homelessness by 40 per cent, moving current assessments of point-in-time homelessness from 550,000 to exceeding 600,000 (Glynn et al, 2018). More generally, utilisation-based measures muddy longitudinal measures of programme success, and increased visibility and outreach may bring more people to receive services regardless of programme efficacy. This was certainly true of evaluations of the VA's efforts to reduce homelessness. Efforts to improve identification and outreach to homeless veterans – ensuring that more people received greater access to evidence-based VA homeless services

– means that the 50 per cent reduction in veteran homelessness from 2010 to 2017 is a likely understatement of the efficacy of its expanded prevention, rapid rehousing, and supported housing programmes.

This limitation similarly confounds efforts to measure the success of programmes designed to prevent or end homelessness by tracking individuals through a single jurisdiction's records. A notable limitation of Byrne et al's (2015) effort to document the efficacy of the VA's prevention and rapid rehousing programme is that success is determined by whether or not a programme recipient appears in subsequent VA homeless programme records; someone who leaves the programme and seeks community-based shelter is incorrectly marked as successfully avoiding future homelessness. This is true more broadly as well, as local systems are unaware of homelessness after a programme exit if an individual uses shelter in another jurisdiction or even sleeps on the street down the block.

This remains true as administrative data are increasingly integrated across agencies and systems to understand the expanse and intersection of needs of people experiencing homelessness. As homelessness data are increasingly linked to records from other social service and healthcare providers, the absence of a matching record should not be conflated with absence of a condition. The absence of child welfare records does not equate to an absence of childhood adversity, for example, and just because a shelter user does not have a matching record in healthcare records does not mean that they do not have a diagnosable health condition, only that they have not received attention for that condition. Even for quantitative analyses, primary data allow researchers to collect data outside of the scope of administrative data, and Marybeth Shinn's iterative attempts at predicting homelessness among high-risk populations is an example of its value (Shinn et al, 2001; Shinn et al, 2013). By interviewing families and single adults seeking homelessness prevention services, she and her team have produced algorithms that combine existing agency records with self-reported data about household characteristics like residential instability, household discord and adverse childhood experiences that would not be apparent through any agency's system.

More broadly, quantitative analyses, particularly those reliant on administrative data exclusively, lack the depth provided by qualitative methods. Our understanding of the experiences of people affected by homelessness – the long-term and proximal causes, the trauma of homelessness itself and the quality of life post-homelessness – has been informed by interviews in which research subjects are valued as experts. The growth of quantitative analysis stemming from administrative data have neither ended nor reduced the value of these methods, although they may have stolen the spotlight. The qualitative analyses of the Family Options study offered nuance in the traumas imposed by homelessness and the trajectories created through the tested interventions, but those findings have been overshadowed by quantitative assessments of success and failure (Gubits et al, 2016). The proliferation and growing confidence in administrative data will undoubtedly produce quantitative analysis of growing complexity and value, but researchers and policy-makers alike must be attuned to its limitations and continue to invest in the qualitative tools that inform our understanding of homelessness's human experience.

Future priorities and shared opportunities

Despite these strong contrasts between the UK and US research and policy traditions and priorities, it is clear that there are also some common priorities and opportunities for future development, many of which are shared by other developed nations.

For example, while there is widespread agreement that 'prevention is better than cure' with respect to homelessness, and many other social harms (Coote, 2012), most countries across the developed world struggle to turn this aspiration into reality. A lack of credible data to focus preventative efforts is a major part of the problem. The sort of statistical and forecasting evidence that is now developing in the UK is especially important in developing tools for more 'universal' or 'upstream' forms of homelessness prevention, to identify the welfare, housing and other structural 'levers' that must be activated to lower overall population-level risks (Bramley, 2017). While such evidence on its own is unlikely to drive policy reform, it can help to reset the parameters of public debate, providing useful ammunition for those seeking progressive change and guiding them on their key lobbying priorities. A clearer set of definitions and improved data to capture marginalised groups not currently well represented in conventional surveys and statistics is a necessary prerequisite to better monitoring, forecasting and policy impact assessments (Bramley et al, 2018).

US policy-makers have similarly struggled to move resources upstream. While some researchers have been pushing for a shift toward a prevention-centred approach since the early 1990s (Culhane, 1993), and Shinn and a series of colleagues wrote a series of papers over two decades fine-tuning targeting of prevention services, supporting research has largely lagged behind policy expansion (Shinn et al, 2001, 2013, 1998). Municipalities like Philadelphia and New York developed homelessness prevention efforts in 1998, and in 2009 the American Recovery and Reinvestment Act, more commonly known as President Obama's economic stimulus bill, pushed the nation as a whole in that direction (Culhane et al, 2011). The bill included $1.5 billion for three years of funding for homelessness prevention and rapid rehousing and, while that funding ended in 2012, the federal government has continued that approach.

Most broadly, the 2009 HEARTH Act changed the Emergency Shelter Grant programme to the Emergency Solutions Grant programme, through which prevention is an allowable expense. In addition, the VA's Supportive Services for Veteran Families programme – which grew from $60 million in 62 per cent of communities in its pilot year to $414 million in 98 per cent of communities in fiscal year 2017 – is the largest single homelessness prevention and rapid rehousing programme (US Department of Veterans Affairs, 2018). The evidence supporting homelessness prevention is still relatively scant. Byrne and colleagues demonstrated strong housing stability rates among veteran households served by prevention services and the quasi-experimental and RCT of New York City's Homebase homelessness prevention programme showed that those who received services enter shelter less frequently, and spent less time in shelter, than a control group (Byrne et al, 2015; Goodmany et al, 2016; Rolston et al, 2013).

International evaluations and comparative research also has a potentially major role to play in identifying the policy and structural factors that drive homelessness, particularly at national level. It has been hypothesised by a range of authors that countries with benign social and economic conditions – well functioning housing and labour markets and generous social security policies – will have a low overall prevalence of homelessness, but that a high proportion of their (relatively) small homeless populations will have complex personal problems (Stephens and Fitzpatrick, 2007; Shinn, 2007). The reverse has been posited to hold true (high prevalence/lower proportion with support needs) in countries with a more difficult structural context. The available comparative evidence is limited but tends to support this hypothesis (Toro, 2007; Stephens et al, 2010). For example, Benjaminsen and Bastholm Andrade (2015) found that Denmark, with its robust welfare state, had levels of shelter use that were substantially lower than those in the US, but also that the 'transitionally homeless' in Denmark were more likely than those in the US to suffer from mental illness and substance misuse. But systematic cross-national research such as this is all too rare in the homelessness sector.

Another fruitful way forward may be to exploit the 'natural experiment' conditions that now pertain in the UK, with homelessness law and policy diverging strongly across the four UK nations in the post-devolution period. Testing and comparing approaches and outcomes systematically across these home jurisdictions could reveal the homelessness impacts of housing, welfare and associated policies and build a more informed reform agenda. An especially exciting comparative opportunity now presents itself in the shape of the significant innovations in homelessness prevention legislation across Great Britain in the past few years, albeit that inter-jurisdictional data diversity makes direct comparison of the outcomes challenging (Fitzpatrick et al, 2019). The US, with its disparate governance structures, holds similar promise for natural experiments. Unlike most social policy experimentation in the US, in which the concentration of power at the state level has been used to assess relative impacts of changes in cash assistance and Medicaid eligibility policies, for example, issues of homelessness often bypass the state and sit largely between the US Department of Housing and Urban Development and the more than 400 continuums of care (CoC) representing geographies as small as a city or as large as a state. While variation in CoC characteristics like size, rurality, climate, political and demographic landscape can make comparisons difficult, Byrne and colleagues (2014) and Corinth (2017) have assessed relationships between local investment in permanent supportive housing and homeless populations, and opportunities exist for others to follow suit.

Another common thread is the potential contribution of administrative data linkage for understanding and addressing the complex, cross-system needs of people who experience homelessness. The US, with its richer history of administrative data linkage in the social service sector, has a head start on its British counterpart. Among the first studies using administrative records, examining the shelter use among Medicaid-reimbursed users of behavioural healthcare, relied on linking disparate data sets (Culhane et al, 1998), and linked records have been integral in establishing the high rate of institution use among homeless adults, particularly focused on hospitals, jails, cash assistance rolls and psychiatric institutions. They have also been integral in programme evaluation as policy-makers seek to understand the full impacts of permanent supportive housing and prevention programmes on related systems and conduct cost–benefit analyses that include all related costs (Culhane et al, 2002; Rolston et al, 2013).

Increasingly, data are being linked in real-time programme administration, allowing shelter caseworkers to coordinate and track healthcare appointments. All told, though, researchers, policy-makers, and practitioners have been slow to capture the potential for cross-system linkages, as these data-sharing projects are confined to agencies with entrepreneurial leaders. Improved data governance guidance, particularly focused on data sharing, is critical to expanding these cross-system collaborations that we know open our eyes to the myriad causes and effects of homelessness and lower the costs of rigorous evaluation. For programme coordination, technology is no longer the barrier, and additional use cases spurred on by entrepreneurial leaders will be required before these arrangements become the norm.

In the meantime, in the UK, there are myriad as yet unrealised opportunities for administrative data linkage to support longitudinal evaluations of homelessness and related interventions at much lower cost than repeat large-scale surveys. The use of data-matching methods on the Troubled Families evaluation described by Aldridge (this volume) illustrates what can be achieved, yet Waugh et al's (2018) study linking health and homelessness data in Scotland remains an exceedingly rare example in our field, certainly at national level. Ideally, one would want such data linkage exercises to include benefits, tax, education, criminal justice and other public systems in tracking relevant outcomes over time. The barriers seem more political and bureaucratic than technical in nature and, frustratingly, persist despite major government investment in 'administrative data research centres' (ADRCs) throughout the UK.

At a local level, growing interest in 'predictive analytics', that enable the identification of 'at-risk' groups, is facilitating more small-scale but nonetheless illuminating administrative data linkage exercises (Watts et al, 2019). This approach may be especially fruitful in the UK where administrative datasets underpinning the statutory homelessness system – including HL1 in Scotland, and H-CLIC in England – potentially capture a large proportion of all those experiencing even 'hidden' forms of homelessness, and can technically be linked to a wide variety of other administrative datasets managed by public authorities. However, data protection-related barriers may prove challenging, so it would be extremely helpful if all such common data systems could have built-in consent for bona fide research using anonymised linkage.

Conclusion

This review of the contrasting homelessness research traditions in the UK and US demonstrates that there is already much to build on, as well as challenges ahead, with some of these challenges apparent on both sides of the Atlantic. But we must not lose sight of the importance of evidence in shaping the way forward in improving homelessness prevention and alleviation.

One key reason why evidence is so important is to overcome inertia and innovation barriers associated with 'path dependency' among existing homelessness policies and services. In other words, once people, resources and organisations are invested in a particular model of intervention, it is very difficult to change tack, even if there is little sign that the intended outcomes are being achieved. Good evidence can assist in a constructive change management process that empowers people and institutions to move in a different, more effective direction without engaging in a blame culture. It is critical to enable, as well as challenge, both statutory and third-sector organisations to move away from their 'institutional stake' in existing ineffective approaches.

The contribution that robust evidence can make to bringing about sometimes radical change, even in the face of strong path dependency, is demonstrated by the remarkable speed with which Housing First has taken root across the developed world in recent years, as noted previously in this chapter (Padgett et al, 2016). However, a contrasting example of a very 'political' policy process can be found in the ready embrace of the very different, but also US-originating, 'common ground' model of homeless accommodation across Australia. Federal backing of this approach proceeded in the face of a complete absence of supporting evaluative evidence, but with the enthusiastic backing of an 'advocacy coalition' that enjoyed high level political support (from the Australian prime minister's wife) (Parsell et al, 2013).

Good evidence is also vital in dispelling falsehoods such as the idea that 'any of us can become homeless' (Bramley and Fitzpatrick, 2017). While such 'inclusive' narratives may appear progressive on the surface, they do serious damage by distracting attention from the structural inequalities that in reality drive homelessness risks. They also play to self-serving ideological agendas on the part of politicians far more comfortable with the notion of complexity and heterogeneity in homelessness than the reality of identifiable and preventable risk, amenable to public policy interventions. Evidence is likewise crucial in challenging public misconceptions that charitable efforts to help people experiencing homelessness, whatever form they take, are necessarily a good thing, or at least can do no harm. The practical consequences of all such voluntary actions should instead be subject to critical, evidence-based scrutiny (Parsell and Watts, 2017).

One final point to acknowledge is that systematic reviews and meta-analyses potentially have much to offer in the homelessness field, as in so many others, in determining and championing 'what works' (White, this volume). But the necessary underlying empirical evidence base – which is currently underdeveloped in homelessness – must exist for these synthesising methods to deliver maximum value. Leaving aside Housing First and certain health-specific interventions, quantitative evaluations that would meet the usual 'gold standard' evidence thresholds for systematic reviews are rare in the homelessness field outside the US. Thus, investment in more robust primary evaluations – both quantitative ('experimental') and qualitative ('realistic') in nature – needs to be a priority in the UK and elsewhere.

Acknowledgements

Thank you to Professor Glen Bramley, Dr Beth Watts, Dr Jenny Wood and Professor Sarah Johnsen for very helpful comments on an earlier draft of this chapter.

Note

[1] https://www.homelessnessimpact.org/evidence-finder.

References

Aldridge, R.W., Story, A., Hwang, S.W., Nordentoft, M., Luchenski, S., Hartwell, G., Tweed, E.J., Lewer, D., Katikireddi, S.V. and Hayward, A. 2018. Morbidity and mortality in homeless individuals, prisoners, sex workers, and individuals with substance use disorders in high-income countries: a systematic review and meta-analysis. *Lancet*. https://www.thelancet.com/journals/lancet/article/PIIS0140–6736(17)31869-X/fulltext.

Alma Economics. 2019a. *Causes of Homelessness and Rough Sleeping: Rapid Evidence Assessment*. London: MHCLG/DWP.

Alma Economics. 2019b. *Causes of Homelessness and Rough Sleeping: Review of Models of Homelessness.* London: MHCLG/DWP.

Alma Economics. 2019c. *Causes of Homelessness and Rough Sleeping: Feasibility Study.* London: MHCLG/DWP.

Benjaminsen, L. and Bastholm Andrade, S. 2015 Testing a typology of homelessness across welfare regimes: shelter use in Denmark and the USA. *Housing Studies*, 30(6): 858–76.

Bramley, G. 1988. *Homelessness and the London Housing Market (Occasional Paper).* Bristol: Policy Press.

Bramley, G. 2017. *Homelessness Projections: Core homelessness in Great Britain.* London: Crisis.

Bramley, G. and Fitzpatrick, S. 2017. Homelessness in the UK: who is most at risk? *Housing Studies*, 33:1: 96–116.

Bramley, G., Sosenko, F., and Wood, J. (2018) *Scoping Project to Investigate the Alternatives for Including Non-Household Populations in Estimates of Personal Well-Being and Destitution*: Final 3 Interim Research Report to Joseph Rowntree Foundation and ONS. Edinburgh: Heriot-Watt University. https://doi.org/10.17861/0KN0–0Z21.

Byrne, T., Fargo, J., Montgomery, A.E., Munley, E. & Culhane, D.P. 2014. The relationship between community investment in permanent supportive housing and chronic homelessness. *Social Service Review*, 88(2): 234-263.

Byrne, T., Treglia, D., Kuhn, J., Kane, V. and Culhane, D.P. 2015. Predictors of homelessness following exit from homelessness prevention and rapid re-housing programs: evidence from the Department of Veterans Affairs Supportive Services for Veteran Families Program. *Housing Policy Debate*: 1–24.

Centre for Homelessness Impact (2019) *Evidence and Gap Map of Effectiveness Studies.* London: https://www.homelessnessimpact.org/gap-maps

Coote, A. 2012. *The Wisdom of Prevention.* London: New Economics Foundation.

Corinth, K. 2017. The Impact of Permanent Supportive Housing on Homeless Populations. *Journal of Housing Economics.* 35 (C): 69–84.

Cowan, D. 2019. Reducing homelessness or re-ordering the deckchairs?. *Modern Law Review*, 82: 105–28.

Cragg, M. and O'Flaherty, B. 1999. Do homeless shelter conditions determine shelter population? The case of the Dinkins Deluge. *Journal of Urban Economics*. https://doi.org/10.1006/juec.1998.2128.

Culhane, D.P. 1993, December 19. Shelters Lead Nowhere. *New York Times*. Section 4, Page 13.

Culhane, D.P., Avery, J.M. and Hadley, T.R. 1998. Prevalence of treated behavioral disorders among adult shelter users: a longitudinal study. *American Journal of Orthopsychiatry*. https://doi.org/10.1037/h0080271.

Culhane, D.P., Dejowski, E.F., Ibanez, J., Needham, E. and Macchia, I. 1994. Public shelter admission rates in Philadelphia and New York City: the implications of turnover for sheltered population counts. *Housing Policy Debate*, 5(2): 107–40. https://doi.org/10.1080/10511482.1994.9521158.

Culhane, D.P., Lee, C.M. and Wachter, S.M. 1996. Where the homeless come from: a study of the prior address distribution of families admitted to public shelters in New York City and Philadelphia. *Housing Policy Debate*. https://doi.org/10.1080/10511482.1996.9521224.

Culhane, D.P., Metraux, S. and Byrne, T. 2011. A prevention-centered approach to homelessness assistance: a paradigm shift? *Housing Policy Debate*, 21(May): 295–315. https://doi.org/10.1080/10511482.2010.536246.

Culhane, D.P., Metraux, S. and Hadley, T. 2002. Public service reductions associated with placement of homeless persons with severe mental illness in supportive housing. *Housing Policy Debate*. https://doi.org/10.1080/10511482.2002.9521437.

Culhane, D.P., Metraux, S., Park, J.M., Schretzman, M., and Valente, J. 2007. Testing a typology of family homelessness based on patterns of public shelter utilization in four US jurisdictions: implications for policy and program planning. *Housing Policy Debate*, 18(1): 1–28.

Fitzpatrick, S. 2005. Explaining Homelessness: a Critical Realist Perspective, *Housing, Theory and Society*, 22(1): 1-17.

Fitzpatrick, S. and Christian, J. 2006. Comparing homelessness research in the US and Britain. *European Journal of Housing Policy*, 6(3): 313–33.

Fitzpatrick, S., Kemp, P.A. and Klinker, S. 2000. *Single Homelessness – An Overview of Research in Britain*. York: JRF.

Fitzpatrick, S., Mackie, P. and Wood, J. 2019. *Policy Briefing: Homelessness Prevention in the UK*. Glasgow: UK Collaborative Centre for Housing Evidence (CaCHE).

Fitzpatrick, S., Pawson, H., Bramley, G. and Wilcox, S. 2011. *The Homelessness Monitor*. London: Crisis.

Glynn, C., Byrne, T.H., and Culhane, D.P. 2018. *Inflection Points in Community-level Homeless Rates*. http://files.zillowstatic.com/research/public/StaticFiles/Homelessness/Inflection_Points.pdf.

Goodman, S., Messeri, P. and O'Flaherty, B. 2016. Homelessness prevention in New York City: On average, it works. *Journal of Housing Economics*. https://doi.org/10.1016/j.jhe.2015.12.001.

Gubits, D., Shinn, M., Wood, M., Bell, S., Dastrup, S., Solari, C.D., … Kattel, U. 2016. *Family Options Study: 3-Year Impacts of Housing and Services Interventions for Homeless Families*. https://www.huduser.gov/portal/sites/default/files/pdf/Family-Options-Study-Full-Report.pdf.

Hopper, K., Shinn, M., Laska, E., Meisner, M. and Wanderling, J. 2008. Estimating numbers of unsheltered homeless people through plant-capture and postcount survey methods. *American Journal of Public Health*. https://doi.org/10.2105/AJPH.2005.083600.

Kuhn, R. and Culhane, D.P. 1998. Applying cluster analysis to test a typology of homelessness by pattern of shelter utilization: results from the analysis of administrative data. *American Journal of Community Psychology*, 26(2): 207–32. https://doi.org/10.1023/A:1022176402357.

Lancione, M. 2013. Homeless people and the city of abstract machine. Assemblage thinking and the performative approach to homelessness. *Area*, 45:3, 358–64.

Lee, B.A., Tyler, K.A. and Wright, J.D. 2010. The new homelessness revisited. *Annual Review of Sociology*, 36: 501–521. https://doi.org/10.1146/annurev-soc-070308–115940.

Luchenski, S., Maguire, N., Aldridge, R.W., Hayward, A., Story, A., Perri, P. Withers, J., Clint, S., Fitzpatrick, S. and Hewett, N. 2018. What works in inclusion health: overview of effective interventions for marginalised and excluded populations. *Lancet*. https://doi.org/10.1016/S0140–6736(17)31959–1.

Mackie, P., Johnsen, S. and Wood, J. 2017. *Ending Rough Sleeping: What Works? An International Evidence Review*. London: Crisis.

MHCLG (Ministry of Housing, Communities & Local Government). 2019. *Impact Evaluation of the Rough Sleeping Initiative*. London: MHCLG.

Montgomery, A.E. 2016. Characteristics and needs of women veterans experiencing homelessness. In *Homeless Evidence and Research Roundtable Series: Women Veterans and Homelessness*. https://www.va.gov/HOMELESS/nchav/docs/HERS-Womens-Proceedings.pdf.

National Alliance to End Homelessness. 2019. Data snapshot: racial disparities in homelessness – national alliance to end homelessness. https://endhomelessness.org/resource/data-snapshot-racial-disparities-in-homelessness/.

O'Flaherty, B. and Wu, T. 2006. Fewer subsidized exits and a recession: how New York City's family homeless shelter population became immense. *Journal of Housing Economics*, 15: 99–125. https://doi.org/10.1016/j.jhe.2006.08.003.

Padgett, D.K, Henwood, B.F. and Tsemberis, S.J. 2016. *Housing First: Ending Homelessness, Transforming Systems, and Changing Lives*. Oxford: Oxford University Press.

Parsell, C., Fitzpatrick, S. and Busch-Geertsema, V. 2013. Common ground in Australia: an object lesson in evidence hierarchies and policy transfer. *Housing Studies*, 29(1): 69–87.

Parsell, C. and Watts, B. 2017. Charity and justice: a reflection on new forms of homelessness provision in Australia. *European Journal of Homelessness*, 11(2): 65–76.

Poulin, S., Metraux, S. and Culhane, D.P. 2008. The history and future of information systems. In R.H. McNamara (ed.), *Homelessness in America* (3rd ed., pp. 171–9). Westport, CT: Praeger Perspectives.

Rolston, H., Geyer, J. and Locke, G. 2013. *Final Report: Evaluation of the Homebase Community Prevention Program*. Bethesda, MD: ABT Associates.

Shinn, M. 2007. International homelessness: policy, socio-cultural, and individual perspectives. *Journal of Social Issues*, 63(3): 657–77.

Shinn, M., Baumohl, J. and Hopper, K. 2001. The prevention of homelessness revisited. *Analyses of Social Issues and Public Policy*, 1: 95–127. https://doi.org/10.1111/1530-2415.00006.

Shinn, M., Greer, A.L., Bainbridge, J., Kwon, J. and Zuiderveen, S. 2013. Efficient targeting of homelessness prevention services for families. *American Journal of Public Health*, 103: 324–30. https://doi.org/10.2105/AJPH.2013.301468.

Shinn, M., Weitzman, B.C., Stojanovic, D., Knickman, J.R., Jiménez, L., Duchon, L., James, S. and Krantz, D.H. (1998). Predictors of homelessness among families in New York City: from shelter request to housing stability. *American Journal of Public Health*, 88: 1651–7. https://doi.org/10.2105/AJPH.88.11.1651.

Shlay, A. and Rossi, P. H. 1992. Social science research and contemporary studies of homelessness. *Annual Review of Sociology*. https://doi.org/10.1146/annurev.soc.18.1.129.

Stephens, M. and Fitzpatrick, S. 2007. Welfare regimes, housing systems and homelessness: how are they linked?. *European Journal of Homelessness*, 1: 201–12.

Stephens, M., Fitzpatrick, S., Elsinga, M., Steen, G.V. and Chzhen, Y. 2010. *Study on Housing Exclusion: Welfare Policies, Labour Market and Housing Provision*. Brussels: European Commission.

Toro, P.A. 2007. Toward an international understanding of homelessness. *Journal of Social Issues*, 63(3): 461–81.

US Department of Housing and Urban Development. 2017. *The 2017 Annual Homeless Assessment Report (AHAR) to Congress*. https://files.hudexchange.info/resources/documents/2017-AHAR-Part-1.pdf.

US Department of Veterans Affairs. 2018. *FY 2017 ANNUAL REPORT: Supportive Services For Veteran Families (SSVF)*. https://www.va.gov/homeless/ssvf/docs/SSVF_FY2017_AnnualReport_508.pdf.

Watts, B., Fitzpatrick, S. and Johnsen, S. 2017. Controlling homeless people? Power, interventionism and legitimacy. *Journal of Social Policy*, pp. 1–18. https://doi.org/10.1017/S0047279417000289.

Watts, E.L., Goldacre, R., Key, T.J., Allen, N.E., Travis, R.C. and Perez-Cornago, A. 2019. Hormone-related diseases and prostate cancer: An English national record linkage study. *International Journal of Cancer*, https://doi.org/10.1002/ijc.32808.

Waugh, A., Clarke, A., Knowles, J. and Rowley, D. 2018. *Health and Homelessness in Scotland*. Edinburgh: The Scottish Government.

White, H., Wood, J. and Fitzpatrick, S. 2018. *Evidence and Gap Maps on Homelessness. A Launch Pad for Strategic Evidence Production and Use: Part 2: Global Evidence and Gap Map of Implementation Issues*. London: Centre for Homelessness Impact.

Why evidence matters

Jonathan Breckon and Emma Taylor-Collins

It is tempting to think that homelessness is something to file under the 'Too Difficult Box' of social conundrums, an issue that cannot be addressed at the street level, only at the level of government policies on affordable housing, social security and poverty reduction.

Of course, social trends and national policies are at the heart of problems relating to homelessness and we need answers that look at whole systems, such as youth justice, mental health and child protection.[1] And those on the frontline – public servants, charity workers and commissioners – need to make urgent decisions to help people experiencing homelessness. That means they need access to the best available evidence to use alongside their professional judgement and practitioner experience, and a culture of rigorous evaluation to ensure continual learning and improvement. Problems may be systemic and complicated, but that cannot distract us from trying to work out which programmes and interventions might do the most good.

In the field of homelessness, we are currently missing a strong evidence base on homelessness interventions. Until fairly recently, this was the case in education, too – it was not until the late 1990s that the concept of 'evidence-informed practice' really started to emerge in the UK (Hanley et al, 2016). Now, thanks to initiatives like researchED and the Education Endowment Foundation (EEF), the picture is vastly different, and more than half the schools in England have been involved in one of EEF's randomised controlled trials (RCTs) (Nevill, 2019). Whole ecosystems of organisations, individuals and networks grow around these kinds of movements, which we have also seen in other policy areas – some of them planned and wide-ranging, like the Campbell Collaboration or the National Institute for Health and Care Excellence; others more sporadic, single-issue grassroot outfits, such as the Society for Evidence-Based Policing, researchED Evidence for the Frontline and Coalition for Evidence-Based Education. We now have a rich tapestry of different organisations providing and advocating for evidence of what works across social policy. The Centre for Homelessness Impact (CHI) is a full member of the growing UK What Works Network. It shows us that a shift towards evidence-informed practice is possible in the homelessness field, too.

Evidence might not provide easy answers but can provide better bets on what direction to go in – a smarter way of working than simply throwing money and resources at problems. Some of our best efforts to improve people's lives may do nothing to help, waste money or even do harm. In health, 156 medical practices were flagged up to be unsafe or ineffective in a study funded by the Australian Department of Health and Ageing (Elshaug et al, 2012). Conversely, we may have the opposite problem: all interventions seem to work equally well – the so-called 'dodo bird effect', discussed in more detail later in this chapter (Forrester, 2015).

If this is the case, then which initiative to choose? Can we find out more on what works for whom, where and why? At the very least, can we see if the benefits outweigh the costs? In an age of severe budgetary pressures, value for money is important. Something may be effective, but unaffordable. This may mean diverting funds from one service to another.

Economists have created ways of capturing value through cost–benefit analysis or cost–effectiveness studies. What is of most value, however, is what is useful for decision-makers. We need evidence that improves the decision-making of those who have to deliver services or help, on issues that matter to them and in language that makes sense and is free from academic jargon. This chapter will make the case for the kind of evidence we need in homelessness prevention, and why.

Why what works? The importance of evidence of effectiveness

There are a whole host of reasons why it is important to use evidence to inform decision-making, particularly for service delivery. Fundamentally, however, evidence of effectiveness, or 'what works', can help discover whether a service is doing any harm. Two examples highlight the pitfalls of what happens when we do not have the right evidence to show that a programme or service is achieving the objectives we hope it will.

Probably the most well-known example of this is Scared Straight, a crime prevention intervention for young people considered at risk of delinquency, initiated in the 1970s in the US. It involves young people visiting prisons and hearing prisoners speak about their life there, with the aim of 'scaring' them away from committing crime. TV documentaries such as *Beyond Scared Straight* claimed that Scared Straight achieved its intended effects (A&E, 2011). But RCTs showed that this was not the case and, when the Cochrane Collaboration conducted a systematic review of RCTs on Scared Straight in the early 2000s, they found that Scared Straight was not only having a negative effect on delinquency, but that young people on the Scared Straight programme were more likely to increase offending behaviour than those who had not been on the programme (Petrosino et al, 2013). Possible reasons mooted include that young people feel that prison offers a sense of belonging they are otherwise missing, that it romanticises prison life, or that young people feel the need to commit crime in order to prove that they were not scared by the programme (Petrosino et al, 2000).

A lesser known example comes from Australia. 'Infant simulator-based programmes', in which teenage girls are given robot dolls that mimic real babies, aim to prevent teenage pregnancies. Following a pilot that showed that girls on the programme were more likely to want to delay pregnancy after taking part, the programme was rolled out in Western Australia. However, it was not until a school-based, cluster RCT that followed participants until the age of 20 was carried out some time later that it was discovered that the girls who had taken part in the programme were more likely to get pregnant before the age of 20 than girls who were not on the programme (Brinkman et al, 2016). The robot dolls made having a baby more attractive. Researchers surmise this could be because participants liked the attention they received while caring for the infant simulator or because they thought a real baby would be easier to care for (Brinkman et al, 2016).

While these are rather extreme examples, they highlight how important it is that the right kind of evidence is used in the right way to make decisions, especially when those decisions affect the lives of vulnerable people.

Depressingly, the infant simulator programme is not uncommon, and some of our best efforts to improve other people's lives may do nothing, waste money, or worse. The field of health and medicine is sometimes seen as a beacon of good evidence-informed practice. In areas like crime or education, policy fads and fashions can have little effect, from boot camps to reduce reoffending, to 'learning styles' in classroom teaching. Evidence can help debunk these ideas.

Evidence of 'what works' is a moral issue. We have a duty to understand if something is working or not. Are we wasting the money of taxpayers and donors to charities? Perhaps we are. Perhaps we are making things worse for vulnerable people, as seen in the example of teenage pregnancy. Being open to evidence is also partly about humility. It is wrong to think doing what is right does not need to be grounded in evidence. We cannot claim to be doing the right thing unless we are prepared continually to test our assumptions. Evidence does not run counter to morality. A passion for reducing homelessness is worthy, but it still needs testing and auditing against reality: are all the millions of charitable pounds going into programmes to reduce homelessness making things better or maintaining the status quo? Good intentions are not enough. We must be judged by our actions and our impact, not by our moral standing alone.

What do we mean by evidence of effectiveness?

When we say we need evidence of what works, we are not talking about simply any type of research or evaluation. Only some types of studies can help answer questions about 'what works', such as RCTs, differences-in-differences, propensity score matching, and natural experiments.[2]

One way of trying to understand these approaches is to create formal frameworks of evidence, as CHI has done.[3] These frameworks, known as standards of evidence, are important communication tools: they set out what sort of evidence is needed, for specialist evaluators and research reviewers and for non-specialist practitioners and policy-makers who need to get to grips with it. There are 18 such frameworks in UK social policy – growing on average by two a year – according to a mapping exercise by the Alliance for Useful Evidence (Puttick, 2018; see Figure 8.1).

One common feature of the current crop of evidence frameworks is the need for multiple studies, not just single studies. Ideally, we would like to see a study replicated many times, to check that it did not just work in one time or place. This is especially important when we import US-based innovations that might not work in the UK context. For example, Mentor UK wanted to know whether the Good Behaviour Game (GBG) – a US intervention designed to improve classroom behaviour and academic success – could be as effective in the UK as it has been found to be in the US. GBG has been running for over 40 years and, in that time, numerous robust studies, including longitudinal designs and RCTs, have found positive outcomes. The intervention therefore is listed and recommended on the US-based National Registry of Evidence Based Programs and Practices and has been tested in multiple other countries, including the Netherlands, Canada and Chile. It might therefore have been reasonable for Mentor UK to expect that GBG would also work effectively in the UK and yet there are examples of where this has not been the case (Williams, 2017). As such, Mentor UK and the EEF conducted RCTs in 77 schools in England, testing the effectiveness of the GBG. They found that while there was some 'tentative'

Figure 8.1: Standards of evidence timeline

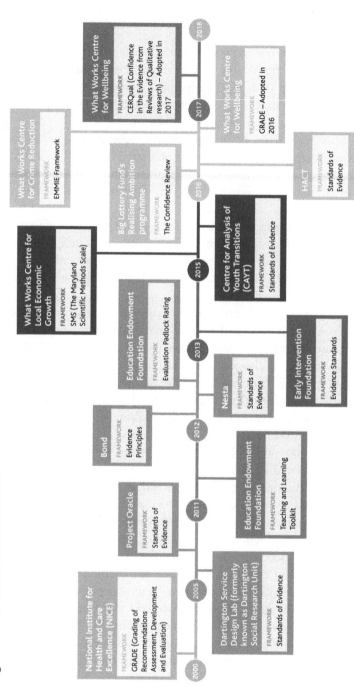

Source: Puttick, 2018, p 8

evidence that the GBG benefited boys identified as at risk of developing behavioural problems, on the whole the GBG did not generally improve pupils' reading nor their behaviour. What worked in the US and elsewhere did not work at these schools in England.

Importantly for the evidence use field more widely, these results have been published[4] and are freely available online – publication bias, in which studies showing null effects are less likely to be published, means that that is not always the case. What this example also shows is the importance of testing interventions robustly before scaling – just because they have worked elsewhere does not mean they work in every context.

The dodo effect v Rossi's law; what if everything or nothing works?

Some of that humility may be about accepting that it is very hard to make much of a difference. When it comes to evaluating social programmes, the sociologist Peter Rossi set out an iron law (or 'stainless steel' law, as he called it), which states that it is really hard to find any net impact (Rossi, 1987). Rossi declared that: 'The better designed the impact assessment of a social program, the more likely is the resulting estimate of net impact to be zero' (Rossi, 1987). This law means that the more technically rigorous – such as thorough RCTs – the more likely are its results to show no effect. The point here is that there is no golden bullet that will fix social problems. Nobody should be trusted who over-promises on a new or existing programme or initiative. Many of the benefits may be marginal or limited, though the cumulative effect of a range of interventions may be positive.

Conversely, we may have the opposite problem to Rossi's law of limited impact: what if all interventions seem to work equally well? This so-called 'dodo effect' is taken from the bird who runs a race with no start or finish in Lewis Carroll's novel *Alice's Adventures in Wonderland*, and finishes by proclaiming 'everybody has won, and all must have prizes'.

The effect can be described as follows: when credible interventions are compared to 'service as usual' they produce significantly better outcomes; but when they are compared to one another they produce similar – often almost identical – effects. This dodo effect has been found in the substance misuse field, alcohol reduction programmes, treatments for depression and parenting initiatives (Forrester, 2015) and, more recently, in homelessness – of those few interventions that have been rigorously tested, most seem to be effective.[5] If this is the case, then which initiative should a policy-maker choose?[6]

One way to address this is to recognise that there may be some common elements that underpin many interventions, such as empathy, engendering hope for change or building on strengths (Chorpita and Daleiden, 2009). It has been a welcome development in the UK that there has been less of an obsession with manualised pre-packaged programmes, complete with how-to manuals and legal copyright, which are much more common in the US. Organisations like the EEF look at what works in the classroom – such as repeating a year, school uniforms or class sizes – rather than manualised programmes alone. Another What Works Centre, the Early Intervention Foundation, did start by focusing on evidence around programmes, and has an invaluable handbook of over 100 programmes that have been shown to improve child outcomes. They have, however, begun to take a new direction by including proven and promising early interventions that do not fit neatly into a packaged programme.

The message from both Rossi's 'law' and the dodo effect is that you will not find simple answers from evidence. But it is still important to ask the right questions and dig more deeply into the interventions (are there 'common elements' that work in homelessness reduction?). We need to be honest and open to failure and to marginal successes (as set out in Rossi's law). As the Australian government minister and former professor of economics, Andrew Leigh, summed it up: 'Rossi's Law doesn't mean we should give up hope in changing the world for the better. But we ought to be sceptical of anyone peddling panaceas' (Leigh, 2018). The dodo effect stresses the importance of understanding what is going on within new mechanisms for change, rather than just looking at the 'black box' of testing effects without understanding the internal wiring that made the effect (or lack thereof) possible. This understanding of these processes is covered in the next section.

Evidence that travels: what works where and why

In homelessness as in any field of social policy, it is a wholly legitimate exercise to ask if both new and existing service models work or not. Even if they seem to be working in one place, we need to know if they work in another place and time, as we saw with the GBG. For example, Nordic homelessness strategies, in particular in Finland but also in Denmark and Norway, follow similar patterns, combining preventative services with new forms of service provision. They also have some of the most supportive welfare systems in the world and generally have a strong commitment to social equality, which of course plays a part (St Mungo's, 2018). But these factors aside, can Nordic initiatives work outside the Nordics? Many working in the homelessness sector will have heard of these initiatives, such as Housing First and Critical-Time Intervention, and the hype around them. But how strong is the evidence to back them up? Now, thanks to organisations like CHI, we can find out through user-friendly maps.[7] Too often in the past, evidence was hidden behind academic journal paywalls, lost in long and complicated articles or data sets, and not curated into a single, free and useful resource. CHI – and the other UK What Works Centres – have rectified that problem, and we can now navigate around what we know (and do not know) on the evidence for dealing with homelessness (see for example Schwan et al, 2018). With only 12 RCTs on homelessness interventions conducted so far in the UK, we have got some way to go until we have a strong evidence base.

This global evidence is a vital step in figuring out whether programme and policies will work here. We need to learn from others before applying things in the UK. One advantage of the UK being slow to catch up with other countries on the much-hyped Housing First policy for rough sleeping and chronic homelessness is that we can learn from others. A growing body of research compares housing first with existing 'treatment as usual' services for homeless people with high and complex needs, and consistently reports that Housing First is more effective at reducing homelessness (Padgett et al, 2016). Much has been done in France, most of the Scandinavian countries, Canada, and the US. In recent years, the evidence base has been strengthened considerably by large-scale experimental trials in Canada (Goering et al, 2014) and in France (DIHAL, 2016). However, we should not slavishly implement those policies just because they have worked there. It is right to ask whether these policies work in the UK context, such as through the pilots by the West Midlands Combined Authority, Greater Manchester Combined Authority, and the Liverpool City Region. However strong the evidence internationally, we still need to see if the programme travels.

We also need to address the question of *why* things work, not just whether they work. As two leading Anglo-US critics of RCTs, Princeton Nobel Economist Angus Deaton and the philosopher Nancy Cartwright, put it: 'RCTs can play a role in building scientific knowledge and useful predictions but they can only do so as part of a cumulative program, combining with other methods, including conceptual and theoretical development, to discover not "what works", but "why things work"' (Deaton and Cartwright, 2018). One approach to these 'why' questions is to engage in more qualitative and mixed-methods approaches, in conjunction with trials, and also do experiments on mechanisms, not just policy experiments.

Is it worth it? The importance of evidence on costs and benefits

In this age of austerity, value for money is also important. Something may be effective, but unaffordable. This may mean diverting funds from one service to another. Economists have created ways of capturing value through cost–benefit analysis or cost-effectiveness studies, and these have been used by other UK What Works Centres such as the EEF and What Works Centre for Crime Reduction. CHI is now trying to ascertain the cost-effectiveness of different homelessness interventions but has found there is little existing evidence on this. The hope is that by bundling up measures of value – particularly on effectiveness – the What Works Centres will save governments money.

What Works Centres point to how to save money by cutting things that do not work,[8] but they also show how money can be saved in other ways: spending taxpayers' money on successful things that are also cheaper than other options. For instance, reading comprehension strategies are both cheap and effective in schools, according to extensive evidence – though the evidence is stronger in the US than the UK.[9] Other successful approaches are just too expensive: one-to-one mentoring, for instance, is reasonably effective, but uses up too much time and money. School budgets just cannot stretch that far.

Evidence for the frontline: answering questions that are relevant to professionals

What we can also learn from the education sector is the need for an evidence ecosystem – a rich tapestry of different organisations helping to fund research and do reviews. Some of this comes from the classroom 'chalkface' of teachers.

A central element to the success of what works is making sure we provide evidence that works to the frontline – for the staff, commissioners and leaders trying to turn back the tide of homelessness. If the research we produce is only of interest to academics and evaluators, we will have failed.

One way to do this is to listen to our audiences, like CHI did with their feasibility study when they were first getting started (Teixeira, 2017). The What Works Centre for Children's Social Care, launched in 2017 by the Department for Education and incubated at Nesta, consulted on the production of their 'evidence store'. They have worked in over half of all English local authorities, with joint projects and events as well as ethnographic work following in the footsteps of social workers, to empathise and understand evidence use on the ground. Sometimes there can be surprising areas of 'what works' evidence that meets user needs. For instance, the Centre is running trials on a 'happy and healthy workforce' to counteract the stresses and severe retention issues in social work.

The evidence we produce must be *with* professionals, not on them. Our evidence will not be taken up if we just push it at people. We need to foster an appetite and demand for the evidence, such as through collaboratively producing research.

What is helpful here is understanding exactly what we mean by evidence-informed decision-making. It can help by first stating what it is not. As Professor Jonathan Sharples put it in his report *Evidence for the Frontline*, it is:

> not 'cook book' teaching or policing, nor should it be about prescribing what goes on from a position of unchallenged authority. It is about integrating professional expertise with the best external evidence from research to improve the quality of practice. ... there is a huge amount of experiential knowledge that is not captured by research, and, therefore, that an absence of evidence certainly does not mean absence of effectiveness. (Sharples, 2013)

The following Venn diagram (see Figure 8.2) shows the sources of information that make up decision-making. Essentially, it is about the conscientious and judicious use of current best evidence, in conjunction with professional expertise, contextual information (such as knowledge about the local area) and the values of stakeholders – such as those experiencing homelessness and the communities in which we work.

A critical element in understanding decision-making is acknowledging that we have to work with the grain of human psychology. The evidence we provide of 'what works' will only land if we are sensitive to cognitive biases and mental shortcuts. As a report on medical and health clinicians by the Behavioural Insights Team described it:

> A key insight of behavioral science research is that human decision-making is often influenced by heuristics and biases – that is, mental shortcuts that simplify decision-making but which can lead to errors of judgment. This means that people's decisions are not always the product of a purely calculated,

reasoned process. Instead, they can be influenced by people's emotional or psychological state, by contextual factors surrounding the decision, or by the way information is presented. (Egan et al, 2018)

Working with this grain means tailoring and targeting your communications, and really obsessing about the demand for your evidence, not the supply. For instance, the Wales Centre for Public Policy's model is to coproduce evidence with the Welsh Government and public service leaders in Wales, ensuring that the evidence is both demand-led and tailored to the needs of policy-makers. It might also mean making sure that an online repository of research is designed with users in mind: avoiding technical jargon, or academic categories that only make sense to other academics. For instance, clinical decision support (CDS) systems can automatically remind a frontline health worker of specific actions or dosages, such as through alerts, reminders or

Figure 8.2: Evidence-informed decision-making in social policy

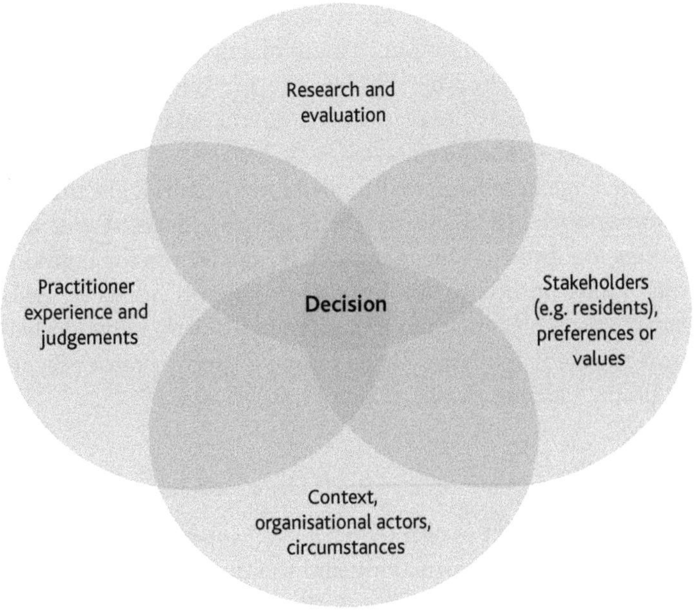

Source: Adapted from Briner (2019)

drug-dose calculations. They can be used through computers, tablets, smart phones or other hand-held digital devices. Instead of wading through reams of guidance or research, the practitioner is given the best relevant knowledge that is 'content germane to a specific patient to facilitate decision making at the point of care or for a specific care situation' (Bright et al, 2012). Tools like CDS or evidence toolkits are not enough in isolation: we need a cocktail of different measures to improve the opportunities, motivation and capability to use evidence.[10] But the important point is that we need to focus as much effort and energy on working with our users as we do on producing our research.

The importance of being part of a wider evidence movement

The CHI has joined an important club of 13 What Works Centres. They have had a lot of interest both in the UK and internationally – with similar institutions being set up in Australia, Canada and France. But they are also part of a wider UK evidence landscape. There have also been many other promising initiatives, set out in an interactive map of the social policy sector created by the Alliance for Useful Evidence.[11] Organisations on the map cover all the eight knowledge mobilisation archetypes (Davies et al, 2015).

They range from large well-funded intermediaries like the UK Administrative Data Research Partnership, to localised evidence brokers like Project Oracle, funded by the Mayor for London; from hands-on bodies like Evaluation Support Scotland, who help charities measure their impact, to bottom-up networks like the Society for Evidence-Based Policing run by police officers for police officers.

Conclusion

We have shown in this chapter what can happen when evidence is not used in decision-making and the unintended harm that can cause. We have looked at wading through different types of evidence and identifying shared ground in what might seem like conflicting evidence. We have talked about the need to understand both whether an intervention works, but also why and how. And through all of this, we have shown how important it is that we think about evidence in a way that makes sense to practitioners. This is not about dismissing professional judgement and expertise, but rather about affirming the importance evidence of effectiveness also plays in decisions made about homelessness.

There is a growing appetite towards an evidence movement in homelessness, as the support for CHI shows. It is vital that we capitalise on this, identifying what we already do and do not know about homelessness prevention, and how we will fill the evidence gaps.

Notes

1   See for example http://awayhome.ca/wp-content/uploads/2018/11/Report-2-Systems-Prevention_26.11.18.pdf.

2   Evidence and Gap Maps on Homelessness. A launch pad for strategic evidence production and use Dr. Howard White Part 1: Global Evidence and Gap Map of Effectiveness Studies https://uploads-ssl.webflow.com/59f07e67422cdf0001904c14/5aea3a8feb6f2594f99576c8_evidence-and-gap-maps-on-homelessness_2018.pdf.

3   https://uploads-ssl.webflow.com/59f07e67422cdf0001904c14/5aea3a8feb6f2594f99576c8_evidence-and-gap-maps-on-homelessness_2018.pdf.

4   Education Endowment Foundation, The Good Behaviour Game: https://educationendowmentfoundation.org.uk/projects-and-evaluation/projects/the-good-behaviour-game/.

5   Centre for Homelessness Impact, Evidence Gap Maps, accessed at https://www.homelessnessimpact.org/gap-maps.

6   Chorpita and Daleiden (2009) have carried out exhaustive reviews of what works for whom and why. They identify many shared characteristics in effective ways of helping. If any of us thinks about what is likely to help people, it is immediately apparent that there are some commonalities across different ways of working. These would include: the helper appearing to care; demonstrating an understanding of the demonstrating an understanding of the person's point of view (empathy); engendering hope for change; building on strengths; developing a plan for change; and so on, with important variations according to the type of presenting difficulty.

7   https://uploads-ssl.webflow.com/59f07e67422cdf0001904c14/5aea3a8feb6f2594f99576c8_evidence-and-gap-maps-on-homelessness_2018.pdf.

8   The centres provide a variety of products to communicate their evidence. The crime reduction toolkit, the EIF guidebook, EEF's teaching and learning toolkit and the early years toolkit, the growth toolkits, and the

wellbeing evidence comparison tool all provide the summaries of findings across a range of topic of concern to the centre. All of these provide information on impact, cost and strength of evidence. The crime reduction toolkit in addition provides evidence on the process by which the intervention has its effect which can assist with interpreting the evidence in relation to different use contexts.

9   Education Endowment Foundation, 'Reading comprehension strategies', Teaching and Learning Toolkit, accessed at https://educationendowmentfoundation.org.uk/evidence-summaries/teaching-learning-toolkit/reading-comprehension-strategies/.

10 https://www.alliance4usefulevidence.org/evidence-exchange/the-science-of-using-science-evidence/

11 https://www.alliance4usefulevidence.org/network/#root.

References

A&E. 2011. *Beyond Scared Straight*. Golden West Television.

Bright T.J., Wong, A., Dhurjati R, Bristow, E., Bastian, L., Coeytaux, R.R., Samsa, G., Hasselblad, V., Williams, J.W., Musty, M.D., Wing, L., Kendrick, A.S., Sanders, G.D., Lobach, D. 2012. Effect of clinical decision-support systems. A systematic review. *Ann Intern Med*, 157: 29–43.

Briner, R. 2019. The basics of evidence-based practice. *People + Strategy*, 42: 16–20.

Brinkman, S.A., Johnson, S.E., Codde, J.P., Hart, M.B., Straton, J.A., Mittinty, M.M. and Silburn, S.R. 2016. Efficacy of infant simulator programmes to prevent teenage pregnancy: a school-based cluster randomised controlled trial in Western Australia. *Lancet*: 388.

Chorpita, B.F. and Daleiden, E.L. 2009. Mapping evidence-based treatments for children and adolescents: application of the distillation and matching model to 615 treatments from 322 randomized trials. *Journal of Consulting and Clinical Psychology*, 77: 566–79.

Davies, H., Powell, A.E. and Nutley, S.M. 2015. Mobilising knowledge to improve UK health care: learning from other countries and other sectors – a multimethod mapping study. *Health Services and Delivery Research*, No. 3: 27.

Deaton, A. and Cartwright, N. 2018. Understanding and misunderstanding randomized controlled trials. *Social Science & Medicine*, 210: 2–21. www.sciencedirect.com/science/article/pii/S0277953617307359.

DIHAL. 2016. The experimental programme "Un chezsoi d'abord" housing first main results – 2011/2015. Paris: DIHAL. http://housingfirst.wp.tri.haus/assets/files/2016/04/unchez-soi-dabord-EN.pdf.

Egan, D., Brazier, A., Mottershaw, A., Ter Meer, J., Hallsworth, M., Fontana, G., Parston, G., Darzi, A. 2018. *Global Diffusion of Healthcare Innovation: Using Behavioral Insights to Accelerate Adoption.* Doha, Qatar: World Innovation Summit for Health. https://www.wish.org.qa/wp-content/uploads/2018/11/IMPJ6078-WISH-2018-GDHI-181016-2.pdf.

Elshaug, A., Watt, A., Mundy, L. and Willis, C. (2012). Over 150 potentially low-value health care practices: an Australian study. *The Medical Journal of Australia.* 197(10). 556–60. 10.5694/mja12.11083.

Forrester, D. 2015. What works in helping people and why? *Social Work and Social Sciences Review,* 16(2): 88–102. https://journals.whitingbirch.net/index.php/SWSSR/article/view/530/569.

Goering, P., Veldhuizen, S., Watson, A., Adair, C., Kopp, B., Latimer, E., Nelson, G., MacNaughton, E., Streiner, D. and Aubry, T. 2014. *National at Home/Chez Soi Final Report.* Calgary, AB: Mental Health Commission of Canada. 31.

Hanley, P., Chambers, B., and Haslam, J. 2016. Reassessing RCTs as the 'gold standard': synergy not separatism in evaluation designs'. *International Journal of Research & Method in Education,* 39(3): 287–98.

Leigh, A. 2018. *Randomistas; How Radical Researchers Are Changing Our World.* New Haven, CT: Yale University Press: 190.

Nevill, C. 2019. How do we make EEF trials as informative as possible?. *EEF Blog.* https://educationendowmentfoundation.org.uk/news/eef-blog-how-do-we-make-eef-trials-as-informative-as-possible/.

Padgett, D.K., Henwood, B.F. and Tsemberis, S. 2016. *Housing First: Ending Homelessness, Transforming Systems and Changing Lives.* Oxford: Oxford University Press.

Petrosino, A., Turpin-Petrosino, C. and Finckenauer, J.O. 2000. Well-meaning programs can have harmful effects: Lessons from experiments of programs such as Scared Straight. *Crime & Delinquency*, 46: 354–79.

Petrosino, A., Turpin-Petrosino, C., Hollis-Peel, M.E. and Lavenberg, J.G. 2013. 'Scared Straight' and other juvenile awareness programs for preventing juvenile delinquency. Cochrane Database of Systematic Reviews.

Puttick, R. 2018. *Mapping the Standards of Evidence Used in UK Social Policy*. London: Alliance for Useful Evidence.

Rossi, P.H. 1987. The iron law of evaluation and other metallic rules. *Research in Social Problems and Public Policy*, 4: 3–20.

Schwan, S., French, D., Gaetz, S., Ward, A., Akerman, J. and Redman, M. 2018. Preventing youth homelessness: an international review of evidence. *Wales Centre for Public Policy*. https://www.wcpp.org.uk/wp-content/uploads/2018/10/Preventing-Youth-Homelessness-full-report.pdf

Sharples, J. 2013. *Evidence for the Frontline: A Report for the Alliance for Useful Evidence*. https://www.alliance4usefulevidence.org/assets/EVIDENCE-FOR-THE-FRONTLINE-FINAL-5-June-2013.pdf p.7.

St Mungo's. 2018. *Using Housing First in Integrated Homelessness Strategies. A Review of the Evidence*. York: University of York. www.mungos.org/publication/using-housing-first-integrated-homelessness-strategies/.

Teixeira, L. 2017. *Ending Homelessness Faster by Focusing on 'What Works'*, https://uploads-ssl.webflow.com/59f07e67422cdf0001904c14/5aeae4f86bdb475b190ba352_ending_homelessness_faster_by_focusing_on_what_works_2017.pdf.

Williams, M.J. 2017. *External Validity and Policy Adaptation: From Impact Evaluation to Policy Design*. BSG working paper series. Oxford: University of Oxford.

9

A public health approach to homelessness

Louise Marshall and Jo Bibby

In common with many population health challenges, homelessness is a complex social problem that arises from a system of multiple interrelated causes and consequences. Both public health and homelessness require a preventive approach that considers the complex systems of determinants that lead to each issue. Both need a strong evidence base to inform policy and practice.

> A complex systems model of public health conceptualises poor health and health inequalities as outcomes of a multitude of interdependent elements within a connected whole. These elements affect each other in sometimes subtle ways, with changes potentially reverberating throughout the system. A complex systems approach uses a broad spectrum of methods to design, implement, and evaluate interventions for changing these systems to improve public health (Rutter et al, 2017).

There is a long tradition of exploring the causes and consequences of homelessness, and there is consensus in the sector that population-level prevention is crucial. However, a gap exists in translating this into action, and political and practical action is too often focussed on rough sleeping and individual-level interventions (MHCLG 2018a, 2018b).

Despite the focus on individual-level action, there is a lack of good evidence and investment in the research required to understand effective strategies to support people at risk of, or experiencing, homelessness (Centre for Homelessness Impact, 2018).[1] The causal evidence that does exist is largely from the US and focuses on interventions around healthcare or supported housing for people already experiencing or at imminent risk of homelessness.

Given the impact of homelessness on people's long-term life chances and health outcomes, there is an urgent need for more investment in research to support evidence-informed policy-making and practice. In this chapter, we share our thoughts on evidence and evidence-informed policy-making and practice in the context of complexity from the field of public health, considering how these relate to homelessness.

Perspectives from public health: evidence-informed policy and practice in complex systems

In public health, there is a long history of evidence-informed practice and policy-making. Starting with the control and eradication of infectious diseases, evidence has been at the centre of decision-making. More recently, the rise of non-communicable diseases has required methods of building evidence to evolve, to take better account of a complex system of causes and consequences of health problems and inequalities in health (see Figure 9.1) (Rutter et al, 2017).

Major contemporary public health challenges (including obesity, diabetes, depression, anxiety and many cancers) occur in the population because of interrelated social, environmental, economic and commercial determinants, known in public health as the 'wider determinants' of health. They do not have a single risk or causal factor, and so cannot generally be tackled by simply changing or eliminating one aspect of behaviour or environment.

Figure 9.1: Characteristics of complex systems

Definition	Example
Emergence Properties of a complex system that cannot be directly predicted from the elements within it, and are more than the sum of their parts	The changing distribution of obesity across the population can be conceptualised as an emergent property of the food, employment, transport, economic, and other systems that shape the energy intake and expenditure of individuals.
Feedback Situations in which change reinforces or balances further change	If a smoking ban in public places reduces the visibility and convenience of smoking, and this makes it less appealing, fewer young people might then start smoking, further reducing its visibility, and so on in a reinforcing loop.
Adaptation Adjustments in behaviour in response to interventions or other changes	A tobacco company may lower the price of cigarettes in response to a public smoking ban.

Source: Adapted from Rutter et al (2017)

Despite this, research into these health issues has tended to focus on treating them once they have already occurred or preventing them by changing the most proximal risk factors in isolation. This generally includes individuals' actions, such as smoking or dietary intake. There has been far less research attention paid to understanding the factors that shape these actions – the wider determinants of health and the complex relationships between them – and the strategies needed to effect change.

This mismatch between the focus of evidence and the action needed to improve health and reduce health inequalities at the population level is in part due to the predominant evidence paradigm for public health research. Public health evidence that is sought to inform policy and practice is generated largely through research and translation methodologies that were developed in the field of biomedical science to understand the effectiveness of clinical interventions. These include: randomised controlled trials (RCTs), systematic reviews and evidence-based guidelines. They are based on cause and effect and are highly effective in investigating the effect of a single intervention in a controlled context, where nothing else changes.

In contrast, the identification, implementation and evaluation of effective responses to population health challenges require a different approach to evidence, focused on the complex systems from which they emerge (Rutter, 2017). Ensuring research is translated into effective practice and policy also requires a focus on building understanding of complex systems among researchers, practitioners and policy-makers, and the need for a complementary set of methods.

Case study: obesity

There is robust evidence to support the effectiveness of bariatric surgery in treating obesity and reversing some of the health consequences in obese individuals (NICE, 2015). However, no one would argue that this should be our sole approach to tackling the problem or a means of achieving a population of healthy weight. We also know that, under controlled experimental conditions, changes to individuals' dietary intakes and activity levels can lead to weight loss. In contrast, much less is known about the effectiveness of actions to reshape the complex system of environmental and societal factors that drive obesity in the population (Government Office for Science, 2007), including those determining the food people eat or how active they are able to be.

More than a decade ago, the UK government's Foresight project looked at how a sustainable response to obesity could be implemented in the UK (Government Office for Science, 2007). The project drew on scientific evidence from a wide range of disciplines and involved a large number of diverse stakeholders, to identify the broad range of factors that drive obesity. The project aimed to create a shared understanding of the relationships between factors, their relative importance and to design effective interventions to address rising rates of obesity. The resultant system map has been instrumental in depicting the complexity of obesity and the need for a whole system approach to tackle it. It illustrates how what we eat and our individual levels of activity are not just based on individual choice, but are a result of the food system and activity environment.

Until recently, research, policy and practice have largely focussed on single initiatives, delivered at an individual level (Jebb, 2017). However, there are signs that understanding systems is starting to drive a wider set of system-level actions, such as the reformulation of food products, advertising restrictions and active transport systems.

Recently, there has been success in reducing smoking rates in the UK. In 2011, 19.8 per cent of adults in England were smokers; by 2017, this figure was down to 14.9 per cent (Selbie, 2018). This came about through a series of population-level interventions, including increasing levels of taxation, the plain packaging of tobacco products, larger and more graphic warnings on tobacco packaging and bans on smoking in cars and public places. The synergy between these separate interventions has made it increasingly expensive and inconvenient to smoke and has changed the social norms around smoking. As fewer people smoke, smoking is less visible and it becomes less attractive to take up. In addition, with the introduction of each measure, and as social norms progressively changed, the introduction of further policy measures that might once have been unthinkable became increasingly acceptable to the public and politicians.

This experience shows that it is possible to reshape the interacting factors within a system to achieve a desirable outcome. The policy interventions were not planned or implemented simultaneously, but gradually as the system adapted and was reshaped. Valuable lessons can be learned from this and applied to other complex challenges.

A remaining challenge is to address the rising inequality in smoking rates. While rates in the population as a whole are at an all-time low, there are striking differences in rates between socioeconomic groups. For example: people with no qualifications are four times as likely to smoke as those with a degree; one in four people in routine and manual occupations smoke, compared with one in ten in managerial and professional roles; and a three-fold difference exists between geographical areas with the highest and lowest rates. If not addressed, this will contribute to rising health inequalities in the future. A systems perspective is needed to understand why approaches have or have not worked in different areas and effective strategies to reduce rates in these segments of the population.

Health and homelessness: products of complex systems

As with many other population health challenges, homelessness is a product of a complex system of multiple and interrelated factors. There is no single causal factor and, as such, simple, linear models of cause and effect are insufficient to create solutions for prevention. This is widely understood in the homelessness sector, and the Centre for Homelessness Impact have carried out system mapping. As in public health, however, a significant gap exists in the use of this evidence to inform whole systems approaches to policy and practice.

Poverty, especially during childhood, is the biggest single predictor of homelessness, accounting for 25–50 per cent of the chance of experiencing homelessness as an adult (Boswell et al, 2018). This is compounded by issues in the housing market. There has been a reduction in social housing stock, accompanied by an increase in private rental housing – much of which excludes people on housing benefits. Housing benefits are also inadequate to cover the cost of rent in most of the country. These elements, together with many other personal, social, economic and cultural risk and protective factors, determine a person's risk of being or becoming homeless. Many of these risk factors are closely related, occurring together and affecting each other (Bramley et al, 2015).

The impact of clustering and accumulation of risk factors over time and the resulting risk of someone experiencing homelessness is starkly illustrated later in this chapter, comparing two individuals with very different life stories (adapted from Boswell et al, 2018). This example highlights that homelessness does not 'just happen' to anyone: it is determined by events that occur throughout our lives (see Figure 7.1).

This evidence about the determinants of homelessness must be applied in its prevention, both addressing the risk factors and targeting support at a far earlier stage to individuals at high risk. Building this understanding into policy and practice can also help promote a longer-term, population-level approach. For example, child poverty has risen at an alarming rate in many parts of the UK in recent years; what does this mean for future prevalence of homelessness and how can risks be mitigated now?

Understanding the risk factors that put and keep people in poverty and increase their chances of becoming homeless can help identify multiple points of action and intervention to reshape the system. This understanding can also help identify appropriate measures to monitor progress and help predict whether positive outcomes are likely to be achieved in the longer term.

Evidence-informed policy-making and practice for homelessness

Better evidence-informed policy-making and practice is urgently needed to end homelessness sustainably. A culture of experimentation must be adopted, with appropriately designed evaluation consistently embedded to increase understanding about what is effective, or is not, and why. Critically, mechanisms must be developed for feeding back learning into policy and practice.

There is a lack of good evidence from well-designed studies examining what is effective in preventing and tackling homelessness (Culhane, Fitzpatrick and Treglia, this volume). There is not a tradition of rigorous evaluation in the homeless sector. Most effectiveness studies are from the US; only 12 have been conducted in the UK, and all focus on healthcare action to support people who are already homeless. This evidence is mostly about relatively straightforward, single interventions, delivered at an individual level to small subpopulations experiencing specific conditions (Centre for Homelessness Impact, 2018).[2]

In most cases, very little is known about the quality and effectiveness of some of the most common interventions used in homelessness (Centre for Homelessness Impact, 2018).[3] There is huge scope to better understand how to help people who are homeless or at risk of homelessness. Understanding the effectiveness of an intervention is a key step in evidence-informed decision-making, and more robust evidence from well-designed research studies is needed (Craig et al, 2018; Culhane, Fitzpatrick and Treglia, this volume).

The aim must be to end, rather than manage, homelessness, and greater attention also needs to be paid to prevention by researchers, policy-makers and practitioners. This means building evidence about what is effective to favourably reshape the complex system of determinants of homelessness and ensure this informs policy and practice. This requires a wider approach to generating and translating evidence, and a better understanding of how to interpret and use this in policy-making and practice. Complexity is not a reason not to build and use good evidence. Rather, it means that a wide range of methods needs to be deployed.

Taking a complex systems approach

The public health and homelessness sectors both recognise that a system-wide perspective is needed to effectively prevent their respective problems. This is a sound foundation on which to build. Now, systems thinking needs to become integral to the design of research and to the translation of the resulting evidence to policy and practice.

While there is good understanding of the major drivers of homelessness, less is known about how these cluster or interact and how they influence the risk of homelessness. Less still is known about how to address these broad factors in an aligned way, as part of a system-wide approach. Developing a comprehensive understanding of the system and system dynamics can enable better design of research into what works in tackling homelessness.

Taking a systems approach involves building a shared understanding of the system of causes and consequences, using appropriate research methods including ongoing monitoring and evaluation, and – importantly – building an understanding of these among practitioners and policy-makers to support translation.

System mapping

The Centre for Homelessness Impact recently convened a broad range of stakeholders to map the system of factors influencing homelessness. System mapping involves identifying as many factors as possible from all perspectives within a sector, and then mapping these out alongside the connections between them. This is typically done in workshops involving as many relevant stakeholders as possible.

When carefully constructed, system mapping workshops are commonly characterised by a positive energy and openness among participants, who find value in stepping away from their day-to-day focus to take a birds' eye view of a problem and discover where their work links – or should link – with that of others. The value to be gained from convening people working with a shared goal, who may have never met or spoken before, is not to be underestimated. This can be an important intervention in and of itself. Involving those who may not have realised the important role their part of the system can potentially play in an issue can effectively act to engage them with the issue.

Mapping the system in this way can be an important step in developing a system-informed approach to action and evaluation. Building a visual representation of a system around an issue, with interconnections, pathways and feedback loops, can provide insight to help policymakers, practitioners and researchers make better informed decisions. The quality and usefulness of such maps, however, depends on the process of their creation. A system map reflects only the perspectives of those involved in its development. Getting this right and involving relevant organisations and people, including those with lived experience of an issue, is therefore crucial to provide views from all parts of the system.

A system map can enable identification of areas where evidence exists or where there are gaps, against where there is currently action or investment, or indeed, a lack of it. It can also be enlightening that evidence, practice, and perspectives about what might work, are not always entirely aligned (NIHR School for Public Health Research, 2019). The system map can also help in understanding the contextual factors that need to be in place for an action to be as effective as possible, as well as the potential wider consequences – both intended and unintended. This can help identify measures for evaluation, to help understand processes and pathways, and ensure no harm is caused as a consequence of unanticipated effects.

System mapping can identify a broad range of system-wide process, output and outcome measures that need to be measured in the evaluation of any action to reshape the system, in order to fully understand whether, why and how it is effective. This is important whether evaluating a system-wide programme of action, or a single, individual-level intervention. Taking this wider perspective even to very specific interventions is important for their application in practice. The system view can identify contextual factors that should be measured in evaluation to understand the context within which the intervention is effective and any potential barriers to its effectiveness.

Building evidence in complex systems

Models of evidence to understand and evaluate action in complex systems are currently the subject of much interest and development in the field of public health. There are, however, sources of guidance and well-established, robust methods that already exist and could be applied to homelessness.

The NIHR School of Public Health Research has published guidance on systems approaches to local public health evaluation (Egan et al, 2019a), providing an accessible introduction to thinking about systems and the benefits of this wider perspective, plus considerations for planning and adopting a systems-informed approach to evaluation.

> It does not cost anything to think about activities from a systems perspective, nor does the incorporation of a systems perspective into an evaluation need to be difficult, laborious or expensive. Bringing a systems approach to an evaluation may merely involve thinking slightly differently about the kinds of ways in which an intervention may exert its effects, and how those effects might be assessed (Egan et al, 2019b).

The NIHR guidance outlines the broad uses of systems approaches in understanding problems (mapping the system as described earlier), identifying and assessing potential levers of change and comparing hypothetical scenarios that involve changing part, or parts, of a system (Egan et al, 2019b). It also identifies the potential value of systems approaches whether evaluating actions to change a single point in a system, 'whole system' approaches to changing many points, or those to change relationships within a system (for example that encourage joint working across sectors). Six main types of systems evaluation methods are described that are currently in use in public health, acknowledging the methodological innovation taking place in the sector.

The NIHR guidance describes three levels of complexity that can characterise public health issues and the approaches to them, that may need to be considered by evaluators:

- *Complex interventions:* comprising a number of different activities, flexible forms of delivery and requiring input from different people or organisations. Reshaping complex systems will often require a complex intervention.
- *Complex environments:* made up of people, activities, organisations, rules and places, that all interact as part of a system. Regardless of the level of complexity of the intervention, the environment it is delivered in is highly complex and constantly changing.
- *Complex consequences:* in individuals – who may be affected in several different ways – populations, political and economic conditions, and in the way different agencies interact. Feedback loops, when consequences influence the intervention itself, add further to this complexity.

The Medical Research Council (MRC) has published draft guidance on the planning, development, feasibility testing, evaluation and implementation of complex interventions, aiming to support more 'complexity-informed' research (MRC, 2019). This describes complexity of an intervention as being not only a property of the intervention characteristics, but also the context in which the intervention is located, and the research perspective taken – and of the interaction between these factors. The characteristics of interventions are described as lying along a spectrum from 'simple' to 'complicated', and the research perspective on a continuum from efficacy to systems, including:

- Efficacy perspective: to what extent does the intervention produce the intended outcome(s) in experimental settings?
- Effectiveness perspective: to what extent does the intervention produce the intended outcome in real world settings?
- Realist perspective: what works, for whom, under which circumstances, and why?
- Systems perspective: how does the intervention interact with the system to produce change?

Complexity-informed research, with an awareness of system(s) can encourage: (i) researchers to develop research questions that take into account the wider contextual factors that influence an intervention; and (ii) researchers, funders, practitioners and policy makers to develop, evaluate, and implement interventions using the most appropriate tools and methods.

This MRC draft guidance discusses the range of methods available to researchers and selection of the best available method for the circumstances. Randomised experimental methods are a means of eliminating certain biases in research and should be considered where appropriate. RCTs have been the predominant research method in evidence-based medicine, and widely adopted in public health research since. They are the 'gold standard' method for evaluating the effectiveness of single, individual-level interventions, independent of wider changes or context. For actions delivered at the population level, this may not be possible; in those cases, other methods can be used to build a robust evidence base about what works. This includes other experimental randomised designs, which may be used where it is not appropriate or possible to carry out a conventional RCT, but also natural experimental designs and systems designs, including modelling and case studies.

There is growing interest in natural experiments in the field of public health research. These include events not under the control of a researcher that divide a population into exposed and unexposed groups. The naturally occurring variation in exposure is exploited to identify the impact of the event on outcomes of interest. The evaluation of natural experiments requires careful consideration and design, but a growing range of methods are available, which are described in detail elsewhere (Craig et al, 2017).

Natural experiments are seen as key to evaluating large-scale population health interventions – for example the introduction of a policy or other population-level action – that are not amenable to experimental manipulation (Rutter et al, 2017). One example is the introduction of the soft drinks industry levy (SDIL) in 2018 in the UK. Public health researchers saw the opportunity here, and planned – well in advance to allow collection of baseline data – a comprehensive, system-level natural experiment to evaluate its impact (CEDAR, 2017). The evaluation aims to examine not only whether, how and for whom the levy has an impact on health, but also the process by which the levy came about and the wider changes in public, political, societal and industry attitudes to sugar and the SDIL over the four years before and four years following its introduction. System mapping identified potential mechanisms for action, and thereby the data collection and methodologies necessary to explore them across a broad range of areas. These diverse data sources include: purchasing data of soft drinks and confectionary to examine whether people switch from sugary drinks to sugary foods; market research data; surveys on attitudes to sugar and the levy; and government data on health outcomes including tooth decay and obesity.

This demonstrates the value of a systems approach in identifying ways of assessing and understanding the broader consequences of actions – both intended and unintended – and the processes that may lead to them. Similar approaches can be used to accelerate progress in building evidence for what works in homelessness.

Translating evidence into action

Understanding the system, and careful and appropriate design of research, will only get us so far, and barriers remain to putting the insights generated into practice. These can include political will, cognitive bias, separate budgets, organisational or sectoral performance targets that do not reflect the value of these ways of working, and the immediate benefits of action falling in different parts of the system to those that need to take, or pay for, that action.

The development of a deeper understanding of the principles discussed here among policy-makers, practitioners, commissioners and researchers is of fundamental importance to developing an evidence infrastructure about what it takes to end homelessness sustainably and to translate this knowledge into policy and practice.

It is important to effectively communicate with policy-makers and commissioners to build understanding of systems approaches. This will enable them to judge the quality of evidence produced from a systems approach to research and evaluation.

In Canada, systems planning at a local level is being promoted for the development of system-wide approaches to preventing and ending homelessness. The Systems Planning Collective (SPC), a group of Canadian organisations that have joined forces to support local areas in systems planning, define this as follows:

> Systems planning at the local level is the process of strategically mapping, coordinating and delivering services, supports, and programmes with the rights, needs, desires of the client/user at the centre. Its aim is to create an integrated system of care, in which various actors and systems work together towards solutions to complex social problems. When applied to the issue of homelessness, the unifying high-level goal of systems planning work is to prevent and end homelessness. (Systems Planning Collective, 2019)

A needs assessment for operationalising systems planning for homelessness, carried out by the SPC, found that capabilities for this vary greatly between local areas (Systems Planning Collective, 2019). This highlights a further challenge to implementing evidence-informed, system-wide approaches to homelessness.

Understanding how these approaches can be put into practice is critical to achieving impact and requires evidence on how systems approaches can be implemented in practice. An important aspect of this is evaluation, with a rapid feedback cycle for making changes when an approach is not working, or flexibility and responsiveness is required. The implementation of local area systems approaches to homelessness in Canada creates an important opportunity, to build understanding about this key step of translation into action, if subjected to detailed evaluation.

Conclusions

Homelessness is the result of a complex system of interacting determinants. The prevention of homelessness therefore requires a system-wide perspective and upstream focus in both action and research. This is not to suggest an alternative to learning what works for people already experiencing homelessness, but a more holistic approach to the problem that includes support for these individuals.

Like public health, homelessness needs to embrace a movement for evidence-informed practice to ensure that action is based on the best available evidence. To facilitate this, we need to build stronger evidence of effective strategies to support people who are at risk of, or experiencing, homelessness and to prevent homelessness further upstream. Evaluation must consider the whole system to understand why or how individual or population level interventions work, and the context and conditions necessary for success. It is vital that once an intervention or policy is put into practice, ongoing evaluation and feedback becomes an integral part of learning for evidence-informed approaches to the problem.

A key challenge for the movement will be to explicate the need for evidence-informed, whole system approaches to homelessness among researchers, policy-makers, commissioners and practitioners. Widespread adoption of these principles and research methods will ensure that we achieve the change urgently required to support individuals, and prevent homelessness for good.

Notes

[1] Centre for Homelessness Impact. 2019. Evidence and Gap Maps of Effectiveness and Implementation Studies. CHI: London: https://www.homelessnessimpact.org/gap-maps

[2] Centre for Homelessness Impact. 2019. Evidence and Gap Maps of Effectiveness and Implementation Studies. CHI: London: https://www.homelessnessimpact.org/gap-maps

[3] Teixeira, L. et al. 2019. The Share Framework: a smarter way to end homelessness. CHI: London: https://www.homelessnessimpact.org/share

References

Boswell, K., Tait, R. and Eisenstein, C. 2018. *Tackling the Homelessness Crisis: Why and How You Should Fund Systemically.* NPC. https://www.thinknpc.org/resource-hub/tackling-the-homelessness-crisis-why-and-and-how-you-should-fund-systemically/ (accessed 24 April 2019).

Bramley, G., Fitzpatrick S., Edwards J., Ford D., Johnsen S., Sosenko F. and Watkins D. 2015. *Hard Edges: Mapping Severe and Multiple Disadvantage in England.* Lankelly Chase. https://lankellychase.org.uk/resources/publications/hard-edges/ (accessed 24 April 2019).

CEDAR. 2017. Soft drinks industry levy evaluation. www.cedar.iph.cam.ac.uk/research/dietary-public-health/food-systems-public-health/sdil/ (accessed 24 April 2019).

Centre for Homelessness Impact. Evidence and gap maps. https://www.homelessnessimpact.org/gap-maps (accessed 27 November 2019)

Craig, P., Gibson, M., Campbell, M., Popham, F. and Katikireddi, S.V. 2018. Making the most of natural experiments: what can studies of the withdrawal of public health interventions offer? *Preventive Medicine*, 108: 17–22. https://reader.elsevier.com/reader/sd/pii/S0091743517305133?token=49FF6804CE9F6B4E29785CC3F59B20628D9F46D303B124189451F51F346C1885A8A45E3D0FC79487313471B446D4F101 (accessed 24 April 2019).

Craig P., Katikireddi, S.V., Leyland, A. and Popham, F. 2017. Natural experiments: an overview of methods, approaches, and contributions to public health intervention research. *Annual Review of Public Health*, 38, 39–56. www.annualreviews.org/doi/full/10.1146/annurev-publhealth-031816-044327 (accessed 24 April 2019).

Egan, M., McGill, E., Penney, T., Anderson de Cuevas, R., Er, V., Orton, L., Lock, K., Popay, J., Savona, N., Cummins, S., Rutter, H., Whitehead, M., De Vocht, F., White, M., Smith, R., Andreeva, M., Meier, P., Marks, D. and Petticrew, M. (2019a). *NIHR SPHR Guidance on Systems Approaches to Local Public Health Evaluation. Part 1: Introducing Systems Thinking.* https://sphr.nihr.ac.uk/wp-content/uploads/2018/08/NIHR-SPHR-SYSTEM-GUIDANCE-PART-1-FINAL_SBnavy.pdf (accessed 24 April 2019).

Egan, M., McGill, E., Penney, T., Anderson de Cuevas, R., Er, V., Orton, L., White, M., Lock, K., Cummins, S., Savona, N., Whitehead, M., Popay, J., Smith, R., Meier, P., De Vocht, F., Marks, D., Andreeva, M., Rutter, H. and Petticrew, M. (2019b) *NIHR SPHR Guidance on Systems Approaches to Local Public Health Evaluation. Part 2: What to Consider When Planning a Systems Evaluation.* https://sphr.nihr.ac.uk/wp-content/uploads/2018/08/NIHR-SPHR-SYSTEM-GUIDANCE-PART-2-v2-FINALSBnavy.pdf (accessed 24 April 2019).

Government Office for Science. 2007. *Tackling Obesities: Future Choices.* Foresight. https://assets.publishing.service.gov.uk/government/uploads/system/uploads/attachment_data/file/287937/07-1184x-tackling-obesities-future-choices-report.pdf (accessed 27 November 2019).

Jebb, S. 2017. *Dusting Off Foresight's Obesity Report.* https://foresightprojects.blog.gov.uk/2017/10/04/dusting-off-foresights-obesity-report/ (accessed: 24 April 2019).

MHCLG (Ministry of Housing, Communities & Local Government). 2018a. *The Rough Sleeping Strategy.* www.gov.uk/government/publications/the-rough-sleeping-strategy (accessed: 24 April 2019).

MHCLG (Ministry of Housing, Communities & Local Government). 2018b. *Homelessness Reduction Act: Policy FactSheets*. www.gov.uk/government/publications/homelessness-reduction-bill-policy-factsheets (accessed: 24 April 2019).

MRC. 2019. *Updated Guidance: Developing and Evaluating Complex Interventions* (draft for consultation). www.sphsu.gla.ac.uk/stakeholder-survey-2019/Full%20complex%20guidance%20draft%20for%20consultation%20v1.1%2026.03.19.pdf (accessed 24 April 2019).

NICE. 2015. *Obesity Prevention CG43. Supporting Evidence*. www.nice.org.uk/guidance/cg43/evidence (accessed: 24 April 2019).

NIHR School for Public Health Research. 2019. *Developing a Systems Perspective for the Evaluation of Local Public Health Interventions*. https://sphr.nihr.ac.uk/research/developing-a-systems-perspective-for-the-evaluation-of-local-public-health-interventions-theory-methods-and-practice/ (accessed 24 April 2019).

Rutter, H., Savona, N., Glonti, K., Bibby, J., Cummins, S., Finegood, D.T., Greaves, F., Harper, L., Hawe, P., Moore, L., Petticrew, M., Rehfuess, E., Shiell, A., Thomas, J. and White, M. 2017. The need for a complex systems model of evidence for public health. *Lancet*, 390 (10112): 2602–4.

Selbie, D. 2018. *Turning the Tide on Tobacco: Smoking in England Hits a New Low*. https://publichealthmatters.blog.gov.uk/2018/07/03/turning-the-tide-on-tobacco-smoking-in-england-hits-a-new-low/ (accessed: 24 April 2019).

Systems Planning Collective. 2019. *Systems Planning to Prevent and End Homelessness*. www.homelesshub.ca/sites/default/files/attachments/SPC-HPS-NeedsAssessmentReport.pdf (accessed 24 April 2019).

10

Data and evidence: what is possible in public policy?

Stephen Aldridge

Humans are not good at acting on what they already know. As early as 1601, Captain Admiral James Lancaster of the East India Company stumbled on the fact that lemon juice provided an effective prevention against scurvy.[1] By the middle of the 18th century, James Lind, a naval physician, was putting that information to the test in the first recorded randomised control trial (RCT).

Lind took 12 men suffering from the symptoms of scurvy and divided them into six pairs, treating each with one of a selection of recommended but untested remedies borrowed from other physicians. These included daily doses of a quart of cider; 25 drops of 'elixir of vitriol'; half a pint of sea-water; a nutmeg-sized paste of garlic, mustard seed, horseradish, balsam of Peru and myrrh gum; two spoonfuls of vinegar; and (rather more effectively) two oranges and one lemon. By the end of the week's treatment, the men who had been fed on citrus fruits were the only ones to show signs of improvement in their symptoms.[2]

In spite of this unequivocal evidence, it still took another half century for the Royal Navy to make a portion of citrus fruits a standard addition to sailors' rations – and, even then, only with the campaigning and support of Lind's advocates. In

161

the Seven Years' War (1756–63), Britain raised 185,899 sailors: 1,512 died in action, while 133,708 died of scurvy. However, the Royal Navy was faster at curing scurvy than its main naval opponents – one reason why it was able to win the Battle of Trafalgar against a larger force of scurvy-ridden French and Spanish ships (Leigh, 2018).

It was not until the 1940s that what is commonly accepted as the first RCT in medicine took place on treatments for pulmonary tuberculosis, and only in 1972 that Archie Cochrane's pioneering work, *Evidence and Efficiency: Random Reflections on Health Services*, finally popularised the concept of the RCT.

Cochrane faced incredible early resistance to the idea of using research evidence to test whether medical treatments and practices were actually effective.[3] This seems extraordinary in a modern world in which we can be sure that medical treatments have all been rigorously tested before coming into general use. Yet it is only relatively recently that RCTs have become part of the medical status quo.

This demonstrates some of the natural resistance to ideas that later appear self-evident. We humans do not like change.

As Director for Analysis and Data at the Ministry of Housing, Communities and Local Government (MHCLG), my role is to bring facts, evidence, research and analysis to the heart of both policy-making and delivery. I head a team of analysts and data specialists including economists, social and operational researchers, statisticians, data engineers and other data specialists, providing data and insight across all the department's areas of responsibility.

Over the past year (at the time of writing) we have worked on pieces of analysis as diverse as the appraisal of bids to the Housing Infrastructure Fund, the evaluation of the Troubled Families programme, the local government Needs and Resources Review, building safety, the future of the high street, the modelling of the housing market, and EU exit; produced over 80 statistical releases on housing and land use planning, homelessness and rough sleeping, building safety and local government finance; provided data and analysis for the local government finance settlement; developed and appraised housing measures; published reports of the English Housing

Survey; and much more (MHCLG's statement of areas of research interest (MHCLG, 2018a) gives a good indication of the breadth of the department's research interests).

It is fair to say that managing a programme of analytical work as varied and technical as this is not without its challenges. The data can be vast and the analysis tricky. The evidence can also often be incomplete or difficult to pin down.

Even so, over time, government has become much better at accessing and gathering the data it needs, developing new methods of analysis, and using the resulting findings better to inform and guide public policy. From a place where analysis was once seen as a discipline for a small group of specialists, we are now at a point where more and more of the civil service feel confident in engaging with evidence and understand why it really matters that they do.

Against this backdrop, this chapter:

- sets out how evidence can improve policy-making and policy design – provided it is sound;
- sets out how government has used What Works Centres to improve its evidence base;
- discusses how evidence can help to drive public sector efficiency and improvement;
- uses the evaluation of the Troubled Families Programme to provide a case study of the cutting-edge use of data to assess policy effectiveness;
- provides a high-level summary of work in hand to improve the data and evidence on homelessness and rough sleeping – of key interest to the Centre for Homelessness Impact; and
- takes a broad look at the opportunities to improve the use of data and evidence more generally and the barriers that need to be overcome in doing so.

Evidence can improve policy-making and policy design – but it needs to be sound

Evidence-based policy-making is the principle that good decisions are, or should be, made and informed by the best available evidence.

This is not to say there is no role for political values, public opinion or other drivers of public policy. But evidence and analysis can help us better to understand the causes of economic and social problems and what would be most cost-effective in tackling them, improving outcomes for citizens and service users and ensuring that public money is well spent.

The introduction of the minimum wage in the UK is often cited as a powerful example of the potential positive impact of soundly based evidence and analysis. My own profession – economics – has always had reservations about the minimum wage for fear that it would cost people their jobs. It took a seminal empirical study by Card and Krueger in the US to challenge this conventional wisdom (Card and Krueger, 1994).

Card and Krueger's work – based on a natural experiment comparing different regimes in two adjacent US states – showed that a *carefully set* minimum wage need not have a significant effect on the employment of workers in the fast food industry. This research shifted the conversation and shaped the approach that was taken to the implementation of the minimum wage – a powerful illustration of how evidence and analysis can build the consensus for change.

Naturally, evidence can come in many different forms: basic data; international comparisons; qualitative evidence from surveys or case studies; sophisticated econometrics and much else. In the evaluation field, RCTs are often regarded as the gold standard for good evidence, since they allow direct comparisons over time between a group receiving a public policy intervention and a control group that is not. However, sophisticated quasi-experimental methods, such as propensity score matching and other methods, can be used when an RCT is not possible.

More RCTs of public policy interventions are undoubtedly needed and there has been a significant increase in such studies in recent years. Indeed, the UK Cabinet Office established a Trials Advisory Panel to provide advice and support to RCTs commissioned by government departments.

However, RCTs are not without their limitations. In some cases it is simply not possible to undertake such trials. In other cases, there may be formidable data or methodological challenges to overcome. In practice, a range of methods are, and should be, used to evaluate policy interventions and there is ongoing debate about what weight can be attached to the findings obtained from each.

An example of the challenges that may be posed in finding robust evidence is provided by the work of the What Works Centre for Local Economic Growth. Over three years, the centre carried out a series of systematic evidence reviews of existing studies in order to synthesise what we know about what works in promoting local growth. This involved looking at nearly 15,000 different studies. Not all of these were impact evaluations, but even so just 361 were impact studies that met their minimum standards for robustness.

This does not mean that we should give up. There are many examples of how public policy has been, or can be, improved by paying closer attention to the evidence. But we need more studies and the resulting evidence needs to be built on sound and robust methods.

How government has improved its evidence base

In some spheres of our lives, we take it for granted that an evidence-based approach will have been taken to decide on a course of action. When we go to the doctor or when we take a new drug developed by a pharmaceutical company, we trust that the procedure or medicine is safe and will be effective. That this is the case owes a great deal to the work of the National Institute for Clinical Excellence, now the National Institute for Health and Care Excellence (NICE).

The success of NICE in the medical and pharmaceutical field led many to suggest the establishment of a 'NICE for social policy' (something in which Sir Jeremy Heywood, the late Cabinet Secretary, played a central part). In response the UK Government launched the What Works network in 2013. This network now consists of ten independent centres covering areas of public spending well in excess of £200 billion.[4]

Their basic aim is common and simple: to help ensure that spending decisions in the public sector and public services, and work by practitioners on the ground, is informed by the best available evidence on what works and what is most cost-effective in achieving desired outcomes.

Although each centre is unique and focuses on its own area of policy, they all do this by systematically reviewing the evidence of what works in their respective areas; building understanding of the effectiveness of current professional practice and the ways in which it might be improved; and identifying evidence gaps and options for addressing them.

The centres disseminate findings to policy-makers, practitioners, commissioners and local decision-makers, developing online tools and dashboards to make their work as accessible as possible to the users of their work.[5]

It is worth dwelling for a moment on how transformative this approach has been. To take one example, the Education Endowment Foundation (EEF) – the What Works Centre for Education – is now responsible for more than 10 per cent of all robust education RCTs *in the world*. Despite only being established in 2011, it has commissioned 160 trials, reaching over 10,000 schools in England and over a million young people.[6]

Thanks to the EEF we know that communicating with parents by text message is an effective way of raising pupils' attainment and reducing truancy and that reducing class sizes improves performance by an equivalent of three months of progress per year (when numbers in the class drop below 20). We also know what does not work. Streaming pupils on the basis of ability is detrimental to low-attaining pupils, setting them back by one to two months per year compared with pupils in mixed-ability groups. Repeating a school year is even worse, with pupils making on average four months' less progress than those who move on.

More than two-thirds of head teachers now use the EEF's teaching and learning toolkit to guide how they spend the pupil premium supplement for disadvantaged children. The EEF's latest initiative – Promising Projects – aims to scale up programmes that have proven to be successful to an even larger number of schools.

How evidence helps to drive public sector efficiency and improvement

Much of the work of the What Works movement has taken place against a backdrop of constraints on public spending needed for fiscal sustainability. While it might seem counterintuitive that tightening the purse strings should drive innovation, reduced budgets have certainly aided the What Works agenda – the argument for greater evidence and efficiency in the public sector at a time of tight budget constraints and increased pressure on services is obvious.

Boosting public sector productivity requires an evidence-based understanding of what public services have been able to deliver, the drivers of these outcomes and the likely effectiveness of different options for further improvement. Government output currently makes up between 20–25 per cent of gross domestic product and any effort to boost economy-wide productivity performance clearly needs to embrace the public sector and public services.

There are a number of dimensions to public sector efficiency – the product of the entire process of turning public money into desired outcomes (see Figure 10.1):

- economy: how cheaply inputs are purchased;
- productivity: how much output we get from each unit of input;
- effectiveness: the extent to which outputs are translated into the outcomes we want.

Improving efficiency does not just mean reducing spend; it means delivering better outcomes and more effective government while using public money in the smartest way possible.

Establishing any kind of efficiency metric for the public sector and public services is subject to numerous measurement and methodological challenges. However, these challenges can usually be at least partially overcome provided the limitations are understood and conclusions drawn with care.

Figure 10.1: The public sector and public service production process

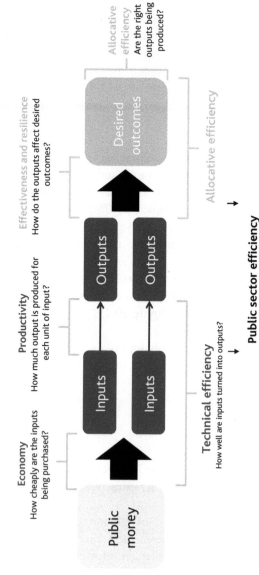

The public sector/service production process

A simplified model of how public money is turned into inputs, outputs and outcomes

Economy
How cheaply are the inputs being purchased?

Productivity
How much output is produced for each unit of input?

Effectiveness and resilience
How do the outputs affect desired outcomes?

Allocative efficiency
Are the right outputs being produced?

Public money

Inputs

Outputs

Desired outcomes

Technical efficiency
How well are inputs turned into outputs?

Allocative efficiency

Public sector efficiency
Relevant to the entire process of turning public money into desired outcomes

Source: Aldridge (2019)

There is though, an important distinction to make between 'technical' and 'allocative' efficiency (see Figure 10.2).

Technical efficiency refers to doing what we do now, but better. It means asking questions like: can we purchase inputs – such as hospital equipment or teaching staff – at a lower cost without affecting quality? Can we produce more outputs – such as medical operations or pupils attaining the highest grades – for the same resources we are putting in?

Allocative efficiency means finding wholly different ways of achieving the outcomes we want. It means asking further, more difficult questions including: are we doing the right things? Allocative efficiency is crucial to effectiveness and service transformation.

The UK has a strong track record in measuring public sector efficiency. Ever since the independent review by Sir Tony Atkinson in 2005, the UK has been at the forefront of the better measurement of the efficiency of government services. The Office for National Statistics, for example, publishes statistics on the productivity of public services as a whole, as well as detailed articles on, for example, healthcare.

More rigorous measurement helps facilitate constructive challenge and helps departments better to understand the efficiency of their services, activities and programmes and to identify where and how they might be improved.

Figure 10.2: The distinction between technical and allocative efficiency

Technical efficiency
'Doing things right'
Doing the things we currently do either at less cost, or getting more outputs from what we currently do at the same cost, or some combination of the two.

Allocative efficiency
'Doing the right things'
Finding wholly different ways of achieving desired outcomes – at less or substantially less cost. Service transformation is crucial to allocative efficiency and unlocking transformational improvements in efficiency.

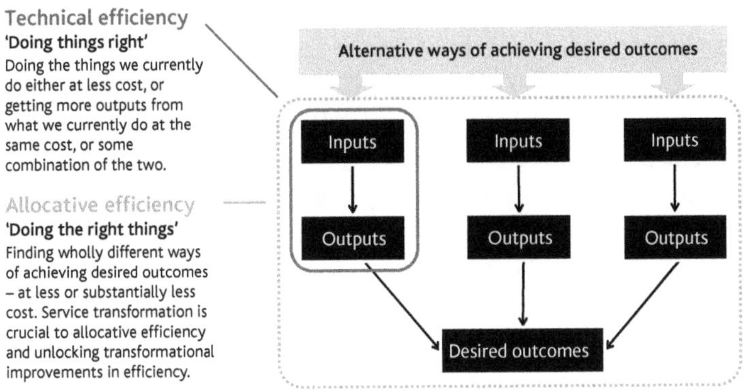

Source: Aldridge (2019)

Historically (see Figure 10.3), based on the available data, private sector productivity has grown faster than public sector productivity. However, since the financial crash in the late 2000s, private sector productivity in the UK has flatlined whilst public service productivity has grown.

It is important to stress here that the components of the index of public service productivity growth in the UK are of mixed robustness. For some services, like defence and policing, outputs are assumed to equal inputs. On the other hand, nearly half of the outputs in the public service productivity index are now quality adjusted.

The UK has particularly good productivity data for health services (see Figure 10.4) with outputs adjusted for quality. This shows steady but modest increases in productivity over time driven by reduced average length of hospital stay and the shifting of activity to day cases.

Growth in health services productivity has picked up since the late 2000s – outperforming the long run trend – driven by a range of factors including pay restraint, better procurement, reduced use of more expensive agency staff, greater use of generic medicines and other changes.

Inputs to publicly funded healthcare have three components: labour, purchases of goods and services, and consumption of fixed capital. Healthcare output is measured by the quantity of healthcare delivered, adjusted for changes in the quality of delivery. Outputs include hospital inpatient, outpatient and day case episodes, family health services, including general practitioner (GP) services, and prescribing – including all drugs prescribed by GPs – and non-NHS provision funded by government. Quality is measured using survival rates and health gain, waiting times and surveys of patient experience.

The comparatively rich data available on health services has, for example, permitted the development of benchmarking tools that allow health service providers to compare their performance with their peers and facilitated assessments of the relative cost-effectiveness of health prevention and treatment (Aldridge, 2019).

Figure 10.3: Total economy, market sector and public service productivity, UK, 1997–2016

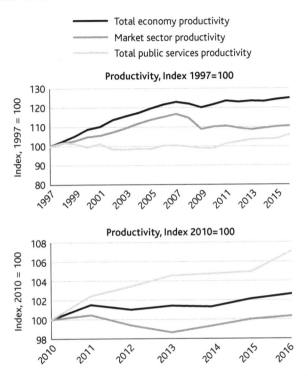

> **Total economy productivity**
> Inputs: Hours worked
> Outputs: Gross Domestic Product
>
> **Market sector productivity**
> Inputs: The volume of labour (adjusted for the skill mix of the workforce), and the volume of capital used.
> Outputs: Total economic output of the market sector (measured by Gross Value Added, GVA).
>
> **Total public services productivity**
> Inputs: Inputs can be broken down into three components. They are labour, intermediate consumption (expenditure on goods and services) and consumption of fixed capital.
> Outputs: are measured in one of 4 ways:
> (a) outputs are assumed to equal inputs (e.g. defence spending) – 38% of total
> (b) quality adjusted outputs equal inputs – 3%
> (c) quantity alone – 12% (e.g. social security administration and children's social care)
> (d) quality adjusted – 47%

Source: Aldridge (2019), based on ONS data

Figure 10.4: Public health care productivity in the UK, 1995/96–2016/17

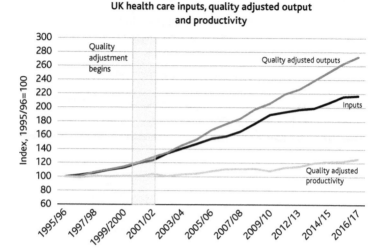

Source: Aldridge (2019), based on ONS data

Beyond health care: a case study of the Troubled Families Programme

In the health sector, there exists a comparatively longstanding infrastructure of measurement, data collection and impact evaluation that allows government to monitor the effects of the resources it spends. In other areas of social policy, this is not yet the case and more complex evaluation is necessary to determine the effectiveness and efficiency of policies and interventions.

In March 2019, MHCLG published an evaluation of the Troubled Families' Programme (MHCLG, 2019a), an initiative that has sought to transform the lives of 400,000 families with multiple, persistent and often severe problems, across six headline issues: worklessness and financial exclusion; school absence; mental and physical health problems; children needing help; domestic violence and abuse; crime and anti-social behaviour. To do so, the programme champions more holistic and proactive approaches to the whole family, joining up services to deliver more comprehensive, earlier and more effective interventions.

The Government wanted a national evaluation that was robust enough to stand up to public scrutiny and to establish whether the programme was achieving its goals and utilising resources effectively. To do this, it used an innovative quasi-experimental approach to assess the added value of the programme, directly linking data from every upper-tier local authority and from the police national computer, the national pupil database, and the Department for Works and Pensions (DWP) and HMRC benefits and employment data. This quasi-experimental design allowed outcomes to be compared for families who joined the programme with those in a matched comparison group.

The evaluation used administrative data from local authorities and government departments to measure outcomes on a scale not attempted before. The data matching provided MHCLG with information on offending, school attendance and attainment, children's social care, and benefits take-up and employment. The result is a very large dataset with over a million cases and over 3,000 variables.

The quantitative net impact evaluation is complemented by a number of other strands of evaluation, in particular qualitative case studies and surveys of Troubled Families staff, both conducted by Ipsos MORI.

The impact evaluation was able to identify that the programme had positive effects on families in the two years after they joined the programme. Compared to the comparison group, the programme was found to have:

- reduced the proportion of children on the programme going into care by a third, from 2.5 per cent to 1.7 per cent;
- reduced the proportion of adults on the programme going to prison by a quarter, from 1.6 per cent to 1.2 per cent, and the number of young people going into prison by more than a third, from 0.8 per cent to 0.5 per cent;
- reduced the proportion of adults with juvenile convictions by 15 per cent, from 4.6 per cent to 3.9 per cent.

Considering all these findings together, they indicate that the programme has had a positive impact. Although in some of these cases the numbers of individuals and families affected may seem relatively small, the importance of these impacts on the lives of these families and on the costs of public services should not be underestimated.

The significance of these impacts relative to the costs of the programme was tested using cost–benefit analysis. The analysis showed that every £1 spent on the programme has delivered approximately £2.28 of benefits, indicating the programme has had a large positive net impact. The cost–benefit analysis also considered the benefits excluding any effects on jobseeker's allowance. Removing these effects gives an economic benefit of £1.94 for every £1 spent.

While the evaluation demonstrates a net positive impact of the Troubled Families Programme, there is nonetheless still more work to be done to determine why the programme was successful, for example what did local authorities do differently that led to the improved outcomes? This is the subject of current work. Nonetheless, the evaluation has been described as a landmark piece of work and setting a new benchmark in data-linking (Behavioural Insights Team, 2019).

What is MHCLG doing to improve the data and evidence on homelessness and individuals who sleep rough?

What about homelessness and rough sleeping – given this book has been initiated by the Centre for Homelessness Impact?

Preventing and tackling homelessness and rough sleeping is a top priority for MHCLG. In 2018, MHCLG published a rough sleeping strategy, a wide-ranging document that laid out the Government's plans to help people who are sleeping rough and to put in place the structures to end rough sleeping (MHCLG, 2018b). This included £100 million of investment over the next two years to tackle rough sleeping.

More broadly, the Homelessness Reduction Act 2017 requires local authorities to provide assistance to everyone who approaches them for help, including single-person households and couples who do not meet the pre-existing vulnerability criteria, not just those in priority need. Households at risk of homelessness are now able to approach authorities for assistance much earlier and every household will get a prevention plan from their council, with agreed steps to address their housing issues.

Better data and evidence will be crucial to tackling homelessness and rough sleeping and to reduce the costs they impose on the public purse. A 2015 report, *Hard Edges*, has estimated that the costs of homelessness to the public purse can range between £14,300 and £21,200 per person per year, with the higher cost being incurred if rough sleeping accompanies substance misuse and offending (Lankelly Chase Foundation, 2015). This is three to four times the average cost of providing public services for an average adult in this country (approximately £4,600).

MHCLG has a comprehensive programme of work to improve the data and evidence on rough sleeping and homelessness, including:

- Putting in place a new case level data collection (H-CLIC – Homelessness Case Level Information Collection) (MHCLG, 2018c). MHCLG is now receiving case-level data on everyone who approaches a local authority for help with their housing. In time this will produce better data on the characteristics of homeless people, routes into and out of homelessness, and the effectiveness of different interventions. In time, too, this data could be linked to other administrative data to help build a better understanding of the impact of homelessness interventions on outcomes such as health, education and crime.
- Collecting better data on the public service use of people who have slept rough or are at risk of sleeping rough. This is being achieved by rolling out a questionnaire to clients of homelessness services throughout 2019.
- Joint research with DWP to review the evidence on the causes of homelessness and rough sleeping and provide options for modelling to understand future trends and appraise policy. This included a rapid evidence assessment of the individual and structural drivers of homelessness and rough sleeping and a review of forecasting models of homelessness (MHCLG, 2019b).

- Monitoring and evaluating the Homelessness Reduction Act 2017. Key objectives of this include understanding how the Act has been implemented and is being delivered in local areas, determining whether any issues need to be addressed to make the Act work more effectively, and highlighting best practice to enable local areas to learn from each other. The commissioned process evaluation should be published around spring 2020 and will provide independent evidence from fieldwork with key stakeholders, including service users and local authorities, using a range of research techniques.

Much has been done, too, to improve the quality of evaluations by putting in place evaluations with comparison groups to understand the net impact of programmes. For example, MHCLG has published:

- An evaluation of the London homelessness social impact bond (SIB) (DCLG, 2017). The London homelessness SIB sought to encourage innovative approaches to reducing rough sleeping in London. The evaluation found that, when compared with a well-matched comparison group, the intervention significantly reduced rough sleeping over a two-year period.
- An evaluation of the Trailblazer Prevention Programme (MHCLG, 2018d) – a programme that sought to improve understanding of what works best in preventing homelessness by comparing outcomes in authorities participating in the programme with a comparison group. The evaluation found the rate of homelessness acceptances in the Trailblazer areas averaged 2.76 per 1,000 households compared to 3.16 in the comparison areas, a difference of 13 per cent. This was attributed to the adoption of new preventative approaches in Trailblazer areas.
- An evaluation of the Rough Sleepers Initiative (MHCLG, 2019d). This initiative was targeted at local authorities with high numbers of people sleeping rough and sought to support people sleeping rough off the streets. The evaluation found the Initiative had reduced the number of people sleeping rough by almost a third had the RSI not been in place.

The Department has also commissioned or has plans in place to evaluate other programmes including:

- An evaluation of housing first pilots. The 2017 autumn budget announced a £28 million housing first pilot (to provide housing immediately and without conditions to take up other support) to be delivered across Liverpool, Manchester and the West Midlands. The evaluation will seek to understand the impact of the housing first pilots in comparison to a matched comparison group of rough sleepers in other areas.
- An evaluation of Somewhere Safe to Stay hubs, announced in the 2018 rough sleeping strategy. The hubs offer shelter as well as rapid assessment of individuals' needs so they can be connected with stable accommodation and appropriate support. This builds on the No Second Night Out rapid assessment model but increases the scope by accepting referrals of individuals who are at imminent risk of rough sleeping as well as those on the streets and allows for repeat visits to the hub. At the time of writing, the Somewhere Safe to Stay hubs are already being delivered in 11 local areas as early adopters with more due to be funded. An impact and process evaluation of the hubs is planned to be completed in 2021.

MHCLG's work to improve the data and evidence available to support interventions to tackle homelessness and rough sleeping is part of its broader commitment to monitoring and evaluation across housing, as set out in a recent strategy document (MHCLG, 2019c). The commitment ranges from the collection of basic data to the application of innovative analytical methods.

The opportunities to use data and evidence more effectively are great

The work summarised in this chapter foreshadows a potential data and evidence revolution not just in MHCLG but across government and public services. It is increasingly possible –

because of advances in information technology – to access datasets that were previously difficult to access; to link different types of administrative data to undertake cutting-edge large-scale evaluations (such as that undertaken for the Troubled Families programme) that were not previously possible; to undertake predictive analytics to improve the targeting of social policy interventions; and to analyse datasets to obtain rich new insights that will improve policy design and the outcomes achieved for citizens more generally.

In time, with new case-level data, we should be able to build a much more comprehensive picture of who is using public services, how their circumstances are changing as a result, and what works best in delivering desired outcomes. Predictive analytics and related methods will also mean we can intervene earlier to prevent or mitigate problems before they pose higher costs on public services and have more serious impacts on peoples' lives.

That applies to policies aimed at tackling homelessness and rough sleeping no less than other public services. Better data, academic research, the evaluation work MHCLG has in hand and the fantastic opportunities offered by the new Centre for Homelessness Impact[7] offer real scope for transformation.

There will of course be challenges to overcome:

- raising awareness of what is possible;
- putting in place mechanisms for data sharing that address legal, ethical, data security or other concerns;
- building capability and capacity – including equipping the public service workforce with the necessary skills;
- embedding evidence-based approaches in professional cultures – in the spirit of Sir Michael Barber's work of creating a culture of continuous improvement to promote public value (Barber, 2017); and
- reducing barriers to the sharing of good practice.

But what is set out here is the future.

There will be fewer and fewer limits to what data and evidence can deliver for public policy and public services.

Notes

1   https://en.wikipedia.org/wiki/James_Lancaster.
2   https://en.wikipedia.org/wiki/James_Lind.
3   https://en.wikipedia.org/wiki/Archie_Cochrane.
4   https://whatworks.blog.gov.uk/about-the-what-works-network/.
5   See, for example, the evidence maps developed by the Centre for Homelessness Impact: https://www.homelessnessimpact.org/gap-maps.
6   https://educationendowmentfoundation.org.uk/news/eef-blog-generating-evidence-is-the-start-scaling-evidence-is-the-goal/.
7   https://www.homelessnessimpact.org/.

References

Aldridge, S. 2019. Public sector efficiency in the UK. Presentation to an Organisation for Economic Cooperation and Development workshop on the Spatial Dimensions of Productivity, Bolzano, Italy, 29 March.

Barber, M. 2017. *Delivering Better Outcomes for Citizens: Practical Steps for Unlocking Public Value.* https://www.gov.uk/government/publications/delivering-better-outcomes-for-citizens-practical-steps-for-unlocking-public-value.

Behavioural Insights Team. 2019. *A Landmark Evaluation of the Troubled Families Programme.* https://www.bi.team/blogs/a-landmark-evaluation-of-the-troubled-families-programme/.

Card, D. and Krueger, A. 1994. Minimum wages and employment: a case study of the fast-food industry in New Jersey and Pennsylvania. *American Economic Review*, September. http://davidcard.berkeley.edu/papers/njmin-aer.pdf.

DCLG. 2017. *The Impact Evaluation of the London Homelessness Social Impact Bond.* https://www.gov.uk/government/publications/london-homelessness-social-impact-bond-evaluation.

Lankelly Chase Foundation. 2015. *Hard Edges: Mapping Severe and Multiple Disadvantage in England.* London: Lankelly Chase Foundation.

Leigh, A. 2018. *Randomistas.* New Haven, CT: Yale University Press.

MHCLG. 2018a. *Areas of Research Interest.* https://www.gov.uk/government/publications/mhclg-areas-of-research-interest.

MHCLG. 2018b. *Rough Sleeping Strategy.* https://www.gov.uk/government/publications/the-rough-sleeping-strategy.

MHCLG. 2018c. *Statutory Homelessness.* https://www.gov.uk/ government/statistics/statutory-homelessness-in-england- april-to-june-2018.

MHCLG. 2018d. *Evaluation of the Homelessness Prevention Trailblazers.* https://assets.publishing.service.gov.uk/ government/uploads/system/uploads/attachment_data/ file/791585/Evaluation_of_Homelessness_Prevention_ Trailblazers.pdf.

MHCLG. 2019a. *National Evaluation of the Troubled Families Programme, 2015–2020.* https://assets.publishing.service.gov. uk/government/uploads/system/uploads/attachment_data/ file/786891/National_evaluation_of_the_Troubled_Families_ Programme_2015_to_2020_family_outcomes___national_ and_local_datasets_part_4.pdf.

MHCLG. 2019b. *Causes of Homelessness and Rough Sleeping Feasibility Study.* https://www.gov.uk/government/ publications/causes-of-homelessness-and-rough-sleeping- feasibility-study.

MHCLG. 2019c. *Housing Monitoring and Evaluation Strategy.* https://www.gov.uk/government/publications/housing- monitoring-and-evaluation-strategy.

MHCLG. 2019d. *Impact Evaluation of the Rough Sleeping Initiative, 2018.* https://www.gov.uk/government/publications/rough- sleeping-initiative-2018-impact-evaluation

11

Using evidence in social policy: from NICE to What Works

Howard White and David Gough

Social research has long informed public policy. At the turn of the 20th century, the descriptions of poverty by Charles Booth in his *Inquiry into Life and Labour in London*, and Benjamin Seebohm Rowntree in his *Poverty: A Study in Town Life*, informed the adoption of the Old Age Pensions Act of 1908 (Taylor, 1988). That tradition still persists. Around the world, data are used to identify social problems with a view to informing potential solutions.

The Centre for Homelessness Impact (CHI) highlighted in 2019 that the deaths of people experiencing homelessness in England and Wales increased by 24 per cent from 2013 to 2017.[1] Unfortunately, they also stressed that simply identifying a problem does not lead to a solution. Policy-makers are prone to adopt *Yes, Prime Minister*'s 'politicians' syllogism': 'Something must be done, this is something, therefore we must do this.'[2] Many of these 'somethings' do not work, however. Indeed, as more evidence becomes available there is a growing recognition of the '80 per cent rule' – that 80 per cent of interventions do not work, including many that seem like 'no-brainers'.

In the US, the Institute of Education Sciences evaluated 90 interventions using randomised controlled trials (RCTs), finding that 90 per cent had weak or no positive effects (Baron, 2018). In a similar exercise by the Department of Labor, 75 per cent of RCTs demonstrated weak or no positive effects (Baron, ibid). In the private sector, over 13,000 RCTs of new products and strategies conducted by Google and Microsoft report no significant effects in over 80 per cent of cases (Baron, ibid). A study by the European Commission found that 85 per cent of projects financed under the Clean Development Mechanism were unlikely to provide additional reductions in carbon emissions (Cames et al, 2016). The Oxford-based effective altruism NGO, 80,000 Hours, has concluded that the 80 per cent rule might in fact be optimistic – it is more likely that a higher percentage of things do not work (Todd et al, 2017).

The rarity of success in RCTs means that it is vital to subject policies and programmes that aim to improve the lives of those experiencing, or at risk of experiencing, homelessness to rigorous evaluation. Different research and evaluation designs can help answer different questions. If the purpose is to evaluate effectiveness – did the programme achieve its intended outcomes compared to outcomes in the absence of the intervention? – then RCTs or other impact evaluation designs are most appropriate.

RCTs of social programmes have been conducted since the 1930s but have become increasingly mainstream over the last 20 years. For example, around ten RCTs of education programmes were being published each year in the early 2000s, growing to over 100 a year by 2012 (Connolly et al, 2018). For social work, the numbers are around ten RCTs a year in the early 2000s to over 50 by 2012 (Thyer, 2015). In homelessness, there were just under two studies a year published prior to 2000, an average of four a year from 2000 to 2009 and nearly ten a year since 2010 (Centre for Homelessness Impact, 2018). This growth of rigorous impact evaluations is part of what is referred to as the 'evidence revolution' (White, forthcoming).

The growing number of studies around the world provides opportunities for us all to learn what has worked in other fields and other nations to enable evidence-informed decision making. Summarising study findings in literature reviews is a mainstay of research, but these reviews have many sources of bias; selectivity in which papers are included, which results are reported from those papers and the conclusions drawn from that evidence. To address these biases, there is increasing recognition that systematic reviews – which are pieces of research with formal and transparent methods – are an appropriate response.

Even so, once knowledge is synthesised it still needs to be used, which requires an additional effort of curating, translating and brokering. In the UK, the What Works Centres have emerged to address this need[3] and to enable policy-makers, commissioners and practitioners to make decisions based upon strong evidence of what works and to provide cost-efficient, useful services. To do this well, they need a strategy to support the uptake of the research evidence they broker.

In this chapter we consider how evidence is produced and used as well as how a new What Works Centre like CHI can enhance the use of evidence in the homelessness evidence 'ecosystem'.

The evidence ecosystem

The evidence ecosystem includes both the production and use of research evidence. In order for it to be used, there needs to be some form of engagement between the research produced and its intended users. Figure 11.1 shows the different components of research production, use and engagement as an ecosystem, where the different parts have to function together and exist within a broader context. This relationship demonstrates why What Works Centres have taken a proactive role not only in the development of evidence tools, but in engaging their intended users.

The evidence ecosystem has many complex known and unknown factors at play that may be specific to the use of research or aspects of the wider environment. The most commonly reported barrier to the use of evidence is poor access to good quality, timely and relevant research (Oliver et al, 2014).

But research evidence is only one of the many factors that influence decision-making. Another is that the type of research findings considered relevant by a policy-maker are determined by their individual values and assumptions.

Figure 11.1: Evidence use ecosystem analytical framework

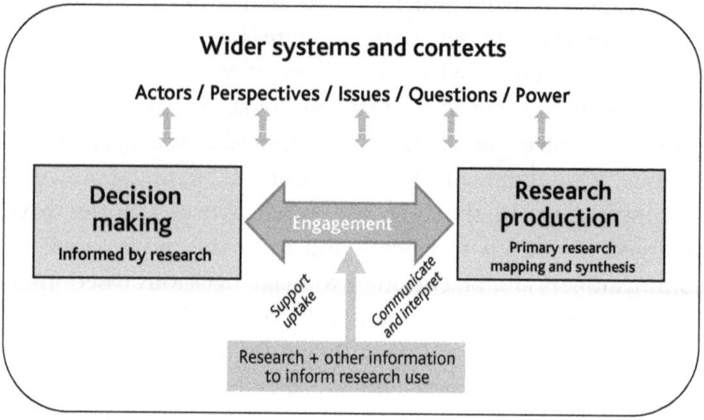

Source: Adapted from Gough et al (2018)

People with different views about housing policy, for example, would be interested in different types of explanation and data about housing. A final factor is that research findings need to be interpreted in order to impact on a decision and people presented with exactly the same research findings may come to different decisions. The interaction between research production and research use is crucial. Only by looking at the ecosystem as a whole can we understand how to make it function more effectively, a challenge that must be addressed in the field of homelessness.

Evidence-based medicine: the origins of systematic reviews and evidence-based policy

The spread of evidence-based policy has its origins in evidence-based medicine. While there has been growth in the use of RCTs in education and social welfare, there are many more studies in the medical field since clinical trials in the UK became well-established from the mid-1940s (Bhatt, 2010). The use of RCTs was championed by Archie Cochrane, who in the 1970s commented that it was a failure of the medical profession not to be producing summaries of all available RCTs on a particular topic (Cochrane, 1972).

Shortly after, America Statistician Gene Glass became the first to use the term meta-analysis; in his presidential address to the American Educational Research Association in 1976. The next year, Glass published a meta-analysis of 375 studies of psychotherapy which – by showing the clear effectiveness of psychotherapy – was one of the founding papers of evidence-based psychiatry (Smith and Glass, 1977). Meta-analysis is at the heart of systematic reviews of studies of the effectiveness of interventions. The development of these methods provided the basis for carrying out Cochrane's vision.

So when Iain Chalmers and others began to organise the production, understanding and use of systematic reviews in health, they named the organisation in honour of Archie Cochrane. Thus the Cochrane Collaboration was born. Since its formation in 1993 it has grown to an international network of researchers from 130 countries around the world, with over 8,000 reviews published in the Cochrane Library.

Cochrane reviews are now well integrated into the decision-making of the health sector. For instance, the World Health Organization (WHO) requires that its various guidelines are based on high-quality systematic reviews, with constant engagement with Cochrane to ensure this. Similarly, the National Institute of Health and Care Excellence (NICE) in the UK draws on Cochrane reviews in its guidelines and to inform its rulings on the use of National Health Service resources, while the National Institute of Health Research (NIHR) funds various Cochrane groups and has different mechanisms for funding Cochrane reviews. Both WHO and NICE guidelines follow a process that takes into account contextual factors in interpreting the evidence to form recommendations for specific policies and interventions.

Although Cochrane's focus was initially on medical reviews, it has broadened over time. In spite of this, there are few reviews of relevance for homelessness. One exception is a study of Interventions to modify sexual risk behaviours for preventing HIV in young people who are homeless, which found three RCTs, but concluded the interventions they evaluated were too heterogeneous to allow synthesis (Naranbhai et al, 2011). A 2006 review examined the evidence for 'Independent living programmes for improving outcomes for young people leaving the care system', finding that there are no rigorous studies for us to know whether these programmes are effective or not (Donkoh et al, 2006). The need to fill these gaps is clear.

In 1992, at the Social Science Research Unit, Institute of Education, University of London, Ann Oakley set up a project to develop a database of well-designed evaluations of interventions in the fields of education and social welfare.[4] In 1995 the Department of Health commissioned a series of reviews in the area of health promotion in the field of non-clinical health issues to mirror the work of Cochrane. Thus, the EPPI Centre was born.

The growth and success of evidence-based medicine eventually prompted social scientists to wonder why a similar approach could not be used to address social problems. Indeed, in 1996 the president of the UK Royal Statistical Society asked:

> What's so special about medicine? We are...
> confronted daily with controversy and debate across a
> whole spectrum of public policy issues. But typically,
> we have no access to any form of systematic "evidence
> base"... Obvious topical examples include education
> – what does work in the classroom?– and penal policy
> – what is effective in preventing re-offending? (Smith,
> 1996, cited in Petrosino, 2013: 10)

As discussed later in this chapter, What Works Centres in both these areas have been set up within the last decade.

The need for a more strategic approach to the accumulation and use of educational research was presented that same year by David Hargreaves, then adviser to government ministers on education, in his famous TDA lecture.[5] This fitted well with the EPPI Centre's approach to user-led systematic reviews concerned with all questions and types of research evidence and led to an expansion of its remit.

It was further broadened in 2000 by gaining support from the Department for Education and Skills to support groups wishing to undertake reviews in the field of education. Some work was also funded by the Training and Development Agency for Schools. The centre now also undertakes reviews in a wide range of areas including public health, social care, crime reduction, education and international development. The EPPI Centre engages with new topics to help stimulate the development of review methodology which has included systematic maps in 1996, multi-component mixed-methods reviews in 2004, qualitative comparative analysis in reviews in 2014, the use of automation in reviews through its EPPI Reviewer software and the publication of a methods textbook (Gough et al, 2017). The centre has also been increasing its focus on studying the use of research in policy, practice and personal decision-making.

In 1999, a meeting was organised at the School of Public Policy at University College London to assess interest in establishing a body for systematic reviews of social interventions. A follow-up meeting in Pennsylvania the following year led to the formal establishment of the Campbell Collaboration, named after the psychologist Donald Campbell, who promoted 'social experimentation'. Like Cochrane, Campbell is an international research network supported by a small secretariat, through which researchers from around the world manage the editorial process for reviews submitted for publication in the Campbell Library.

The first review published by Campbell was an example of interventions that do not work. Anthony Peterosino and colleagues assessed studies of Scared Straight, an intervention for juveniles at risk of criminal behaviour, which exposes them to the reality of prison life. Despite its popularity in the UK and US over the past 30 years, not only does the intervention not work, it makes youth more likely to commit criminal acts (Petrosino, 2013). Another review on teenage pregnancy found that a range of interventions, such as sex education and promoting abstinence, have no effect on either sexual activity or pregnancy (Scher et al, 2006).

At the time of writing, Campbell has published over 150 reviews in a range of social policy fields, including a recent review assessing the range of interventions to improving housing stability (Munthe-Kaas et al, 2018). A challenge for Campbell has been policy uptake of the findings of its reviews, which has become a stronger focus in recent years. This has also been a concern of other researchers in evidence synthesis.

To address this, Campbell has been expanding its range of evidence products and the research questions addressed by its reviews. It is not just a question of 'what works' but also 'how to make it work', the answer to which is often found in process evaluations containing both quantitative and qualitative data. Campbell now publishes an increasing number of 'mixed-method reviews', which synthesise evidence across the causal chain, and will in future publish reviews solely of qualitative evidence where appropriate.

Campbell also supports the production of evidence maps, which show what evidence is available in a given field. Working with CHI, Campbell produced two maps: one of effectiveness studies (what works) and one of process evaluations (how it works) which between them contain around 500 individual pieces of research (White, 2018). Making these studies more discoverable and accessible is one way in which CHI is promoting the use of evidence, since many evaluations remain unused despite their value.

It is notable that of the 238 effectiveness studies contained in the maps only 12 were conducted in the UK. The large number of effectiveness studies – mainly RCTs – that have been carried out in the US show that it is not impossible to do such analysis of interventions for those experiencing homelessness, but that UK researchers have mostly not been oriented toward this type of research. It is also clear that the field is 'under-reviewed'; there is a low ratio of systematic reviews to primary studies and what reviews there are exist mostly in the health field.

Building evidence architecture in the UK: the What Works Network

The last decade or so has seen increased recognition that bridging the gap between research and policy takes an explicit effort. Knowledge brokering seeks to address the 'market failure' in evidence use. The What Works movement began with the What Works Clearing Houses in the US, notably the Institute of Education Science's What Works Clearing House for Education, and the last six years have seen the establishment of a similar movement in the UK.

The centres are called 'What Works' as they are particularly – though not exclusively – concerned with supporting the use of evidence on the effectiveness of policy and practice interventions.[6] Currently there are 13 such centres based in England working in different areas of social policy ranging from education to crime reduction, plus two affiliate centres working in Scotland and Wales. CHI is a full member of the network and its remit, unlike the others, is UK-wide.

The What Works Centres operate in many parts of the evidence ecosystem. They could be involved in all or some of the following:

• the implementation of policy and practice informed by research;
• policy and practice guidance informed by research;
• access to summary quality assured research findings on particular topics;
• the synthesis of research findings;
• primary research;
• awareness of a social issue in the wider societal context.

Most of the centres put the majority of their energy into the synthesis and communication of research findings, although over time they have been broadening their work into guidance and use of research. For example, the Education Endowment Foundation (EEF) identified 34 school-level interventions that may improve learning outcomes, commissioning systematic reviews of each of them in order to inform its teacher and learning toolkit.[7]

As they are independent from government, each of the What Works Centres has to find its own pathway into policy influence. Until recently, the centres have been taking a predominantly research production (push) approach to the use of research, rather than a problem-solving, demand-led (pull) approach. Apart from EEF they have not been engaged in much primary research as they lack the resources to make a significant contribution to the research base. One exception to the production model is NICE, which has a very particular role in providing practice guidance to health and welfare practice-driven questions.

While the centres are clearly focusing on particular parts of their evidence ecosystems, the extent to which they are working to embed their work within existing systems and processes or to create new systems to disrupt existing systems is less clear.

Monitoring of centre activities and their intermediate and long-term outcomes have similarly been limited so far. This is perhaps not surprising as centres have limited funding for such self-evaluation and the time needed to be able to demonstrate their effectiveness may be longer than their current funding would allow.

Promoting engagement between research and decision-making

How can the use of research in decision-making be increased? A recent systematic review presents a three-part framework for examining the evidence of the effectiveness of different approaches to increase the use of evidence-based decision-making (see Figure 11.2).[8]

- First, it examines the level at which the approach strategy to increase research is applied: interventions can be focused on the individual, organisational or national basis.
- Second, it looks at the mechanisms by which the approach is thought to have an effect. Examples of common mechanisms are providing decision-makers with easy access to research findings, developing good relationships between producers and users of research and training decision-makers in the research skills to make use of evidence.
- Third, it assesses the behavioural aspects of approaches and the extent to which these increase capacity, opportunity or motivation of decision-makers.

If there is a clearly defined process for using research evidence then there is more likely to be the capacity, opportunity and motivation to use it. These processes require knowledge translation and brokering. This raises issues of who is to do such

Figure 11.2: Enabling evidence use: SOUS Conceptual Framework

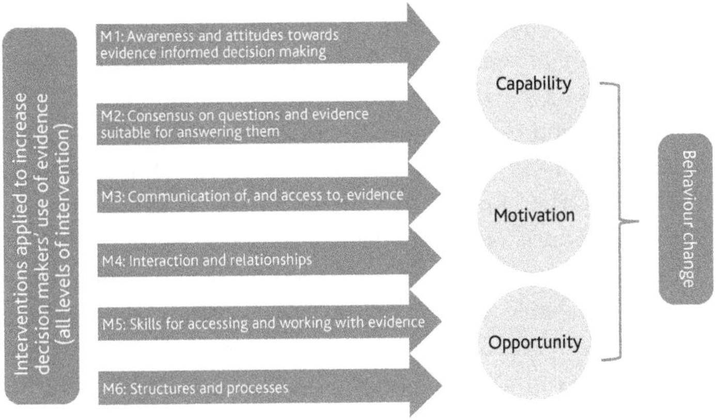

Source: Langer et al (2016)

brokering, the process by which they will conduct this brokering and whether users will have confidence in the findings with which they are presented.

Conclusions: Building the evidence architecture for homelessness

So what does this all mean for those planning or developing an intermediary evidence organisation such as the CHI? What are the issues to be considered by those promoting the use of evidence?

A first issue is to recognise the importance of values, assumptions and priorities. Although research findings are objective, research questions, methods and the interpretation and use of findings are driven by values. So it is best to be explicit about these values, state what your priorities are and any assumptions being made. Such a statement is important to locate yourself in the evidence ecosystem.

It is important to recognise that any new initiative will be entering an existing ecosystem. However poorly the ecosystem is functioning, it exists, and so it is sensible to assess that system and what is and is not working well and why. The analysis of the pre-existing system will need to continue to inform the development of a strategy to change the system and enable the increased use of research evidence. This may involve acting in all, some or just one part of the ecosystem or also in the wider system in which the evidence ecosystem exists. Many What Works Centres, for example, work predominantly in synthesising and communicating evidence, while others take a more demand-led approach in developing stakeholder-driven guidance. Other knowledge brokers may focus on specific evidence products such as guidelines, or online evidence portals.

Following on from this, it can be best to work through others as much as possible to magnify impact or to add something very new. It may want to align with or disrupt pre-existing work. The strategy can also include a more detailed specification of the knowledge brokers' boundaries in terms of topic or sector.

It is also important to be clear about the activities that will be undertaken to achieve the overall strategy and the theory of change of how those activities will achieve the desired results. It is clear that simply providing evidence tools will in itself not be sufficient. Engagement matters. Hence part of the theory of change for a knowledge broker should include clarity about who the broker will work with, including relevant stakeholders, who will be the users of research and who will be the ultimate beneficiaries of the work. They also need to consider to what extent these groups are defined or worked with as individuals or groups or organisations.

Just as it is important to be clear about activities, it is also important to be clear about the type of research evidence answering what types of research questions and the nature of the evidence standards used for making evidence claims in addressing these questions (to inform the use of evidence in policy, practice and personal decision-making). Explicit attention needs to be paid to developing and applying evidence standards and ensuring that these standards are transparent.

A final point is the importance of monitoring and evaluating the extent to which you are achieving your aims. If evidence intermediaries are advocating the usefulness of using research findings, they will be expected to apply the same logic to themselves and use research evidence to appraise their own work.

The development of intermediary processes and organisations between decision-making and research findings is a relatively new area and likely to develop in the coming years. Previously there was an assumption that the implicit evidence ecosystem would work just with better access of research and better relationships between researchers and users of research. This now seems unduly optimistic. We need more institutions and infrastructure beyond those provided separately for researchers and policy-makers and practitioners. In the information age, intermediary evidence organisations are a necessary infrastructure. What Works Centres such as CHI are very welcome additions to the evidence ecosystem, even if the road to impact will not be easy or straightforward.

Notes

1 www.homelessnessimpact.org/post/preventing-premature-deaths-among-people-experiencing-homelessness.
2 'Power to the People' *Yes Minister* Series 2 Episode 5, first broadcast 7 January 1988.
3 www.gov.uk/guidance/what-works-network.
4 For a full account of the early evolution of systematic research synthesis and the EPPI-Centre, see Oakley et al (2005).
5 http://eppi.ioe.ac.uk/cms/Portals/0/PDF%20reviews%20and%20summaries/TTA%20Hargreaves%20lecture.pdf.
6 This section is based on Gough et al (2018).
7 https://educationendowmentfoundation.org.uk/evidence-summaries/teaching-learning-toolkit/.
8 This section is based on Langer et al (2016); and see Figure 11.2.

References

Baron, J. 2018. How to solve U.S. social problems when most rigorous program evaluations find disappointing effects. https://www.straighttalkonevidence.org/2018/03/21/how-to-solve-u-s-social-problems-when-most-rigorous-program-evaluations-find-disappointing-effects-part-one-in-a-series/.
Bhatt A. 2010. Evolution of clinical research: a history before and beyond James Lind. *Perspectives in Clinical Research*, 1(1): 6–10.
Cames, M., Harthan, O., Füssler, J., Lee, C.M., Erickson, P. and Spalding-Fecher, R. 2016. *How Additional is the Clean Development Mechanism? Analysis of the Application of Current Tools and Proposed Alternatives.* Berlin: Öko-Institute.V.

Centre for Homelessness Impact. 2018. *Evidence and Gap Maps: A Launchpad for Strategic Evidence Creation and Use.* https://www. homelessnessimpact.org/post/research-agenda-evidence-base.

Cochrane, A.L. 1972. *Effectiveness and Efficiency: Random Reflections on Health Services.* London: Nuffield Trust.

Connolly, P., Keenan, C. and Urbanska, K. 2018. The trials of evidence-based practice in education: a systematic review of randomised controlled trials in education research 1980–2016. *Educational Research,* 60(3): 276–91. DOI: 10.1080/00131881.2018.1493353.

Donkoh, C., Underhill, K., Montgomery, P. 2006. Independent living programmes for improving outcomes for young people leaving the care system. *Cochrane Database of Systematic Reviews 2006,* Issue 3. Art. No.: CD005558. DOI: 10.1002/14651858. CD005558.pub2.

Gough, D., Oliver, S. and Thomas, J. 2017. *An Introduction to Systematic Reviews.* 2nd edn. London: Sage.

Gough, D., Maidment, C. and Sharples, J. 2018. *UK What Works Centres: Aims, Methods and Contexts.* London: EPPI-Centre, University College London.

Langer, L., Tripney, J. and Gough, D. 2016. *The Science of Using Science: Researching the Use of Research Evidence in Decision-Making.* London: EPPI-Centre, Social Science Research Unit, UCL Institute of Education, University College London.

Littell, J.H. and White, H. 2018. The Campbell Collaboration: providing better evidence for a better world. *Research on Social Work Practice,* 28(1): 6–12. https://doi. org/10.1177/1049731517703748.

Munthe-Kaas, H.M., Berg, R.C. and Blaasvær, N. 2018. Effectiveness of interventions to reduce homelessness: a systematic review and meta-analysis. *Campbell Systematic Reviews,* 14: 1–281. doi:10.4073/csr.2018.3

Naranbhai, V., Abdool Karim, Q., Meyer-Weitz, A. 2011. Interventions to modify sexual risk behaviours for preventing HIV in homeless youth. *Cochrane Database of Systematic Reviews 2011,* Issue 1. Art. No.: CD007501. DOI: 10.1002/14651858. CD007501.pub2.

Oakley, A., Gough, D., Oliver, S. and Thomas, J. 2005. The politics of evidence and methodology: lessons from the EPPI-Centre. *Evidence and Policy*, 1(1): 5–31.

Oliver, K., Innvar, S., Lorenc, T., Woodman, J. and Thomas, J. 2014. A systematic review of barriers to and facilitators of the use of evidence by policymakers. *BMC Health Serv Res*, 14(2). doi:10.1186/1472-6963-14-2

Petrosino, A. 2013. Reflections on the Genesis of the Campbell Collaboration. *The Experimental Criminologist*, 8: 9–12.

Scher, L., Maynard, R. and Stagner, M. 2006. Interventions intended to reduce pregnancyrelated outcomes among adolescents. *Campbell Systematic Reviews, 2006*:12 DOI: 10.4073/csr.2006.12.

Smith, A. 1996. Mad cows and ecstasy. *Journal of the Royal Statistical Society*, 159(3): 367–83.

Smith, M.L. and Glass, G.V. 1977. Meta-analysis of psychotherapy outcome studies. *American Psychologist*, 32(9), 752–60. http://dx.doi.org/10.1037/0003-066X.32.9.752.

Taylor, D. 1988. The social reforms of the Liberal Government 1906–14. In: D. Taylor (ed.), *Mastering Economic and Social History*. London: Macmillan Education Ltd.

Thyer, B. 2015. A bibliography of randomized controlled experiments in social work (1949–2013). *Research on Social Work Practice*, 25(7): 753–93.

Todd, B. and the 80,000 hours team. 2017. Is it fair to say that most social programmes don't work? https://80000hours.org/articles/effective-social-program/ (accessed: 11 April 2019).

White, H. 2018. *Evidence and Gap Maps on Homelessness. A Launch Pad for Strategic Evidence Production and Use. Part 1: Global Evidence and Gap Map of Effectiveness Studies*. London: Centre for Homelessness Impact.

White, H. forthcoming. *The Twenty-First Century Experimenting Society: The Four Waves of the Evidence Revolution*. London: Palgrave Communications, Springer Nature.

12

Charities and donors in evidence systems

Caroline Fiennes

Research is a behaviour change exercise, albeit often in disguise. Its goal is to improve people's lives – in this case, the lives of people who might become homeless, who are currently homeless, who have been homeless and those around them – by changing the behaviour of agencies, public policy-makers and funders.[1] It is dangerous to think that simply producing more evidence will change behaviour by itself. This is rarely or never the case, so we need to understand how evidence influences behaviours, and to plan around each stage.

Evidence systems

An 'evidence system' comprises the four stages by which research is produced and influences behaviour:[2] production, synthesis, dissemination, and use of the evidence (see Figure 12.1). Creating change requires work at all four stages. It is clearly not sufficient to produce research and then hope that practitioners will magically find it, understand it, know how to apply it and have the resources and rights to do so. Normally, different organisations and skills are needed at each stage: the best people to produce research are often not the best people to sit with

Figure 12.1: Elements of an evidence ecosystem

Source: Adapted from Shepherd (2007)

practitioners and help them understand what they should do within their particular context and constraints.

Organisations such as What Works Centres need to influence organisations across these 'evidence systems', including research producers, synthesisers, disseminators and implementing organisations, such as charities, frontline agencies, funders and policy-makers. In some cases, relevant organisations may not yet exist and need to be established.

At each stage, it is essential to understand what gets done, who does it, why they do it, how it is funded, what does not get done and what aids and hinders useful activity. My own work at Giving Evidence has for years been about encouraging and enabling charitable *giving* based on sound *evidence*. Giving Evidence's focus is on donors and charities in many sectors, but many of the observations that follow and which come from them also apply elsewhere.

Yes-Land v No-Land

There are two types of issue in the world:

• Those for which there is reliable evidence about what interventions are effective. Let's call this 'Yes-Land'.
• Those for which there is not yet reliable evidence about what interventions are effective. Let's call this 'No-Land'.

Ascertaining whether and where we are in Yes-Land versus in No-Land is the primary purpose of an evidence and gap map (EGM). The EGM by the Centre for Homelessness Impact (CHI) shows that, in homelessness, No-Land is very extensive and that Yes-Land is still very small.

In Yes-Land

Yes-Land is defined as where there is reliable evidence about the effect of interventions on the outcome of interest. That evidence can have various forms: it may show positive effects, negative effects, no effects, or may be mixed or inconclusive. We are not in Yes-Land if there is only a *single* study of an issue or intervention – there need to be several. When in Yes-Land, the first step is to synthesise the existing studies to find out what they say. The collective evidence may suggest that some intervention is effective, or that one is harmful and therefore should be stopped; it may suggest that a different course of action would be more effective or cost-effective.

In Yes-Land, the main tasks are synthesis, dissemination and use.

In No-Land

Here there is not yet reliable evidence about interventions' effectiveness. There are three main strategies in No-Land:

1. Produce or fund the production of evidence in order to get to Yes-Land.

2. Go to somewhere in Yes-Land where there is evidence. (This is an acceptable strategy for some donors, not all of whom are interested in the production of research.)
3. Guess and hope. Many donors, policy-makers and others assume that they 'just know' what to do. (Spoiler alert: this is a terrible strategy!)

Sandbanks

In fact, there are also areas that are neither Yes-Land nor No-Land: places where there is evidence but not about the precise place or context in which it is required. Let us call these 'sandbanks'. On a sandbank, the task is to determine whether you are really in No-Land or Yes-Land. That requires identifying the mechanism that made the intervention work in its original context and gauge whether it will still work in this new context. Complex systems have many sandbanks.

Sometimes you can figure out that the mechanism is unlikely to work in a new place without a new impact evaluation but rather just from simpler information, as long as you understand the original theory of change. A good example is from the No Lean Season programme run by Evidence Action. During the annual 'lean season' in the countryside in northern Bangladesh, work is available in cities. No Lean Season gives people money for a bus ticket to migrate to the cities for that period to work and send money home. It *seemed* to be effective in tackling seasonal poverty and hunger. The researchers then got interested in whether No Lean Season would also work in Malawi: it had not been studied there, so that was No-Land. Simply by using maps and some interviews, they ascertained fairly easily that in Malawi there were no cities whose labour markets could absorb rural migrants during lean periods. The programme is therefore unlikely to work there.

Most donors want it simple

Nobel laureate Professor Richard Thaler has formulated two 'mantras' for promoting evidence-based policy and practice:

- 'You can't make evidence-based policy decisions without evidence.'
- 'If you want to encourage some activity, make it easy' (Thaler, 2012).

In the charitable world, most donations are given by normal individuals, not by billionaires or foundations (see Figure 12.2). When they give their £20, they are not looking to do a PhD in the complex social issue of interest. Nonetheless, some donors are interested in giving well.

Nobody has yet provided donors with evidence-based recommendations about which UK charities are effective, but in international development, independent analysts GiveWell have identified what it thinks are high-performing charities. Its recommendations are easy for donors to find and use and it has influenced a material and growing sum (GiveWell, 2018).

This implies that if somebody credible and independent identified and promoted high-performing UK charities, donors might support them.

Figure 12.2: GiveWell's annual money moved to recommended charities

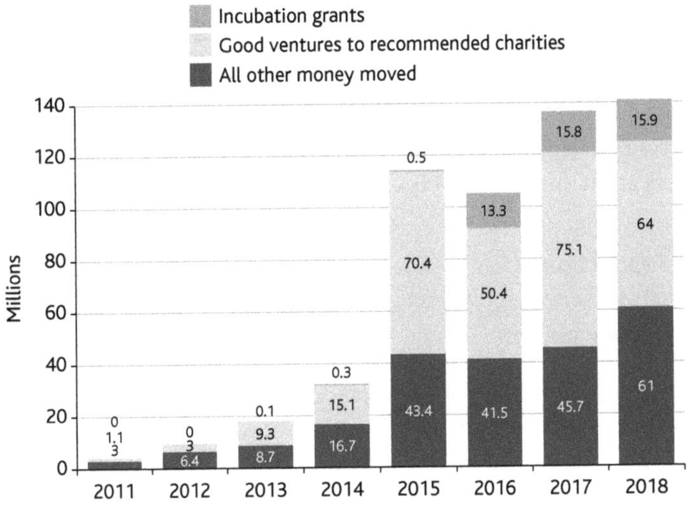

Source: GiveWell Metrics Report, 2018

Psychologist Professor Daniel Kahneman describes in his best-selling book *Thinking Fast and Slow* how it is useful to think of the human brain as having two modes of thinking, which he calls System 1 and System 2 (Kahneman, 2012). System 1 thinking is quick, reflexive, easy. System 2 is what we use for more complicated tasks. Kahneman cites considerable high quality empirical research that shows that people do not like System 2 thinking – our pulse quickens, pupils contract and we try to avoid it.

For most people, giving is voluntary and they want it to be easy; they like to give while only needing System 1. This is true not just of 'small-scale' donors. I have quite often worked with people who have made considerable fortunes in analytical jobs such as finance who – perhaps surprisingly – do not want to wade through masses of data when choosing causes or organisations to give to.

In the language of the evidence system, most donors will just 'use' easily packaged evidence: few will engage with the other stages. Of course, that means that funding the production, synthesis and dissemination of evidence can be great leverage for those donors who are willing to do it.

Roles of charities and donors at each stage of the evidence system

Although charities and charitable funders improve and enlarge activity at each stage of the evidence system, which improves lives at the frontline, their work is not always obvious or visible.

1. Production

Producing research

Funding the production of research is a common role for donors. For example, giving unconditional cash transfers to people experiencing poverty in the Global South has been shown to be effective in alleviating poverty (ODI, 2016). The NGO Give Directly, which specialises in these 'cash transfers', is keen to see whether they are similarly useful in refugee situations. Its pilot impact evaluation on this was funded by the IKEA Foundation and many individual donors via Comic Relief, among others (Give Directly, 2018).

To be clear, useful research is not solely about the effectiveness of interventions. It is often, valuably, to understand the nature and extent of a problem and the views of the people affected. A huge example is the Annual Status of Education Report (ASER)[3] in India, run by the NGO Pratham. ASER is an India-wide household survey that shows the learning levels of a representative sample of children aged 3–16, irrespective of whether they are enrolled in school or not. It tests over half a million children and is used by education providers and government to identify problems and to plan what services to provide and where. ASER is funded entirely by donors.[4]

Sadly, the research produced or funded by charities and donors is not always high quality, not least because few donors think of themselves as 'research funders'. So, although there are checklists for how research should be designed, reported and conducted – and using them vastly improves both the quality of research and its usefulness – non-specialists rarely know about them and so may not know to insist that they be used. (Some checklists are discussed later in this chapter.)

Prioritising research topics

Where No-Land is extensive – as CHI's EGM has found it to be in UK homelessness – research topics need to be prioritised. CHI has done work on this already. In medicine, there is often a striking mismatch between the questions studied by researchers and those that patients and frontline clinicians would like answered (Crowe et al, 2015). This is for various reasons, including that research incentives for academics largely focus on getting papers in high-impact-factor journals, which do not always relate to practice. Researchers' choices may be driven by norms or trends in their disciplines or by what will get them a conference slot. That pattern may hold in homelessness too.

In medicine, to solve this and get research produced on topics that matter to practice, there has arisen a process for structured consultations with patients, their carers and clinicians. It was developed by the James Lind Alliance, which has run 'priority setting partnerships' on almost 60 conditions internationally, such as Parkinson's, depression, autism and dementia. They are often funded at least partly by patient charities such as Parkinson's UK and Asthma UK.

Reporting guidelines

If people are to use the research, they need to be able to see precisely what intervention was tested and how the research was done. This may sound self-evident, but many research reports do not have this detail, which renders them virtually useless.

Medicine is perhaps the discipline most sophisticated discipline in terms of production and use of evidence. It has various guidelines for reporting these details about research. We will focus here on two guidelines:

First *what intervention did you run?* Charities' reports of their research often give only scant detail about what the intervention actually was. Without that, the intervention cannot be replicated and the research cannot be used. I once saw a UK mental health charity describe its intervention only as 'a 12-week programme', giving no details of what happened during those 12 weeks. To make research reports more useful, medicine has developed a 12-point checklist for describing interventions. The template for intervention description and replication (TIDieR) could easily and usefully be adapted for charities, including those in homelessness. Funders should become more vigilant about requiring that research by charities in all the fields that they fund reports the kinds of details listed in TIDieR.

Second, *what research did you do?* Again, medicine has developed checklists for reporting research of various types, over 200 in total.[5] The checklist for medical RCTs is CONSORT[6] (Consolidated Standards of Reporting Trials); for observational studies, it's STROBE (STrengthening the Reporting of OBservational studies in Epidemiology);[7] for systematic reviews and meta-analyses, it's PRISMA (Preferred Reporting Items for Systematic Reviews and Meta-Analyses).[8] A version of CONSORT has been developed to cover RCTs in social and psychological interventions[9] including crime reduction, education, public health and social work, which is highly relevant to many charities.

Growing evidence suggests that reporting guidelines make research better, less biased and more useful (Moher et al, 2010).

Research produced by charities, including monitoring and evaluation

Some research produced by operational charities (and part-funded philanthropically) is academic standard and designed to be useful to the whole field. This could be:

- Maps of the current situation. An example is *Homelessness Monitor:* a longitudinal study that looks at the levels and patterns of homelessness in England, Wales and Scotland. It is funded by Crisis and the Joseph Rowntree Foundation (Crisis, 2019). ASER is in this category.
- Studies of effectiveness of intervention(s). An example is a study done by the universities of Bristol and Durham and funded by the NSPCC, which claims to be 'the largest randomised controlled trial of a service for children affected by sexual abuse' (NSPCC, 2018). It evaluated the effectiveness of an intervention called Letting the Future In.

Other research by charities includes 'monitoring and evaluation' of their own work, which can often be problematic.

First, let us be clear about the difference between monitoring and evaluation. The two terms are often used interchangeably but they are two completely different things:

1. *Monitoring* measures the inputs (cost, people involved, materials and equipment used and so on), outputs (for example the number of workshops run, number of leaflets distributed, number of children vaccinated), and/or outcomes (incidence of measles, number of people who vote, pollution levels among others). It can include gathering feedback from the individuals or communities that an NGO seeks to serve.

2. *Evaluation:*
   - *Impact evaluation* is 'a serious attempt to establish causation'. In other words, evaluation aims to show whether/when the inputs cause the outcomes. Does increasing the amount of input increase the amount of outcome? Are the outcomes observed caused by the inputs, or by something else?
   - *Other types of evaluation*, such as process evaluation, which asks how the process actually ran, what intervention was actually received, how close that was to the intention, and why any variations arose.

Monitoring is rarely designed to be useful to other implementing organisations. It is often used for reporting and/or accountability. The exception is process-related data, which are often useful to other implementing organisations to give an idea of the resources and time that an intervention needs.

Charity-generated impact evaluations could in principle be useful to other organisations, though rarely are. This is because of the following five serious problems with them:

1. *Skills.* Doing social science research is complicated and few operational charities have those specialist skills. Their staff are specialists in something else. Operational charities are not research houses and (in general) should not be expected to produce good social science research.
2. *Funding.* Doing reliable social science research can be expensive and often charities have insufficient funds for it.
3. *Sample size.* Reliable research often requires a large sample size to be conclusive. Many charities simply serve too few people to allow rigorous research (Justice Data Lab, 2018).
4. *Incentives.* The request for charities to investigate their own impact often comes from funders who use that information to inform future funding decisions. More rigorous research is likely to be less flattering than weak research is. Asking charities to evaluate themselves creates an incentive for them to produce poor quality evaluation.
5. *Poor reporting.* Often charities' reports of their evaluations are not detailed enough to be useful. It would helpful if

they contained more of the types of information required in TIDieR, CONSORT or the checklists for other types of study.

2. Synthesis

Producing/funding production of synthesis

Often multiple studies of the same thing (for example several studies of the effects of a particular intervention) will find different answers. This can be because the sample size differed between the studies (smaller studies are more likely to get 'weird' answers than are large ones) or because the people studied differed between the studies, or just by random chance. Synthesising studies gets closest to the 'true answer'. Systematic reviews are a rigorous form of research synthesis: they search for all studies of a particular type and then synthesise them. To misquote Isaac Newton, systematic reviews allow the user to stand on the shoulders of all the relevant giants.

Charitable funders sometimes fund the production of some systematic reviews in order to inform their own funding. A very few operational charities produce systematic reviews, either to inform their own practice and/or that of the wider field. The Flemish Red Cross in Belgium is an example: its Centre for Evidence-Based Practice (Rode Kruis Vlaanderen, 2019) has produced peer-reviewed systematic reviews on topics such as whether it is safe for people with epilepsy to donate blood, how first aiders should respond to snakebites, and the amount of water that should be provided per person after disasters and emergencies (Fiennes, 2019).

Reporting synthesis

As with primary research, there are standards and checklists for producing and reporting synthesis, which are not known to all charities and funders. For instance, synthesis studies should, like primary studies, be pre-registered to prevent publication bias, and it should be described fully when published. PRISMA is a checklist for reporting syntheses.

3. Dissemination

Publishing the full research detail

Most academic journals are paywalled, which is a major (and obvious!) barrier to the usefulness of their research. Philanthropic donors are involved in several responses.

First, there is open access. The Gates Foundation is one of several funders that requires that the research that it funds, including the underlying data-sets, be published on an open access basis (Gates Foundation, 2019). It will pay the publisher's fees to ensure this.

Second, there are new journals. Believing that the existing journals were inadequate, three nonprofits – the Howard Hughes Medical Institute, the Max Planck Society and the Wellcome Trust – set up a new journal, *eLife*, for biomedical and life sciences research, in which the entire content is freely available for all to read, use and reproduce (Wellcome, 2011).

And third, smaller-scale foundations sometimes pay for researchers or practitioners to have journal access and/or to attend conferences.

Publishing/disseminating the findings in easier-to-use formats

Returning to Richard Thaler's mantra, if we want people to use evidence, we should make it easy. Toolkits by various UK What Works Centres, including CHI's intervention tool and the Education Endowment Foundation's toolkit, summarise the reliability and findings of the evidence about various interventions.

4. Use: barriers to uptake of evidence

Several factors prevent individuals and organisations from using evidence and anybody attempting to increase evidence-based practice needs strategies for each of them (Banerjee and Duflo, 2012).

- *Ignorance about what to do.* The purpose of conducting, reporting and disseminating research is to overcome this, but is often insufficient. Simply 'disseminating' research ('at' people) will not ensure that it is used.

- *Ignorance about how to do it*. Policy-makers and practitioners often need help to find, interpret and apply the research in their particular situation. A senior policy-maker in India told researchers working on poverty alleviation programmes: 'Don't just tell me what the best strategy is, come and help me implement it' (Dhaliwal and Tulloch, 2012). That practical support to policy-makers and practitioners is often funded by donors.

- *Ideology*. Even if research finds conclusively that an intervention is effective, it may be politically unacceptable to implement it. For instance, even if research finds that offering parents an incentive payment will keep their children in school, it may be unacceptable to be seen to 'bribe' them.

- *Inertia*. Policy-makers and the delivery system may be too preoccupied with other issues or may find the intervention too difficult or the existing system too hard to change.

- *Incentives*. Evidence that threatens commercial interests is rarely welcomed by those who stand to lose out. Regulation and legislation can be necessary to force compliance. Equally, if an organisation or person has previously promoted a particular thing, it can be tough for them to publicly change their position and pivot away from it.

- *Resources/decision-rights*. Even if all the above are solved, sometimes the individual accessing the evidence simply does not have the right or the funds or the other resources necessary. In these situations, the task is to help the policy-maker find the best answer given the resources and rights that they have: that may be the least-bad answer for their context.

Donor and charity reactions to research/evidence

'The great discovery that launched the Scientific Revolution was the discovery that humans do not know the answers to their most important questions', says Professor Yuval Noah Harari in his book *Sapiens* (Harari, 2015). Intuition gave way to empirical investigation.

We still do not yet know the best way to solve many social problems – and CHI's EGMs show that homelessness is among them. Even if we have a good understanding of the root causes, we may not know how (best) to tackle them. Central to our task is encouraging people in the homelessness system to 'discover their ignorance' about what is effective and to be curious to find out.

Humans do not always welcome their ignorance being exposed: most of us like to think that we have a reasonable idea of what we are doing.

Worse, though progress in many fields is easy to define and see, in most areas where charities and donors operate progress is really hard to see, especially for donors. Warren Buffett talks about how 'business is easy because the market tells you whether you're right or wrong. But with philanthropy, you can keep doing something that doesn't make any sense and there's no playback from the market' (nextavenue, 2019). This is what Katherine Fulton, then president of the Monitor Institute, meant by:[10] 'The problems of philanthropy are not experienced as problems by philanthropists.' Donors may not realise that Yes-Land is distinct from No-Land, or may mistakenly think that their experience of giving means that they are in Yes-Land.

Reactions to the results of experiments

Donors are often disappointed by small results. Perhaps this is because, as Harvard surgeon Atul Gawande notes:

> [W]e have been fooled by Penicillin. Discovered in 1929, it was almost 20 years before it was mass produced and could stop disease. And [then] it was like a miracle ... this treatment that could eliminate whole classes of disease – a whole body of bacterial infections that we basically thought you couldn't do much of anything about. It came as a miracle because it was so easy. That made us imagine that this was the future of medicine; that we would just have an injection for cancers, for heart disease, for stroke. But ... very little has turned out to be like Penicillin. (Gawande, 2014)

We often hear claims that some new social programme is a 'magic bullet'. For instance, micro-credit was described by[11] no less a body than the Nobel Prize committee as having 'proved to be an important liberating force in societies where women in particular have to struggle against repressive social and economic conditions. [T]o eliminate poverty in the world…micro-credit must play a major part.'

This turns out to be false. A detailed summary by the European Bank of Reconstruction and Development of evidence from across the world found 'that giving poor people access to microcredit does not lead to a substantial increase in household income (European Bank of Reconstruction and Development, 2015). There also appear to be no significant benefits in terms of education or female empowerment … Microcredit is a useful financial tool but not a powerful anti-poverty strategy.'

Many social programmes only have a small effect, but that need not deter us. Many (perhaps most) medical interventions have only tiny effects, but if (and only if) they are implemented consistently, they can nonetheless have dramatic effects on prevalence and outcomes.

Negative/null results

Some programmes have no effect and some even create harm. These results are not always welcome.

For example, two programmes funded by the Big Lottery Fund (BLF; now the National Lottery Community Fund) were evaluated using RCTs and both were found to have no effect. A 'think piece' published jointly in 2018 by BLF reflected on that experience. One of the implementing organisations appeared to dismiss the findings, saying 'I still believe that the programme makes a difference, I've seen it with my own eyes' (Young Foundation, 2018).

This denial is perhaps just people defending the 'sunk cost' of their effort or money. Donors do not want to hear that the effects of their investment have failed or, worse, exacerbated a problem. For private donors, this is money that could have been used to more obvious personal gain elsewhere − like buying another house. Most major donors put a lot of themselves into their giving. Many want to think of their giving as part of their personal legacy and it can thus be an existential issue. Donors' reluctance to hear about failures is understandable and we should deal with it sensitively.

Bring on the charm offensive

Evidence, and the particular interventions that it recommends, can usefully be viewed as an innovation. Those of us interested in evidence-based practice are seeking to encourage adoption of that innovation and so we can learn from (for example) the theory of how innovations diffuse across a population, originally posited by Everett Rogers in 1962 (Rogers, 1995). We can look for early adopters, and people who influence many others.

And we can learn from Dr David Sackett, a founder of evidence-based medicine. His method was salutary: having found the medical establishment to be 'negative, condescending and dismissive' to the evidence-based approach, he engaged with people – not by publishing 'the right answer' in some journal – but rather through constant face-to-face engagement. He made teaching visits to more than 200 district general hospitals in the UK and to scores in Europe (Guardian, 2015).

All of us who aim to increase the use of evidence in homelessness and elsewhere should avoid assuming that the magic impact fairy will take our research and turn it into change on the frontline. We should remember that – whether we are trying to influence donors, policy-makers, practitioners or whomever else – perhaps ultimately this is a ground offensive, and a charm offensive.

Notes

[1] For concision, this chapter uses the term 'funder' and 'donor' interchangeably other than where specified.

[2] Adapted from Shepherd (2007).

[3] ASER Centre (2019) Home page, available at: www.asercentre.org (accessed: 11 March 2019).

[4] Ibid.

[5] US National Library of Medicine. *Research Reporting Guidelines and Initiatives: By Organization.* [Online] (accessed: 24 September 2014).

[6] Consort. *The Consort Statement.* [Online] (accessed: 24 September 2014).

7   Strobe. STROBE Statement. [Online] (accessed: 2 October 2014).
8   Prisma. [Online] (accessed: 2 October 2014).
9   https://trialsjournal.biomedcentral.com/articles/10.1186/s13063-018-2735-z (accessed: 5 March 2019).
10 From an unpublished but rather brilliant paper by Katherine Fulton, (then) president of the Monitor Institute.
11 The Nobel Peace Prize for 2006. NobelPrize.org. Nobel Media AB 2019. Tue. 12 Mar 2019. www.nobelprize.org/prizes/peace/2006/press-release/.

References
Banerjee, A. and Duflo, E. 2012. *Poor Economics: Barefoot Hedge-fund Managers, DIY Doctors and the Surprising Truth about Life on less than $1 a Day*. London: Penguin.

Crisis. 2019. *Homelessness Monitor*. www.crisis.org.uk/ending-homelessness/homelessness-knowledge-hub/homelessness-monitor/ (accessed: 5 March 2019).

Crowe, S., Fenton, M., Hall, M., Cowan, K. and Chalmers, I. 2015. Patients', clinicians' and the research communities' priorities for treatment research: there is an important mismatch. *Research Involvement and Engagement*, 1(2). doi:10.1186/s40900-015-0003-x.

Dhaliwal, I. and Tulloch, C. 2012. *From Research to Policy: Using Evidence from Impact Evaluations to Inform Development Policy*. https://www.povertyactionlab.org/sites/default/files/publications/With%20JDE%20Revisions%20and%20Footnotes%202012.09.03.pdf.

European Bank of Reconstruction and Development. 2015. *The Impact of Microcredit: Evidence from Across the World*. www.ebrd.com/publications/impact-of-microcredit (accessed: 11 March 2019).

Fiennes, C. 2019. Why I've joined a board of the Flemish Red Cross. *Giving Evidence* blog. https://giving-evidence.com/2019/11/26/flemish

Gates Foundation. 2019. *How We Work – Bill & Melinda Gates Foundation Open Access Policy*. www.gatesfoundation.org/How-We-Work/General-Information/Open-Access-Policy (accessed: 1 March 2019).

Gawande, A. 2014. *The Future of Medicine*. Reith Lectures. BBC Radio 4. https://www.bbc.co.uk/programmes/b04bsgqn (accessed: 6 March 2019).

Give Directly. 2018. *From Subsistence to Refuge.* https://givedirectly. org/pdf/CashTransfersToRefugeeCommunitiesWhitePaper. pdf (accessed: 11 March 2019).

GiveWell. 2018. *Impact.* www.givewell.org/about/impact (accessed: 11 March 2019).

Guardian. 2015. *David Sackett Obituary.* www.theguardian.com/ education/2015/may/29/david-sackett (accessed: 11 March 2019).

Harari, Y.N. 2015. *Sapiens: A Brief History of Humankind.* London: Vintage.

Justice Data Lab. 2018. *User Guidance.* https://assets.publishing. service.gov.uk/government/uploads/system/uploads/ attachment_data/file/794249/User_Journey_Document_ Update_PDF.pdf

Kahneman, D. 2012. *Thinking Fast and Slow.* London: Penguin.

Moher, D., Schulz, K.F., Simera, I. and Altman, D.G. 2010. Guidance for developers of health research reporting guidelines. *PLoS Medicine,* 7(2): 8.

nextavenue. 2019. *How Warren Buffet Made Me Smarter About Charity.* nextavenue.org/how-warren-buffett-made-me-smarter-about-charity/ (accessed: 6 March 2019).

NSPCC. 2018. *Evaluation of the Letting the Future In service.* https://learning.nspcc.org.uk/research-resources/2016/ evaluation-of-the-letting-the-future-in-service/ (accessed: 5 March 2019).

ODI. 2016. *Cash Transfers: What Does the Evidence Say? A Rigorous Review of Impacts and the Role of Design and Implementation Features.* www.odi.org/publications/10505-cash-transfers-what-does-evidence-say-rigorous-review-impacts-and-role-design-and-implementation (accessed: 11 March 2019).

Rode Kruis Vlaanderen. 2019. *Publications.* www.rodekruis.be/ en/who-are-we/research/centre-for-evidence-based-practice/ publications/ (accessed: 10 March 2019).

Rogers, E. 1995. *Diffusions of Innovation.* 4th ed. London: The Free Press.

Shepherd, J. 2007. The production and management of evidence for public service reform. *Evidence and Policy,* 3(2): 231–51.

Thaler, R.H. 2012. Watching behavior before writing the rules. *The New York Times*, 7 July. www.nytimes.com/2012/07/08/business/behavioral-science-can-help-guide-policy-economic-view.html?_r=2and (accessed: 14 November 2013).

Young Foundation. 2018. *Realising Ambition Programme Insights: Issue 11*. https://youngfoundation.org/wp-content/uploads/2018/02/Programme-Insight-11.pdf (accessed: 11 March 2019).

13

Why transparency matters to knowledge mobilisation

Tracey Brown

The focus of the evidence movement in policy has always been on improving the quality of evidence available and ensuring its dissemination and use. But this assumes that we have a picture of what is currently going on in a given area of policy, that we have a baseline of current practice and that we know what good looks like. Without evidence transparency, we do not.

There are some other reasons to pay attention to evidence transparency. Without it, there is little clarity about what government or contributors to a field of policy have looked at, making it very difficult for anyone to understand the motivations for a proposal – to decide whether they agree with it, to participate in its development or to consider whether an intervention is working. Researchers and specialist contributors cannot see what they could add to the field and government and delivery bodies are less able to build on their own previous work, let alone determine whether initiatives are improving the evidence base for policy. A transparent chain of reasoning is, therefore, vital to all aspects of knowledge mobilisation.

Transparency is a prerequisite to assessing quality – rather obviously, you cannot assess something that you cannot see. More importantly, it is also a tool for behaviour change. Knowing that others will see the basis of your conclusions invites you to reflect on how you reached them and perhaps acknowledge their limitations. Such openness offers a more considered and constructive environment in which to determine the best interventions and how to resource them in social care, homelessness, drug policy, crime prevention and many other fields.

The renewed focus on achieving better use of evidence in homelessness policy presents a great opportunity. To improve, everyone must know the baseline. Those involved in this movement will first need to establish what evidence is being used by different policy and delivery actors and how, and to achieve a common understanding of the evidence base that currently, honestly, underpins practice. For this reason, the early experiences of introducing an evidence transparency framework, and assessing against it, are discussed over the coming pages, in order to explore how the same could be achieved in the field of homelessness.

In 2018, Sense about Science published *Transparency of Evidence II*, an assessment of whether 12 UK government departments were transparent about the evidence they used in policy development and how they used it (Sense about Science, 2018). It was the culmination of three years' work with partners and volunteers across the UK, developing a transparency of evidence framework and applying it through two assessments: first to establish what good practice looks like and then to review progress.

The result of this work has been a new focus on evidence transparency. In its first update in 15 years, HM Treasury's Green Book – the government's official guidance on policy evaluation – now refers extensively to the need for transparency about evidence and the public duty to share the reasoning and calculations upon which it is based. The transparency assessments prompted extensive discussions about evidence across civil service professions and across departments, including at cabinet level, as well as requests for workshops, meetings and presentations from those keen to improve their practice. The same methods have been taken on internationally by other government bodies and parts of the European Commission at the EU. These are broad foundations from which people concerned with improvement in specific areas of policy-making can now build, with government-level commitments more clearly articulated and understood, and good practice defined.

Exposing the chain of reasoning in policy

Sense about Science, together with the Institute for Government and the Alliance for Useful Evidence, first developed the evidence transparency framework in 2015, responding to a suggestion by David Halpern, chief executive of the UK Government's Behavioural Insights Team, to compare the way departments used evidence. It was impossible. We could not tell what had been used and how – and we were people with some knowledge of the policy world.

Despite a commitment to transparency in the Civil Service Reform Plan of 2013 (Civil Service, 2013), repeated in the Open Government Action Plan 2016–18, we found that it was hard for even the most motivated citizens to work out what assertions in policy were based on, how evidence had been used or the assumptions behind projected costs and benefits.

Through a series of scoping meetings with evidence advocates we established that in order to evaluate policy evidence and the effectiveness of initiatives to improve it, the government's use of evidence needed to be much more transparent. As described in the Institute for Government's discussion of this approach, *Show Your Workings* (Rutter and Gold, 2015), it is 'a first and necessary step in enabling the quality of a department's evidence-based decision-making to be judged '.

To address this, we set out a transparency framework; an approach to testing evidence transparency that could be applied rapidly, did not require subject expertise, gave meaningful results and allowed comparison between different policy areas. An experimental review of the year to May 2016 enabled us to elaborate on the framework and then apply it to a spot check of policies announced in the year to July 2017 to identify examples of excellence[1] in government departments. The results revealed improvements in departments' efforts to share their evidence base and reasoning with the public and a much broader range of examples of doing so under different policy-making conditions.

The Department for Work and Pensions, for example, had put its policy proposals into a regular format so that the evidential reasoning for them was prompted and easily located, even by people with no familiarity with policy-making. Other departments had experimented in the same way, though with arguably less success. Across all departments, we found an increase in proper citations and far fewer cases of vague gesturing towards source documents. In those policies caught in the spot check, there were very few cases of missing documents and broken links and the sources of the analysis were most usually available.

Despite this, and the improving picture discussed in the following pages, the publication of the evidence behind policy is still a negotiated issue. During the review, departments variously told us that a given policy was not typical because it: was at consultation stage, was dropped, became the focus of public debate, was not a focus of public debate, was developed jointly with other departments, is derived from manifesto commitments, was announced in the budget, is low priority, concerns a specific group of specialists, had to be done in a rush, was inherited from a previous government.

There just are no 'normal' circumstances for policy-making: showing the workings and being clear about the chain of reasoning behind proposals applies to all situations. Certainly, improved publication of evidence depends on greater trust: trust among colleagues in government that they know what to publish and greater trust in the public's ability to handle the fact that policy evidence is rarely complete and definitive. Some of the examples in the next section show that this is possible.

High standards have been achieved under all conditions of policy-making and states of evidence. These are the standards that those who wish to improve the use of evidence in homelessness policy should insist upon as a starting point.

What to look for in an evidence transparency review

Put simply, the question we asked of departments was: could someone outside government see what you are proposing to do and why? The framework assesses this question across four different areas, which provide the basis for both formal analysis of policy reasoning and a more iterative discussion:

- *Diagnosis* (the issue that will be addressed)
  The document(s) should explain: what policy-makers know about the issue, its causes, effects, and scale; how policy-makers have assessed the strengths and weaknesses of that evidence.
- *Proposal* (the chosen intervention)
  The document(s) should explain: why the government has chosen this intervention; what evidence, if any, that choice is based on; how policy-makers have assessed that evidence base, including what has been tried before and whether that worked; whether there are other options and why they have not been chosen; what the government plans to do about any part of the intervention that has not yet been decided upon; what is being assumed in any estimates of costs and benefits.
- *Implementation* (how the intervention will be introduced and run)
  The document(s) should explain: why this method for delivering the intervention has been chosen; what evidence, if any, that decision is based on; whether there are other methods and, if so, the reasons for not choosing them; if the way to deliver the intervention is still being decided, what evidence if any will be used for that; what is being assumed in any estimates of the costs and benefits.
- *Testing and evaluation* (how we will know if the policy has worked or, in the case of consultations and further investigations, how the information gathered will be used)
  The document(s) should explain: any testing that has been or will be done; plans to measure the impact of the policy and the outcomes that will be measured; plans to evaluate the effects of the policy, including a timetable; plans for using further inputs.

Policy engagement

A review will necessarily challenge or there would be little point in doing it. All manner of things conspire in the policy world to create resistance to change: inertia – the fact that doing *something* is harder than doing nothing; lack of knowledge; losing sight of outcomes in favour of system pressures; defensiveness and lack of imagination. However, it is important to remember that there are usually people within a sector or organisation who are working for improvement and are enabled to do so by external commentary.

While few bodies welcome exposure to scrutiny in the first instance, in the end they see that it is impossible to be recognised for good practice without it. Exposing evidence gaps or a lack of transparent reasoning may be taken as criticism where organisations fall short, but ultimately what they most need is for that transparency to offer a way forward.

What we found in our assessment of evidence transparency

Diagnosis

The starting point of a robust policy is an understanding of the problem it is trying to address. This helps people understand the need for the policy and any relevant information they should raise. It also makes it possible to assess whether the policy is likely to have its intended effect and, later, whether it has had that effect. To enable this, departments should describe what they know about an issue – its causes and effects and its scale – and set out the sources from which they have drawn that knowledge.

Overall, the best results were achieved against the diagnosis section of the framework, where departments seemed more likely to pay attention to gaps in relevant knowledge. The Department for Work and Pension's policy, *Support for Young People with a Limited Capability for Work*,[2] for example, did well on this aspect of transparent reasoning because it described the limitations of existing evidence and what it planned to do about this.

> 59. We also know that evidence gaps exist, in particular:
> - how best to support those in work and at risk of falling out of work, including the pat employers can plat;

- understanding how best to help those people in the Employment and Support Allowance Support Group who could and want to work;
- the settings that are most effective to engage people in employment and health support; and
- how musculoskeletal treatment and occupational health interventions improve employment outcomes.

60. We have a range of activity underway that is focused on the evidence gaps we have identified, including access to services and levels of support we should offer. This will help us to develop new models of support to help people into work when they are managing a long-term health condition or disability.

This example is particularly striking because the effect of it is to provide a basis for confidence in the department's approach to evidence gathering. It illustrates the fact that acknowledging the limitations of knowledge is not such a political problem.

One of the hardest things for citizens to follow is when departments are responding to previous reports or proposals. It is often unclear whether government is adopting the contents of those reports. This was the case with Cabinet Office's *Combatting Electoral Fraud*, which left the citizen unsure as to what extent the government was relying upon the evidence previously gathered for the independent review by Sir Eric Pickles.

Some policies are motivated by values. This is reasonable. Transparency includes being clear about this. The mobilisation of knowledge is not a fight against values, but rather a project for *testable* questions. Consider the difference in the following statements:

Liverpool should host the Olympics because it is a prestigious thing to do for our city.

Liverpool should host the Olympics because it will encourage more young people to take up sport and help tackle childhood obesity.

The first is a value statement. The second is a testable question – two in fact!

Consider also Figure 13.1:

Figure 13.1: Testable claims: when is evidence expected?

It is not fair that some rich people don't play by the same rules as everyone else. 'Non-doms' should be taxed.	'Non-doms' should be taxed because it will bring more money to the Exchequer, even if some of them leave as a result.
Supporting children from all backgrounds is a priority for this government, so we need a national network of early years centres to show that commitment.	If we provide early years centres we will measurably improve the education of children who have access to them.

Source: Sense about Science, 2018, Appendix 3

Values include a desire for fairness in principle. This might lead government to close a loophole in regulations even if there is no evidence about whether it is being exploited. An example of this was the Home Office's *Re-employment of Senior Fire Officers*, which tackled the practice of taking retirement to create a tax-free income and then being re-employed and able to transfer earnings tax-free back into a pension. This scored well because it was reasonably clear that it was concerned with the principle as much as the practice.

Readers seeking more examples of good practice might also find it useful to look again at some proposals from the 2016 review: the Cabinet Office's proposal to establish common measures of socio-economic background – a very early stage document that included a thorough discussion of the problem and uncertainties in the evidence base;[3] and the Home Office's consultation on introducing a stalking protection order, which explained and sourced its view on the limitations of existing measures.[4]

Proposal

Once departments have diagnosed a problem, they need to develop a clear hypothesis on how an intervention might address it and deliver the government's objectives. Departments would usually draw on evidence – from past attempts to address a similar problem, evaluations of those attempts, international or other jurisdiction experience or academic research – to justify why there is reason to believe the intervention might work.

Implementation

Once the government has developed a hypothesis on its proposed intervention, it needs to work out how to make that happen. There are often choices on the best way to do it and citizens should be able to see why departments have chosen one way instead of another and what evidence they have used. They should also see cost and benefit calculations, and the assumptions behind them, and some discussion of the opportunity cost of the new intervention if it will divert resources from existing activity. Often implementation issues – which are the root of many policy failures – are not considered when a policy is proposed. This may be why transparency about the evidence behind plans to implement policies was an area of weakness in many policy documents, including those that had scored well on other parts of the framework.

Testing and evaluation

Testing allows policy development to be informed by real-world experience, to gather information and feedback and to incorporate unforeseen influences on the policy's effects before embarking on any major costs and reorganisation. Evaluation promotes a more systematic and objective organisation of information about the policy's effects, which, as well as informing policy development, is an essential part of the accountability of government.

Having now been through two extensive review processes, there are some key observations that may help others to apply the framework across specific areas:

Evidence is often drawn upon without being referenced (contrary to the guidance noted earlier). An aspiration we should all have for documents intended to inform policy, or elaborate its basis, is that testable statements are indeed tested or, at the very least, we understand the extent to which they have been. For example, fines may well reduce use of mobile phones while driving, but referencing the basis for believing this to be so in a proposal for new legislation is essential to understanding whether this is an effect found only at certain monetary levels, in different social groups or whether it has been compared with other penalties.

Evidence that has been collated is very often not published. At minimum this represents a huge waste of effort and money and often lost opportunity. We uncovered really strong evidence synopses that would have been beneficial to many others in the field, such as justice and pensions, had they been published with the policy and made widely available.

At worst, the failure to publish the evidence on which decisions are being made can lead to decisions that damage lives or to a lack of public conviction about beneficial measures. It has been particularly shocking to discover, in a separate initiative, that health authorities are not publishing a large proportion of clinical trials,[5] on everything from vaccines to hospital equipment. How doctors and other frontline workers are supposed to confidently convey choices to patients is anyone's guess.

People should be able to follow the thinking between diagnosis, proposal, implementation, and testing and evaluation. The most transparent proposals demonstrated the chain of reasoning as to what the problem was and why the policy was the chosen response and included discussion about the limitations of the evidence.

Transparency in homelessness policy

A particular challenge for a transparency review of the evidence behind current policy and practice in homelessness is that it may be interpreted as a simple request for volume: is there evidence or is there not? In fact, we would hamper policy innovation severely with a request for everything to pass some kind of evidence threshold. Action in the absence of clear evidence must be possible. Experimentation (with clear testing and reporting plans) needs to be encouraged.

Furthermore, it would be of little use to anyone if the quest for a clear account of the evidence behind different practices and proposals led to 'gaming' the system. A policy proposal that looks busy with footnotes is not necessarily transparent.

In pursuing this, to achieve a common assessment of what we know and how it is being used, advocates should emphasise not just the good practices we have identified in the different aspects of policy, from diagnosis of the problem to impact measurement plans, but also some of the cross-cutting issues.

Transparent can be short and simple

It would be a mistake to imagine that a document crowded with references or extensive extracts is better grounded or more transparent. References should be meaningful and useful, to enable the reader to understand how the source is relevant and to enable them to assess that source for themselves if they wish. The noting and referencing of underlying evidence is not enough to provide a chain of reasoning between policy and evidence. There should be clarity about its relevance to the proposal and how that analysis was used.

Policies can be transparent in the absence of evidence

Governments often have to act where the evidence base is weak or absent. They may not have the luxury of waiting for those gaps to be filled before they introduce proposals. The most transparent policy documents were those that acknowledged this and explained how the department would fill the gap or evaluate the policy at a later point.

Weakness in the evidence base should be acknowledged

The most transparent policy documents acknowledged weaknesses and discussed them. We found more discussion of the strengths and weaknesses of the evidence base in this review but the number of '2's indicates that it was still missing from many otherwise transparent policies.

Values-based policies can be transparent

Particularly at national level, policies are sometimes introduced with a values-based justification, rather than justified just by their intended outcomes and effectiveness. In those cases, there may be less of a role for evidence.

We considered policies to have achieved a basic level of transparency if they were clear about their rationale being values-based rather than evidence-based, so long as they supported any testable claims about the situation they were addressing. They were considered to be fully transparent if they also discussed the evidence and explained why it had been disregarded in developing the policy. There were in fact very few policies that were not based on some testable claims or assumptions.

Acknowledging different influences also helps the public to follow the chain of reasoning behind the policy and to see how evidence has been weighed alongside other pressures. Advocates of policy reform and better use of evidence can then proceed with a discussion about the role that evidence could or should play.

Advocates of improvement to policies to tackle homelessness have been hampered by obfuscation about evidence use, left wondering whether evidence is understood and disregarded, misapplied, or not seriously examined in the first place. A transparency review is an invitation to everyone to take a clear-headed look at what is being used and how. We can see where the gaps are – in the evidence itself, in what is being drawn upon or how its strengths and limitations are understood. This is the foundation for identifying the improvements that the evidence movement can make and for starting to make them.

Notes

[1] This was conducted with a grant from the Nuffield Foundation to support a dedicated researcher; collaboration between Sense about Science, the Institute for Government and the Alliance for Useful Evidence to provide oversight and other inputs; and a group of volunteer citizen scorers whose experience of engaging with policy ranged from some to none.

[2] *Improving Lives: The Work, Health and Disability Green Paper*, Consultation, 31 October 2016, p 5.

3   *Engagement Document: Developing a Common Set of Measures for Employers on the Socio-Economic Backgrounds of their Workforce and Applicants*, May 2016, p 3.
4   *Introducing a Stalking Protection Order – a consultation*, December 2015, p 11 para 5.
5   https://eu.trialstracker.net.

References

Civil Service Reform Plan: One Year On Report, July 2013. www.gov.uk/government/uploads/system/uploads/attachment_data/file/211506/CSR_OYO_LOW_RES_PDF.pdf.

Rutter, J. and Gold, J. 2015. *Show Your Workings. Assessing How the Government Uses Evidence to Make Policy.* www.instituteforgovernment.org.uk/publications/show-your-workings.

Sense about Science. 2018. *Transparency of Evidence: A Spot Check of Government Policy Proposals July 2016 to July 2017.* https://senseaboutscience.org/wp-content/uploads/2018/01/Transparency-of-evidence-spotcheck.pdf.

14

Afterword

Julia Unwin

There is no shortage of evidence about the existence and reach of homelessness. If evidence of need was all that was required, homelessness would be solved by now. Walk through any town centre today and you will see them: the encampments of tents, propped up against shop doorways, providing inadequate shelter for people who have nowhere safe to sleep tonight. These encampments have become so commonplace that they have almost become a part of the landscape. Just as we never talked about food banks until 2010, so I do not recall seeing tents in cities until five or six years ago.

But just as there was hunger before 2010, there was homelessness too, and visible homelessness occupies a longstanding place in our collective consciousness. From the homeless shelters of George Orwell's *Down and Out in Paris and London*, through to the wounded soldiers arriving home to nothing after World War II. From the men, and occasionally women, walking from town to town to *Cathy Come Home*, to the explosion of young people sleeping on the streets of London in the late 1980s. From the rising number of people in our cities and the lack of affordable accommodation to house them, to the perilous uncertainty of so many people experiencing 'hidden homelessness' in precarious situations, homelessness has been part of our landscape for longer than we would like to admit. But this is not inevitable. It does not need to be this way.

Despite the evident need for solutions, it is striking how little is known about what we must do. To achieve a step change in ending homelessness we need to know and understand more. We must focus on what works by finding and funding solutions backed by evidence and data. Currently we often know what problems need to be solved but lack the right kinds of investments to address them because the evidence base is weak, underdeveloped or, often, non-existent.

The absence of causal evidence and the lack of urgency to create tangible change tells us a great deal about the way our society views homelessness and those it affects. We know very little about different homelessness interventions and whether or not they work. We hear very little of the voices of people who are at risk of, or experiencing, homelessness – always the best people to explain the challenges they face. And despite important data and evidence initiatives such as the What Works Cities Programme in the US or the Research Schools Network in the UK, the UK and international homelessness sectors are yet to make comprehensive use of the power of data and empirical experimental methods to take lasting preventive action. The majority still see homelessness as a marginal concern.

As the chapters in this book make crystal clear, homelessness is real and it is damaging for so many. Homelessness affects families struggling to pay their mortgage, terrified of repossession. It affects young people leaving local authority care without adequate planning and provision. It affects returning service people with inadequate support. It affects those with disabilities and those struggling with addiction. It affects children and women fleeing domestic violence. It affects people seeking asylum, and those with no recourse to public funds. And it affects those who are living in overcrowded accommodation and at risk of eviction.

Homelessness blights the lives of families and its damage scars future generations. It makes recovery from addiction, from distress and from illness so very much harder. It poses a vast, and largely unquantified, risk to the health of those who experience it, their wellbeing and, inevitably, their survival. It undermines communities, making it hard for them to develop the resilience and strength needed in challenging times.

Housing needs to be secure, safe and affordable. That has always been the requirement. But the persistence of homelessness can too readily blind us to the other great truth. That new and imaginative strategies can power progress. In other fields, great progress has been made possible by investing in better understanding. Why do we fail to bring the same rigour and analysis to the pressing question of homelessness?

Aiming higher means that everyone involved needs to know more. We need more reliable evaluations of different interventions. We need more data and we need the experiences of those who have experienced, or are experiencing, homelessness to be part of devising solutions to the problem. To succeed, as the Centre for Homelessness Impact always likes to point out, we also need to create a movement that leads to faster learning and experimentation across the field.

Just as we can trace the incidences of homelessness through the decades, so we can track our ability to respond. Just as there is no shortage of evidence of need, there is no shortage of inspiration behind us. The ability to marshal money and houses, to push for wider varieties of intervention, to organise, to get support, to change lives and to make a difference, runs throughout the last century: the drive by the Salvation Army, the Church Army and others to provide a roof over people's heads, however rudimentary; the formation of a whole wave of housing associations – the *Cathy Come Home* generation – started by people who knew that it was simply not right for people to be homeless and have nowhere to go; the establishment of what became Notting Hill Housing Trust by the Reverend Bruce Kenrick in the early 1960s; the creation of Centrepoint by the Reverend Kenneth Leech in 1969 in the crypt of St Anne's, Soho. The establishment of Shelter and Crisis 50 years ago.

Truly we can see so far because we stand on the shoulders of giants.

Every step forward in responding to the needs of people who have nowhere to live has been driven by hope and certainty. Hope that a better life can be achieved and certainty that a safe, secure home is absolutely essential if anyone is to flourish and grow. A core human need is for a place to be for safety, for warmth, for security. It is the recognition of this for all of us that powers so much change and so much activity. It is a recognition that for all of us home is the most precious place, the base from which we launch, the place we want to feel safe, the place we share with those we love.

That is why the continuing presence of homelessness is both an affront to our sense of decency and a challenge to all of us who recognise for ourselves that without the security of home we could achieve nothing. Continuing high levels of homelessness challenge our sense of compassion and solidarity, but also represent a huge waste – of talent, capability, and contribution.

It is now vital to look forward and make full use of opportunities to do better. Early progress has been inhibited because the systems that have developed over time are complex, hard to navigate and often expensive. Entitlements have changed in ways that are frequently difficult to understand and the interplay between a complex benefits system, a shortage of housing and pressures on other support services have all been deeply felt by the most excluded people in society. Homelessness occurs at the interface between many areas of policy and system failure, and the solutions can be found in changes to those systems through focused support and the efforts of people experiencing homelessness themselves.

We hold assets that previous campaigners and policy-makers lacked. First, we have a clear understanding of the limits of our knowledge thanks to the evidence tools created by the Centre for Homelessness Impact. We have a roadmap to improve the global knowledge of what works and what interventions make a difference.

Across the UK we have differing frameworks of legal rights, but that gives us both knowledge and the capacity to challenge. We have history and experience and we have both great institutions and grassroots movements committed to making a change. We know what has worked in the past and we also know where we have fallen short.

And we have enjoyed significant achievements. Scotland is unique in that virtually every homeless person has a legal right to permanent housing. And over recent years in all UK nations there has been a growing awareness that the ideal solution is to prevent people from becoming homeless in the first place. Recent developments in Wales and England – where local authorities now have a duty to help prevent homelessness regardless of priority – are setting an example for other countries to follow.

Other great examples include the changing approach by mortgage lenders minimising the horrors of repossession that blighted so many lives in the 1990s and the programmes of work, including rough-sleepers initiatives, co-ordinated by Whitehall and more recently in Newcastle and in Liverpool.

Looking back over the past few decades, it is possible to identify some of what is needed for us to defeat homelessness sustainably in the UK. We know it will not be easy. It requires the commitment and hope that have inspired so many who have come before us. But the solutions of the past will never be the solutions for the future. The systems and services of the last 20 years are rightly criticised for allowing too little agency to individuals experiencing homelessness and for wrongly and inappropriately treating them as passive recipients of unaccountable and distant services. The pattern of support for the future will need to work much more closely with people experiencing homelessness as partners in identifying solutions. To do this will require intelligent engagement to ensure genuine and lasting impact and not simply the achievement of short-term goals.

Public attitudes matter. So too do the structures of the services that exist to serve people whose voices are too rarely heard and whose needs and contributions are too frequently overlooked. We need to listen to the growing demand from communities across the country that this is not good enough.

That call from the community needs to be met by a commitment that making better use of evidence and data is a priority – from governments across the UK, from local authorities, mayors, police forces and health bodies; from churches, philanthropic organisations and broader civil society; from housing providers whether voluntary, private or local authority; and from businesses, employers and those concerned with economic growth and resilience. A shared commitment is needed that recognises we must do more to help people better. You only need to look at other fields trying to tackle complex problems to see this is the case. We need to have the necessary evidence and data if we are to accelerate progress as others have done.

We need to recognise and value the power of homeless people themselves. No organisation, or group, or caring intervention ever resulted in one person becoming housed. It is always the courage and determination of people who are themselves homeless to build a new future. People experiencing homelessness have voice and agency and we need to listen and serve. Too often we still talk about people with lived experience without recognising that most people affected self-exit.

But most of all we need to change the way we talk about homelessness. The horror of being homeless is experienced by a small group of people. The impact of homelessness is felt across the nation. There is nothing inevitable about it. And we need to respond to the groundswell of indignation about this terrible waste of human lives with a strategy that brings together governments, business and broader civil society to make sure that nobody becomes homeless, but that, if they do, that they can be provided with the support and the housing that they so urgently need.

Current levels of homelessness shame our country and have no place in a modern, successful nation. All of us need to be involved in its prevention – building homes that people can afford, helping those who are struggling, making sure people can stay housed whatever else life throws at them and, most of all, making sure that no one is homeless for more than one night. All of this is as important as helping people back into housing. Better use of evidence can provide the most stable platform for that change.

This work is not simple. But that does not mean it is impossible. As the chapters in this book show we have evidence of need. We have an understanding about the multiplicity of different ways in which homelessness is manifest. And we have an opportunity to accelerate progress by fully embracing the opportunities that data and evidence offer – in particular, to create a learning sector that is prepared to put its assumptions to the test.

By building a great coalition, involving homeless people themselves, communities who care, institutions and governments, we have the opportunity to end homelessness sustainably. We have the opportunity to ensure that everyone has the safety and security of a home, the most fundamental need of all.

The shame of homelessness is felt most sharply by people who are themselves homeless. But the real shame should belong to all of us who have allowed the challenge of ending homelessness to be seen as too difficult, and in so doing have betrayed generation of people who have lacked that most basic and fundamental need. Lessons from other fields show that great progress is possible through faster learning and experimentation. It is time for the homelessness sector to catch up.

Index

council housing 63
Cragg, M. and O'Flaherty, B. 108
credit checks 40
Crisis 3, 21, 27, 76, 77, 91, 94, 205,
    232
    *Everybody In: How to End
    Homelessness in Great Britain*
    (2018) 21–2
critical research 102
critical time intervention (CTI) 88,
    133
cross-party approach 85–96
Culhane et al 109
cultural models 76
currents 78–9

D
Dartington Service Design Lab 130
data
    homelessness and rough sleeping
        174–5
    opportunities for effective use
        177–8
data collection and analysis 11–12,
    175
deaths 54, 56, 60, 90
    causes of 90–1
    demographics 57–8, 90–1
    drug poisoning 58, 90
    learning lessons from 90
    underlying causes 57
    of women 57, 58
Deaton, Angus 134
decision-making 136–7
    and research, promoting
        engagement between 190–1
decision-rights 209
Denmark 64, 114
Department for Education and Skills
    (DfES) 186
Department for Work and Pensions
    (DWP) 105, 175, 220
Department of Health (DoH) 186

Department of Housing and Urban
    Development (HUD, US)
    101, 107–8, 110, 115
Department of Labor 182
Department of Veterans Affairs (VA,
    US) 110, 110–11
    Supportive Services for Veteran
        Families programme 113
destitution 72–3
disabled people 71
discharge arrangements 25
diseases 144
dissemination
    publishing full research detail 208
    publishing in easier-to-use
        formats 208
dodo effect 131–3
domestic abuse 91–3
    housing 92
    vulnerability test 93
Domestic Abuse Bill 91, 93
domestic abuse, survivors 87, 88
donors 201–2
    negative/null results 211–12
    reactions to research/evidence
        209–10
    reactions to results of experiments
        210–12
    roles in evidence systems
        barriers to use of 208–9
        dissemination
            publishing full research
                detail 208
            publishing in easier-to-use
                formats 208
        production
            prioritising research topics
                203–4
            producing research 202–3
            reporting guidelines 204–5
            research produced 205–7
        synthesis
            production/funding 207
            reporting 207